The Strange Death of David Kelly

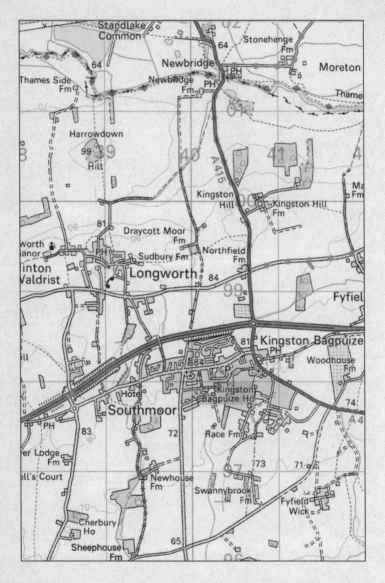

Map of Kingston Bagpuize, Harrowdown Hill and environs
(Ordnance Survey © Crown copyright 2007)

The Strange Death of David Kelly

Norman Baker

Methuen

First published in Great Britain 2007 by
Methuen Publishing Ltd
8 Artillery Row
London
SW1P 1RZ

10 9 8 7 6 5 4 3

A CIP catalogue record for this book is available from the British Library.

ISBN 978-1-84275-217-3

Set in Bembo by SX Composing DTP, Rayleigh, Essex
Printed and bound in Great Britain by CPD, Wales

Contents

Foreword

The death of David Kelly in July 2003 shocked the nation. And when shock had subsided, anger set in. Britain had gone to war in Iraq on what most people regarded as, at best, dubious grounds. The weapons of mass destruction, deployable within 45 minutes, were nowhere to be found. And all through July, the government oozed spin like pus from a boil.

So when Dr Kelly, a patently decent and honest man, was found dead in the woods at Harrowdown Hill, the Blair government found itself in the most serious political crisis of its ten years. The very future of the government looked to be at stake at one point, and commentators and public alike speculated on this, and on the future of the BBC.

In this highly charged atmosphere, the death of Dr Kelly was central, but it was largely taken for granted from day one that he had committed suicide. Indeed, with attention so focused on the turmoil enveloping the government, the questions that would normally have been raised went unasked.

Even at the time, it seemed to me to be unsafe simply to assume that David Kelly had killed himself. While it certainly seemed the most likely explanation, suicides after all can be staged, so I kept an open mind and awaited the Hutton inquiry.

I waited in vain. The process was a travesty, and the final result provoked widespread derision and anger, as Lord Hutton cleared the government of virtually everything, and came down like a landslide on the heads of the BBC. The result was that nobody from a government that had led us into what was almost certainly an illegal war resigned, while the BBC, which had broadcast one exaggerated, but for all that essentially true, report at 6.07 one morning, lost its chairman, its director general and the journalist who filed the report. Like many people, I felt incensed. This was an outrage.

But I had also noticed the letters that had begun to appear in the *Guardian* from leading medical specialists, in which they queried the conclusion that Dr Kelly's death was suicide. The letters were well argued, and I began to wonder if the Hutton report, which was so manifestly loaded in favour of the government in its political conclusions, could be trusted in respect of its analysis of how Dr David Kelly died.

And there the matter lay in abeyance, as my frontbench role for the Liberal Democrats, covering Environment, Food and Rural Affairs, took precedence as the general election approached. I had resolved to myself, however, to look further into the whole business when time allowed and did so early in 2006. I had expected to conclude in my own mind that it was indeed suicide, or at the very least, that there was no evidence that it was not. But my initial enquiries led me to a rather different conclusion – that the suicide explanation was an unsafe one, and that there were a large number of important points Lord Hutton had simply not considered.

At that point, I made a decision. When the next Lib Dem reshuffle took place, I would give up my Environment role to devote a year or so to looking fully into both the political events of this period and Dr Kelly's death itself. (I should add that there were other reasons why I wanted to relinquish my role, but this was a major one.)

I did not have long to wait. The forced resignation of Charles Kennedy precipitated a leadership contest, then, naturally, a new team under Sir Menzies Campbell, whom I had backed for the leadership. I turned down the invitation to carry on in my Environment portfolio, and so began a fascinating journey into the unknown, one that would take many peculiar turns.

Before I decided to announce publicly that I intended to begin this investigation, there were two related matters I needed to consider. First, I had to be sure that my constituency work would not be affected. My first duty, after all, is to the people of the Lewes constituency, whom I am proud to represent in Parliament. I decided therefore that I would allocate to my investigations only the time that I had freed up by relinquishing my frontbench role.

Second, there was the impact my work might have on Dr Kelly's family. Mrs Kelly was on record as saying very clearly that she believed that her husband's death was suicide. Furthermore, it must have been very painful for her not only to lose her husband, but to do so in the glare of the world's media. The last thing I wanted to do was to cause the family any further grief, which I recognised might come from further media coverage.

So for a few days, I actively turned the dilemma over in my mind, and asked friends for their advice. Should I abandon the whole idea? On the one side was the fact that a good man had died in a very public way and nobody had been brought to book, whether it was suicide or murder. There was also the fiasco that was the Hutton inquiry, and the clear public mood that this was unfinished business. On the other side was the potential impact on the family.

I decided to publish an article, carried in July 2006 by the *Mail on Sunday*, in which I set out my concerns and initial thoughts, to see what the reaction would be. It was enormous. I received hundreds upon hundreds of letters, emails and phone calls, all bar three supportive of my decision to publish my concerns, and willing me on. This was by far the largest response I had received to anything I had done in my ten years as an MP.

Amongst the contacts, there were about fifty or so which drew attention to curiosities in the case and suggested leads, and a smaller number, around fifteen, that actually provided specific information not hitherto in the public domain. I had to carry on.

At this stage, I want to make clear that I have not sought to get in touch with Mrs Kelly or her daughters, although I do have their contact details. I have assumed that they would get in touch with me if they wanted to. They have not done so, although other members of the family have made contact to offer to help. However, let me say here that if my investigations have caused any distress to Mrs Kelly or her family, then I apologise for that.

I am immensely grateful to the many who have helped me with this book, but particularly my long-suffering researcher Jana Sparks, my good friend Emma Sanderson-Nash, the indefatigable Rowena Thursby, the medical professionals who first raised concerns, and Alan Gordon Walker and Jonathan Wadman at Politico's Publishing. Most of all, I thank my wife Liz for her support. To her I dedicate this book.

Preface

'Not another conspiracy theory!' The cry will go up as this book hits the shops. It will be heard especially from the smart commentators and senior politicians, who will exude an air of experienced superiority over the naïve and gullible who dare to give the time of day to anything the politicos sneeringly call a conspiracy theory. It is the new insult from the established classes.

It is also bad journalism and bad politics.

A conspiracy theory, according to the *Concise Oxford Dictionary*, is 'a belief that some covert but influential agency or organisation is responsible for an unexplained event'.

Does such a concept deserve to be dismissed out of hand? History teaches us otherwise.

• In 1933 the Reichstag building, the seat of the German government, was set alight. This was blamed on the Communists, the ensuing chaos affording the Nazis the opportunity to seize yet more power. In fact the Nazis themselves were responsible for the fire, precisely in order to achieve the double objectives of discrediting the Communists and benefiting themselves.

• CIA archives show that in 1953, the United States and the UK used a 'false flag' operation, Operation Ajax, to overthrow the regime in Iran led by Dr Mohammed Mossadeq. Mossadeq was western educated and pro-American, but had nationalised the oil fields so it was concluded he had to be removed. The tactics employed in Operation Ajax were to carry out acts of terror and blame them on Mossadeq. These included attacking a mosque, machine-gunning civilians and distributing phoney handbills.

• In 1962, recently declassified files show, the United States planned terrorist-type activity under the banner of Operation Northwoods to provoke a war with Cuba. The Joint Chiefs of Staff were 'to indicate brief but precise description of pretexts which they consider would provide justification for US military intervention in Cuba'. The 'cover and deception plan' suggested incidents which would provide this justification. These included blowing up a US ship in Guantanamo Bay and blaming Cuba; developing a 'Communist Cuban terror campaign' on the US mainland; sinking 'a boatload of Cubans en route to Florida (real or simulated)'; 'exploding a few plastic bombs in carefully chosen spots'; and causing the destruction of a US plane in the air. The United States, of course, has long had an obsession with Cuba, and with Fidel Castro in particular. In 2006 Channel 4 ran a programme entitled *638 Ways to Kill Castro*, which revealed the bizarre, almost unbelievable plans drawn up by the United States to try to assassinate him. These included giving him an exploding cigar intended to blow up in his face, placing high explosive in an underwater shell which could be set off while the Cuban leader was scuba-diving nearby, and preparing bacterial poisons to add to his handkerchief.

• In 1967, during the Six Day War, the CIA intelligence ship *Liberty* was bombed by unmarked Israeli planes in an apparent case of mistaken identity. It is now widely accepted that the attack was ordered by President Lyndon Johnson himself. Other US ships in the area were prevented from assisting the ship. The bombing of the *Liberty*, with the loss of thirty-four crew members and the wounding of 171 others, was designed to look like an Egyptian attack, thus giving the United States a pretext to enter the war. This was only averted and the episode ended when a Soviet spy ship appeared on the scene.

But that was then and this is now. Such things don't happen today, do they? Especially not in Britain. It's not as though a Bulgarian could be murdered at a bus stop with a ricin-tipped umbrella, an Italian with close links to the Vatican be found hanging from Blackfriars Bridge, or a Russian dissident be poisoned with radioactive polonium-210 in a Japanese restaurant, is it?

Yet people seem – illogically – to assume that the explanation of a dramatic event will inevitably be obvious and simple, even if tracing the history of that event may well reveal highly complex social and political processes. So the person offering anything other than a two-dimensional explanation for the end point of a three-dimensional sequence is called a conspiracy theorist – just as in the USA Robert Parry was, by colleagues, political opponents and the media alike, when he began uncovering the Iran–Contra affair.

Naturally, if a so-called conspiracy theory is validated, the term is dropped in respect of that particular event. A conspiracy theory must by definition be absurd, and if it turns out to be true, it must be reclassified. It goes without saying that it is enormously helpful to governments to make any challenge to orthodox official explanations politically difficult.

Of course this certainly does not mean that every event has a sinister explanation, that every wild theory must be right. Most will be wrong. But it does mean that those who dismiss so-called conspiracy theories out of hand without even examining the evidence are as sloppy and unprofessional in their approach as those who soak up every such theory without question.

In my investigations into the circumstances surrounding the death of Dr David Kelly, I have accepted without question neither the official version of events nor any alternative explanation. I have sought to examine the facts, to test the evidence, and only to accept that which can be substantiated.

Let the facts speak for themselves.

1 'No indication of any other party being involved'

On 17 July 2003 Prime Minister Tony Blair was in the United States being feted by the US Congress and President Bush. Their adulation was such that he was being offered the rare honour of a Congressional Gold Medal. Naturally enough, Bush and his administration were hugely grateful for the Prime Minister's decision to join the United States in its invasion of Iraq. That invasion was supposed to lead to the discovery and disposal of weapons of mass destruction and make the world a safer place. In the end of course, no such weapons were found. Iraq, four years on, is a ferment of anarchy and violence and the world is immeasurably less safe than it was prior to the invasion.

Meanwhile, as Blair was lapping up the grateful plaudits from the US Congress, the man who had done more than almost any other individual on earth to contain the threat from WMD lay dead in the woods at Harrowdown Hill in Oxfordshire.

For Dr David Kelly, the UK's leading weapons inspector, there was to be no adulation, no medal, no standing ovation. His life ended in the cold lonely wood where he was found the next morning, his left wrist cut open, and three nearly empty blister packs of coproxamol tablets in his jacket pocket.

His death was of course sensational front page news. Dr Kelly, unknown to almost everybody at the beginning of that July, had in recent days barely been absent from media headlines. Much to his chagrin he had been thrust into the harsh glare of publicity, accused of being the mole who expressed to the BBC deep concerns about the government's 'sexing up' of its dossier on weapons of mass destruction.[1]

Had the government indeed misused, exaggerated or even invented intelligence in order to justify the US–UK invasion of Iraq? For Blair the stakes could not have been higher. This was undoubtedly the greatest crisis of his premiership to date.

To add fuel to the flames, Blair's director of communications, Alastair Campbell, and the government had launched an unprecedented and vitriolic attack on the BBC, questioning its integrity and professionalism in the way it reported the doubts expressed by the BBC's source.

It is not surprising therefore that the news of Dr Kelly's death was seen by the wider world largely as a highly political incident, rather than the tragedy that it was for the individual, his family and friends.

The media, the political establishment, indeed almost everybody accepted as fact the suggestion that Dr Kelly had committed suicide. With the political temperature high, media attention was directed towards the consequences for the government, and indeed the BBC, and away from what has subsequently been shown to have been a rather strange death. In all the column inches devoted to this extraordinary episode in the days following Dr Kelly's death, I have not been able to find one journalist who questioned the conclusion that this was an act of suicide, until Peter Hitchens did so in his article of 27 July 2003 in the *Mail on Sunday*. But his was very much a lone voice. The question for the media was not how David Kelly died, but whether Downing Street, through the pressure it had placed on him, had blood on its hands. The lightning speed with which the Prime Minister acted to establish an inquiry into the whole business under Lord Hutton – within hours of Dr Kelly's body being found – further concentrated attention on the politics, and away from the death itself.[2]

The next morning, a Saturday, Dr Kelly's widow, Janice, along with one of their three daughters, was taken in an unmarked police car to the John Radcliffe Memorial Hospital in Oxford, where at 11.25 Mrs Kelly formally identified her husband. Afterwards, at around 2 p.m., Thames Valley Police issued the following statement:

'A post-mortem has revealed that the cause of death was haemorrhaging from a wound to the left wrist. While our enquiries are continuing, there is no indication at this stage of any other party being involved.'

It seemed an uncontroversial statement. Yet in specifying the alleged cause of death, Thames Valley Police were displaying a certainty that on closer examination could not be justified by the facts. It also has to be asked whether determining the circumstances of the death was not a matter that should have been left to the Oxfordshire coroner, Nicholas

Gardiner, or indeed Lord Hutton, given that he had just been tasked with investigating 'the circumstances surrounding the death of Dr David Kelly CMG'.

The official version of events, then, is that Dr Kelly found himself under tremendous personal pressure as a consequence of suddenly becoming front page news. By his own admission, he had discussed the war in Iraq, and specifically the way the available intelligence had been used to justify the invasion, with a number of BBC journalists, including Andrew Gilligan, who was to play such a major part in the whole David Kelly episode. This had led to a very uncomfortable time in a televised session before the Foreign Affairs Committee in the House of Commons on the Tuesday before his death. The pressure continued in the forty-eight hours after that, including demands for further details of his journalist contacts. Dr Kelly feared he had been caught out lying, and, as a man of considerable integrity, felt wretched. He may also have feared he would lose his job when his managers at the Ministry of Defence (MoD) fully established this. Perhaps a call from the ministry on the Thursday confirmed the worst. Perhaps under all this pressure, he buckled and decided to commit suicide.

Having so decided, the official version continues, he then left his house in Southmoor, Oxfordshire, at about 3 p.m. on Thursday 17 July 2003, taking with him a knife he had had since boyhood and thirty coproxamol tablets. He took a familiar path into an area of woodland he knew well, and then, in a secluded and private spot, cut his wrist and swallowed twenty-nine of the thirty tablets he had brought. His body was officially discovered at around 8.30 the following morning.

Lord Hutton summarised the death thus in his report:

> In the light of the evidence which I have heard I am satisfied that Dr Kelly took his own life in the wood at Harrowdown Hill at a time between 4.15 p.m. on 17 July and 1.15 a.m. on 18 July 2003 and that the principal cause of death was bleeding from incised wounds to the left wrist which Dr Kelly inflicted upon himself with the knife found beside the body. It is probable that the ingestion of an excess amount of Coproxamol tablets coupled with apparently clinically silent coronary artery disease would both have played a part in bringing about death more certainly and more rapidly than would otherwise have been the case. Accordingly the causes of death are:
>
> 1a   Haemorrhage
> 1b   Incised wounds to the left wrist
> 2   Coproxamol ingestion and coronary artery atherosclerosis.[3]

Lord Hutton went on to say that he was satisfied no third party was involved, that it was 'highly unlikely' that a third party could have forced Dr Kelly to swallow a large number of coproxamol tablets, and that Dr Kelly was suffering from no 'significant mental illness' at the time of his death.

That, then, is the official version. It is faulty and suspect in virtually all important respects, as we shall see.

David Christopher Kelly was born in the Rhondda valley on 14 May 1944. His father, the son of a coal miner, was then a signals officer in the RAF. His mother, the daughter of a gravestone sculptor, was a schoolteacher. They were married in Pontypridd just after Christmas in 1940, and later moved to Tunbridge Wells. Within two years, however, his parents were divorced, and David, their only child, was taken back to live in Pontypridd with his mother and his grandmother, Ceinwen Williams. Friends at school remember him talking warmly of his grandmother, but rarely of either parent.

His father married another woman, Flora Dunn, just two weeks after his divorce was made official. She was ten years his junior. Together they settled in Kettering and started a new family. He became head teacher at a local school. Eventually they had three children, and adopted a fourth, but David was never asked to live with them. His father died of lung cancer, aged sixty-six.

His relationship with his mother appears to have been little better. It must still have been traumatic for him, however, when she was found dead at her cottage in Pontypridd on 13 May 1964, the day before his twentieth birthday. Aged just forty-seven, she had taken an overdose of sleeping pills.

The question inevitably arises whether this tragic incident was in Dr Kelly's mind on 17 July 2003. It turns out that the subject of his mother's suicide came up in conversation many years later with a close friend, another weapons inspector, whose brother had recently taken his own life. It was at that point that Dr Kelly revealed that his mother had also died by her own hand. His tone, by all accounts, was slightly dispassionate and quite balanced. No-one can say with certainty that this tragic incident in Dr Kelly's youth did not prey on his mind throughout his life, but his colleague was given no impression that it did so. It had certainly affected him deeply at the time.

David Kelly's answer to his emotionally difficult childhood appears to have been to throw himself into his work, an approach that persisted throughout his life. At grammar school, he rose to become head boy, and his application also led him to excel in athletics. He went on to study bacteriology at Leeds University, where he met his wife to be, Janice, a student teacher. They were married near her family home in Crewe in 1967. He was twenty-three, and she twenty-two. The couple were to have three daughters: Rachel and Ellen, who were twins, and Sian.

Leeds was followed by Birmingham, where David took another degree, followed by time at Oxford, where he studied for his doctorate. The family moved to Oxfordshire in 1974.

His career in the public sector began in 1973, when he was appointed as a senior scientific officer in the Unit of Invertebrate Virology at the National Environment Research Establishment, a post he held for eleven years, including a promotion to the post of principal scientific officer in 1982. During his time there, he specialised in the field of biological control applicable to agriculture, in particular the use of viruses to attack insect pests.

In July 1984 Dr Kelly joined the Ministry of Defence as head of what was then the Chemical Defence Establishment at Porton Down, near Salisbury. He led the research into ways to enhance the defence of troops in battle against biological warfare. This research proved particularly useful in the field in 1991, during the war over Kuwait. He also directed the decontamination of Gruinard Island, off the north-west coast of Scotland, used in the Second World War to test anthrax weapons.

His first involvement in the murky world of weapons inspection came in 1989, when he was used as a technical expert to assess the disturbing data then emanating from the Soviet Union, largely through defectors such as Vladimir Pasechnik. From 1991 onwards, David Kelly began to participate in on-site inspections abroad, and soon proved his worth, through both his expertise and his approach. He was rewarded in 1992 with an individual merit promotion to Grade 5. In simple terms, this gives the recipient the freedom to focus on research without the responsibility for managerial work normally associated with a Grade 5 employee. In July of that year, he was appointed senior adviser in biological defence at Porton Down. From 1992 onwards, Dr Kelly increasingly found himself working on inspection duties for the United

Nations Special Commission, and was appointed senior adviser to that body in 1995.

In April 1996, Dr Kelly was seconded to the MoD's Proliferation and Arms Control Secretariat, also working as an adviser to the non-proliferation department of the Foreign and Commonwealth Office on Iraq's chemical and biological weapons capabilities. He briefed both the Defence Intelligence Staff and MI6 on these matters. Significantly, given subsequent events, he was also expressly tasked with communicating information relating to Iraq's weapons activities to the media. Additionally, Dr Kelly contributed to the work of the United Nations Monitoring Verification and Inspection Commission, advising on chemical and biological weapons and helping to train weapons inspectors.

Less publicly, part of Dr Kelly's work involved liaising with the Rockingham Cell, described by US weapons inspector Scott Ritter as a 'secretive intelligence activity buried inside the Defense Intelligence Staff which dealt with Iraqi weapons of mass destruction and activities of the UN Special Commission'.[4] It has also been referred to by Michael Meacher MP as a 'clearing house' which received and analysed intelligence data on Iraqi capabilities.[5] And according to the *Sunday Times* journalist Nick Rufford, Dr Kelly had 'sometimes [been] an undercover man for the intelligence services'.[6]

David Kelly had come a long way. As we shall see, he had established himself as the leading weapons inspector in the UK, and possibly in the world. He was highly respected both by those he worked alongside and those he challenged, in countries such as Russia and Iraq.

In 1996, his 'service in relation to foreign affairs' led to his becoming a Companion of the Order of St Michael and St George (CMG) in the Queen's Birthday honours list of that year. Before the events of July 2003 overtook him, he was being actively considered for a knighthood.[7] It would have been a fitting crown to his career, as he contemplated retirement. But it was not to be.

Aged fifty-nine, Dr David Kelly was dead, alone on Harrowdown Hill.

2 'Was Kelly murdered?'

The headline screamed out from the London *Evening Standard* on Tuesday 27 January 2004. It followed the publication, with somewhat less fanfare, it has to be said, in that morning's *Guardian* of a letter from three specialist medical professionals, questioning the conclusion that David Kelly had committed suicide. The letter was signed by David Halpin, a specialist in trauma and orthopaedic surgery, Stephen Frost, a specialist in diagnostic radiology, and Searle Sennett, a specialist in anaesthesiology.

Throughout 2004, further letters to the *Guardian* would follow in which other health professionals expressed their doubts about the verdict. These would include John Scurr and Chris Burns-Cox, respectively specialists in vascular surgery in internal general medicine. By the end of the year, the medical experts numbered ten, and they were joined by Michael Powers, a leading QC with particular knowledge of coronial matters, and one Rowena Thursby. Together, they formed a loose association called the Kelly Investigation Group. What links them are the significant doubts they hold about the official explanation given for the death of Dr Kelly, and the affront they feel at the way the whole Hutton inquiry was handled.

The group had originally been assembled by Ms Thursby, who had first raised her doubts about the official process in two articles she had posted on the internet, which attracted the attention of medical professionals. Gradually, the group had increased in size.

Ms Thursby is a remarkable woman. Despite suffering from a painful, chronic neuro-immune condition that means any trip out, even to the local shopping centre, can exhaust her for days afterwards, she has tenaciously probed away into the circumstances surrounding the death, asking questions, posting pieces on the internet, and generally keeping the issue on the radar. She is able to do so successfully, of course, because there are so many loose ends, so many contradictions, so many curiosities in the evidence that has been made public.

The doubts of the medical experts would, however, take centre stage only briefly in the media, for the following day, 28 January, the conclusions of the much awaited Hutton report appeared on the front page of the *Sun*, ahead of the official publication time, and the attention of the media and politicians alike reverted to where it had been during the previous six months, namely fixed on the political implications of Dr Kelly's death for the government and the BBC. Lord Hutton's unbelievably one-sided report, which castigated the BBC and gave the government a clean bill of health, led shortly afterwards to the resignations of the BBC's chairman and its director general, Gavyn Davies and Greg Dyke respectively.[1] Andrew Gilligan, the reporter at the centre of the controversy, would follow shortly afterwards.[2] No minister from the government resigned, or even apologised for any actions they had taken, though it might be argued that Alastair Campbell's resignation the summer before had been precipitated by these events, though that had been officially denied.

There was some suspicion at the time that the publication of the Hutton report's main findings in the *Sun* had been deliberately engineered in order to deflect attention from the *Evening Standard*'s front page the previous evening, or at the very least that it represented some dark trading between Campbell and the government's favourite paper. In fact, neither of these two explanations is true. The scoop was actually secured thanks to an enterprising piece of work by the affable *Sun* journalist Dave Wooding, who thus earned himself a nice bonus. In the paper itself, though, Trevor Kavanagh, the political editor, got the byline and the credit.

The publication of the Hutton report, coming as it did swiftly on the heels of the doubts expressed by the health professionals, was unfortunate in its timing, for the objections that had been raised to Lord Hutton's opinion that Dr Kelly's death was suicide were serious ones and deserved much fuller consideration than they were given. In their letter to the *Guardian*, the three medical experts described as 'highly improbable' the suggestion that Dr Kelly had bled to death by a self-inflicted wound to his left wrist. At the Hutton inquiry, the pathologist employed to carry out the post-mortem, Dr Nicholas Hunt, stated that only one artery had been cut in Dr Kelly's wrist, the ulnar artery. As the letter to the paper pointed out, arteries in the wrist are of matchstick thickness and severing one of them does not lead to life-threatening blood loss.

John Scurr, the specialist in vascular surgery who added his name to what was by then the sixth letter from medical experts to the *Guardian* in 2004, told me that in his opinion, it was just about possible to die from a cut to the ulnar artery, if the artery were sliced away at, but not if it were cut transversely, as we are told was the case here. David Halpin, the former senior orthopaedic and trauma surgeon at Torbay Hospital and at the Princess Elizabeth Orthopaedic Hospital in Exeter, believes even the deepest cut to this artery would not have caused death. 'A transected artery, one that has been completely cut, retracts immediately and thus stops bleeding, even at a relatively high blood pressure,' he told me.

So it is extremely difficult to kill yourself by cutting your wrist. Of course, people can die from wrist or arm cutting, but it requires some basic medical knowledge to be successful. The cut should be lengthwise along the arm rather than across the wrist, and even then it is likely to result in death only if the person concerned is sitting in a warm bath. Others, with less medical knowledge, will tend to slit their wrists crosswise, thereby severing the radial artery. Neither group would actually choose to sever the ulnar artery. The choice of this artery would make sense, however, if the hand were held by another, and the cut administered by that person.

There is a further consideration which argues against the suggestion that the cutting of the ulnar artery would be a chosen method of suicide. The artery in question is hidden deep in the wrist on the little finger side of the hand, and can only be accessed by cutting through nerves and tendons, an extremely painful process. It is not common for those who commit suicide to wish to inflict significant pain upon themselves as part of the execution of that process.

Certainly the incidence of individuals dying from a severed ulnar artery is a rarity according to official statistics. Karen Dunnell, the national statistician, confirmed to me in writing that there had been only six individuals who had died from injury to the ulnar artery between 1997 and 2004. Of these, three were suicides, two accidents, and one had 'an underlying cause of injury of undetermined intent'. Only one such death occurred in 2003, the year of Dr Kelly's death.

The information provided by the national statistician comes from tables provided by the *International Statistical Classification of Diseases*.[3] An examination of these tables shows that in fact the only person to have died in 2003 from injury to the ulnar artery was aged 25–29. There are three individuals aged 55–59 who are shown as having died from 'injuries to the wrist and hand' so it is possible that Dr Kelly's death was categorised thus. There is also one from that age bracket listing as having died from 'superficial injury of wrist and hand, unspecified' and two from 'open wound of wrist and hand part, part unspecified': just six out of a total of 12,286 deaths of men aged 55–59 in 2003.

The official statistics take cause of death from the death certificate and, as we have seen, that gave the primary cause of death as 'haemorrhage' and 'incised wounds to left wrist'. The fact remains that however the death has been categorised, mortalities due to wrist and hand injuries are extremely rare.

For the general public, the suggestion that someone may have died from slashing their wrists will come as no great surprise. It has, after all, been the staple diet of books, films and television programmes over the last century or so. In fact, official figures show that cutting any part of one's body open is a relatively rare method of achieving suicide. In the UK in 2003, there were a total of 4,659 suicides, including 'injuries of undetermined intent', of which just 236 were of men aged 55–59. Of the 4,659, 126 were classified under the heading 'contact with sharp object'. By far the most successful methods chosen were hanging, strangulation and suffocation, responsible for 1,921 suicides, and drug-related poisonings, responsible for 1,159.

Further evidence for the ineffectiveness of wrist or arm cutting as a method of attempting suicide comes form a report produced in 1998 by Geoffrey McKee, 'Lethal versus Nonlethal Suicide Attempts in Jail',[4] which analysed suicide attempt reports from all South Carolina jails between 1985 and 1994. The report shows that, perhaps in line with public misconceptions, wrist or arm cutting was the second most common method chosen by inmates in attempts to end their lives. In fact 275 prisoners, 28.7 per cent of the total, attempted suicide in this way. The figures also show, however, that only one death resulted from these 275 attempts. Other methods chosen, most notably hanging and swallowing substances, were statistically much more successful.

In psychological terms, those who choose to slit their wrists may frequently be making a cry for help, rather than seriously attempting to kill themselves. In Dr Kelly's case, the unlikelihood of the proposition that he would attempt to kill himself by cutting this artery is further compounded by the weapon he apparently chose for this purpose. This was, we are told, a blunt concave pruning knife, one with a little hook or lip towards the top of the blade. The use of such a knife would only have increased the pain and would also have failed to cut the artery cleanly, thereby hastening the clotting process and so limiting the loss of blood further.

The knife in question had in fact been owned by Dr Kelly since his boyhood, so it might just be argued that the use of this particular weapon was chosen for sentimental rather than practical reasons. Nevertheless the sheer inappropriateness of this particular knife makes it difficult to believe that Dr Kelly would have acted in this way. Furthermore, we were to learn from the pathologist, Nicholas Hunt, that the wound to Dr Kelly's wrist showed 'crushed edges', suggesting that the knife was blunt. This made it an even more inappropriate weapon to choose. A further objection is that Dr Kelly undoubtedly knew more about the human anatomy than most people, and the idea that he would have chosen such an uncertain and painful method to commit suicide is not easy to sustain.

It might be argued that Dr Kelly did not leave his house in Southmoor that Thursday afternoon with the intention of committing suicide, but that a black mood came upon him in the woods and the decision was spontaneous. He then found that the only weapon to hand was this knife and used it as best he could to effect that purpose. This theory, however, simply does not hold water, if we are also to believe that Dr Kelly brought with him from his cottage thirty coproxamol tablets, which, according to the official version of events, were used either to dull the pain of the incision or to provide a second parallel method of achieving suicide. The presence of the coproxamol tablets, if they are part of a suicide plan on Dr Kelly's part, clearly implies premeditation.

Coproxamol is itself a frequent cause of death, either by suicide or by unintentional overdosing, often in association with alcohol. Between 1997 and 1999 there were on average 255 deaths per year by coproxamol poisoning in England and Wales. Discounting those deaths where accidental overdosing is thought to be the explanation, coproxamol is still associated with 5 per cent of all suicides in that period. It was in fact the second most commonly used drug in overdose suicides.

Dr Kelly, we are told, removed from his house three blister packs, each containing ten coproxamol tablets, whose active ingredients were 325 milligrams of paracetamol and 32.5 milligrams of dextropropoxyphene. Police investigations confirmed that the tablets came from the same batch as the ones Janice Kelly had at home (although this batch ran to

1,600,000), who had been taking them for her arthritis, so it seems likely that they were taken from their house.

We are told that the police found that twenty-nine of the tablets had been removed from their trays – doubtless the one that David Kelly thoughtfully left helped the police with their enquiries. Dr Kelly had apparently also very considerately replaced the empty blister packs inside the pocket of his wax jacket, found at the scene. The clear implication therefore was that Dr Kelly had consumed the twenty-nine tablets. Subsequent medical tests, however, revealed the presence of only the equivalent of a fifth of one tablet in his stomach. Even allowing for natural metabolising, these two figures cannot easily be reconciled. There were vomit stains visible on his face when the body was found, though as far as we can tell, no analysis of them was carried out to establish the contents of the vomit. In any case, if the tablets had been regurgitated, they can hardly have been a contributory factor in his death.

Alexander Allan, the forensic toxicologist at the Hutton inquiry, gave evidence that although levels of coproxamol in the blood were higher than therapeutic levels, the blood level of each of the drug's two main components – paracetamol and dextropropoxyphene – was less than a third of what would normally be found in a fatal overdose.[5] Furthermore, it is generally accepted that concentrations of a drug in the blood can increase by as much as tenfold after death, leaving open the possibility that Dr Kelly consumed only a thirtieth of the dose of coproxamol necessary to kill him.

But just as there were objections to the alleged choice of weapon by Dr Kelly, so too is there an objection to his apparent use of coproxamol tablets. Mai Pederson, who serves in the US Army, had been a close friend of Dr Kelly's since 1999. She has said on record that Dr Kelly had an aversion to swallowing tablets. If this is right, we are then being asked to believe that Dr Kelly indulged in a further masochistic act in an attempt to take his life.

Rowena Thursby has learned of an occasion when Ms Pederson was at the Kelly house in Southmoor and was actually offered coproxamol tablets by Janice Kelly to help relieve some pains she was experiencing. Ms Pederson accepted, but Dr Kelly criticised his wife for offering tablets prescribed for her alone. If true, this can only reinforce the doubts that exist that Dr Kelly would actually have chosen to ingest twenty-nine of these tablets.

A further objection is that police evidence states that there was a half-litre bottle of Evian water by the body which had not been fully drunk.[6] Common sense tells us that quite a lot of water would be required to swallow twenty-nine tablets, particularly ones such as these, oval with a long axis of about half an inch. It is frankly unlikely, with only a small water bottle to hand, that any water would have been left undrunk. In addition, Roy Green, the forensic biologist who was called to the scene at Harrowdown Hill on the Friday, told the inquiry that 'when people are injured and losing blood they will become thirsty'.[7] He thought it very likely that Dr Kelly would have drunk water after cutting himself, if that is what happened, thereby reducing further the amount that would have been consumed to swallow the twenty-nine tablets. He confirmed that there were blood smears on the water bottle.

Nor is death from coproxamol overdose a quick and painless experience. According to the Medicines and Health Care Products Regulatory Agency, early symptoms include severe respiratory depression and convulsions. Pallor, nausea and vomiting may persist for twenty-four hours and psychotic reactions may occur. After between one and three days, features of hepatic necrosis (death of the liver tissue) may appear, followed by jaundice. It is a slow and painful way to go. Coproxamol is undergoing a phased withdrawal, to be completed by the end of 2007.[8]

At the very least, Dr Kelly would have known that to overdose on coproxamol could have left him alive but medically damaged. Would he have wanted to risk creating such a burden for either himself or his family? Similarly, he would have known that to cut the ulnar artery could well have left him alive, suffering in extreme pain and with a hole in his wrist. Interestingly, the *Times* of Saturday 19 July 2003 quoted 'a police source' as saying that they 'had ruled out an overdose, or use of a gun in the death'. It seems they too were unconvinced by the argument that he could have been killed by coproxamol poisoning.

If David Kelly had genuinely wanted to commit suicide, he would have made sure that his chosen method was an effective one. Are we really expected to believe that someone of the knowledge and maturity of David Kelly would have decided upon such an inept, uncertain and painful way to kill himself?

Medical experts have also seriously questioned the amount of blood which Dr Kelly actually lost. An adult human body contains about eight pints of blood, of which about half has to be lost to cause death. The effects of four pints of blood spurting from a body cannot be hidden. Yet the two searchers who found the body initially did not even notice that Dr Kelly had apparently incised his wrist with a knife. In addition, the two paramedics who arrived on the scene shortly afterwards pointedly referred to the fact that there was remarkably little blood around the body when they subsequently gave evidence to the Hutton inquiry.[9] One of the paramedics, Vanessa Hunt, was not asked about this, but volunteered her view anyway. She told Lord Hutton:

> The amount of blood that was around the scene seemed relatively minimal and there was a small patch on his right knee, but no obvious arterial bleeding. There was no spraying of blood or huge blood loss or any obvious loss on the clothing . . . There was dried blood on the left wrist . . . but no obvious sign of a wound or anything, it was just dried blood.[10]

Ms Hunt's colleague, Dave Bartlett, confirmed her observations, reporting no blood stains on the clothes apart from a one-inch stain on the trousers over the right knee, the likely result of Dr Kelly kneeling in blood.[11]

Dr Bill McQuillan, a former consultant at Edinburgh's Royal Infirmary, ran a clinic on peripheral nerve injuries for twenty years, which dealt with quite a few patients with arterial injuries. He told the *Daily Express*:

> Arterial bleeding is quite dramatic. In surgery you have to divide small arteries from time to time, and blood sprays out like a kid's water pistol. What you see is a pump action with each beat of the heart and I have known it hit the ceiling. If the bleeding was as small as alleged, that is astonishing.[12]

Lord Hutton was to place considerable emphasis on his evidence of Roy Green, the forensic biologist who testified at the inquiry. Mr Green confirmed that a cut to an artery would indeed have led to blood spraying out, as Dr McQuillan would later suggest. He termed the phenomenon 'arterial rain', and said there was evidence of blood deposits on the nearby nettles. It is possible but unlikely that the blood may have spurted out in a fountain-like manner, thereby leaving the clothes relatively untouched.

Nicholas Hunt, the inquiry pathologist, told the inquiry that in his view the injuries to the wrist had been inflicted a matter of minutes before his death. He gauged this by observing what he called 'a well-developed vital reaction',[13] which he explained as the body's response to an area of damage, in this case reddening and swelling around the area of the left wrist. We are thus led to conclude that the blood loss was so enormous, and the rate of loss so fast, that Dr Kelly died in minutes following the cut to the tiny ulnar artery, yet with the paramedics observing how little blood there was around, and with Dr Kelly's clothes largely unspoilt.

David Halpin told me that even if you knew enough about the human body to choose the most effective artery to sever, probably the groin, it would still take well over half an hour to die. It is, he suggested, well-nigh impossible to die by severing the ulnar artery alone, and certainly not within a matter of minutes. 'Surgeons know rather more about arteries than pathologists do,' was how he rather witheringly put it to me.

Yet if this cut was not the cause of death, then the clear implication is that he died from a different cause, with the cut to the wrist merely there to provide a diversion.

The conclusions from this are clear. Either Dr Kelly did not lose very much blood, which is after all consistent with a cut to the ulnar artery, whether before or after death, and so died from a different cause. Or he did lose the required amount to cause death but that this happened elsewhere and his body was moved to the location in which he was found. Both scenarios imply the involvement of another party. Neither was properly considered by the Hutton inquiry.

So concerned were the ambulance crew, Dave Bartlett and Vanessa Hunt, both paramedics for more than fifteen years at the time, that in December 2004 they went on record in an interview with the respected *Observer* journalist Antony Barnett to question the official version of events.

'There wasn't a puddle of blood around,' Ms Hunt told the reporter. 'There was a little bit of blood on the nettles to the left of his left arm. But there was no real blood on the body of the shirt. The only other bit of blood I saw was on his clothing. It was the size of a 50p piece above the right knee on his trousers . . . When somebody cuts an artery, whether accidentally or intentionally, the blood pumps everywhere. I just think it is incredibly unlikely that he died from the wrist wound we saw.' She also revealed that there was no blood at all on his right hand. 'I didn't see any blood on his right hand . . . If he used his right hand to cut his wrist, from an arterial wound you would expect some spray.'

The two paramedics told Mr Barnett that over the years they had raced to the scenes of dozens of suicide attempts where someone had slit their wrists. In only one case had the victim been successful. Referring to that occasion, Ms Hunt said: 'That was like a slaughterhouse. Just think what it would be like with five or six pints of milk splashed everywhere.'[14]

Nor has time changed their views. Mr Bartlett told me that they 'stand by everything we have said 100 per cent'.

The inquiry was not told how much blood Dr Kelly was estimated to have lost, despite this being a key statistic. Indeed, it is not even clear if this figure was established, though it is not particularly difficult to do so. An objective method used is first

25

to measure the blood volume in the body. Next, an analysis of the soil into which the blood would supposedly have soaked can have the haemoglobin leeched out and measured. It is not clear if this was done.

There is one further oddity related to the blood, referred to by Ms Hunt above, namely the blood mark on Dr Kelly's right knee. Roy Green, in his evidence, referred to this as a 'contact blood stain', brought about, he suggested, by Dr Kelly kneeling in a pool of blood. Quite why, having cut his wrist, he would then need to get up from either his lying or his sitting position to kneel is far from clear.

As well as the incision to the wrist and the ingestion of coproxamol tablets, both the official death certificate and Lord Hutton refer in passing to Dr Kelly's alleged heart condition. It is worth noting that Dr Kelly's own GP, Dr Malcolm Warner, who was called to give evidence at the Hutton inquiry, appeared to know nothing about this. To the question 'Were you aware of any serious medical condition from which Dr Kelly suffered?', he answered with a simple 'No'.[15] Indeed, his evidence revealed that Dr Kelly had less than two weeks before his death, on 8 July, undergone a medical for the Ministry of Defence in preparation for yet another trip to Iraq. That medical revealed no problems and he was cleared to go. His general state of health was said to have been good. Dr Warner had not been consulted by David Kelly since 1999. It is indeed a mystery how both Lord Hutton and the coroner were able to discover that Dr Kelly suffered from 'coronary artery atherosclerosis', or hardened arteries, when this fact appeared to have bypassed both his own GP and those carrying out the MoD medical.

Dr Nicholas Hunt was the pathologist chosen by the Oxfordshire coroner, Nicholas Gardiner, to undertake the post-mortem and associated matters, and who advised that the causes of death were those which duly appeared on the death certificate.

Of the forty-three names on the Home Office register of forensic pathologists deemed to have sufficient qualifications, training and experience, to be instructed in cases of suspicious or violent death, Dr Hunt's was one of the most recent additions, having been added only in 2001. The list included many far more experienced pathologists, some of whom had been entered on the register as far back as 1978. It is curious therefore that the Oxfordshire coroner should have made this choice, particularly as this was an extremely high-profile death commanding front-page headlines. Under the circumstances, Mr Gardiner could have been forgiven for employing the most experienced pathologist he could find from the register, or even employing two such people.

Dr Hunt arrived at the spot where Dr Kelly lay at around noon on the Friday, some two and a half hours after the corpse was first discovered. It must be said that, given the sensational and highly political environment surrounding this death, he might perhaps have been expected to arrive rather more promptly. He approached the body and began a visual examination and confirmed death some twenty-five minutes later. He did not carry out a more detailed examination until a further hour and a half had passed, after the fingertip search conducted by the police had been completed. By this point, a scene tent had been erected. The police erected two tents, a blue one over the body and a white one on the edge of the wood, which provided a place to fill in paperwork out of wind or rain.

Dr Hunt told the inquiry that the procedure he adopted was to retrieve as much trace evidence as possible, including looking for fibres, or DNA contamination by a third party. He also at that stage noticed an area of blood staining to the left side of the body, across the undergrowth in the soil. It is not clear how much blood may have caused this area of staining, nor even if it matched Dr Kelly's DNA, though we are implicitly invited to assume it does.

In order to place the time of death accurately, it is standard practice to take the rectal temperature of a body as soon as possible. As the body cools towards the temperature of the surrounding environment, it becomes increasingly difficult to be specific about the time of death. Oddly, having arrived at noon, and begun his detailed examination at around 2 p.m., it was not until 7.15 that Dr Hunt actually took the rectal temperature, just four minutes before he left. As a consequence he was able to provide the inquiry with only a very wide window within which death may have occurred, namely between 4.15 p.m. on the Thursday and 1.15 a.m. on the Friday. Dr Hunt arrived at this window by estimating that death occurred between eighteen and twenty-seven hours prior to taking the rectal temperature. The fact that his estimate is based on this observation serves only to reinforce the importance of this procedure in determining time of death. Why did he not take the temperature as soon as he had access to the body?

Another method to help determine time of death is the test for livor mortis, or post-mortem lividity. Upon death, with the heart no longer pumping, the blood begins to settle in the lower part of the body, and the denser red cells sink through the blood by the force of gravity, causing a purplish-red discolouration of the skin. Livor mortis starts between twenty minutes and three hours after death, and is congealed in the capillaries in four to five hours. Maximum lividity occurs within six to twelve hours.

Dr Hunt told the Hutton inquiry that he found livor mortis to be a clear post-mortem feature. Yet if Dr Kelly died from a massive loss of blood, as we are told he did, then significant livor mortis simply would not have occurred. Put simply, there would not have been enough blood.

We might reasonably expect to draw inferences from the tests normally carried out following a death of uncertain cause. Yet it is not clear whether such standard tests were undertaken, and, if they were, the results were not reported to the Hutton inquiry. Incredibly, nothing is said in evidence in respect of the onset of rigor mortis, though such an indicator is surely standard in such investigations.

Rigor mortis begins to set in after six hours at the latest, and within eight to twelve hours the body is completely stiff. It then remains stiff for a further twelve hours or so, before the process begins to reverse. It follows therefore that a standard assessment of rigor mortis could have helped to narrow down the time of death more accurately. Why was this not done? We do know, however, that the paramedics had to move Dr Kelly's arm off his chest. That would suggest that rigor mortis had not fully set in at that point, placing the time of death early on the Friday morning. If that was the case, where was Dr Kelly in the ten or more hours between leaving his house and his death?

It is also unclear if a full battery of tests were done on the lungs, the blood, the heart or the soil. Dr Hunt's report does not even provide an estimate of the residual blood volume in the body, a key indicator in helping to establish if Dr Kelly did indeed bleed to death. These are all crucial pieces of forensic evidence that are simply missing. Why were they not produced, and why did neither Lord Hutton nor the inquiry QC, James Dingemans, seek to elicit them?

We know that Dr Hunt did retain a lung and some blood to test for volatile substances such as chloroform, in order to establish whether or not Dr Kelly might have been over-powered, but Assistant Chief Constable Michael Page, who also gave evidence at the Hutton inquiry, revealed that the tests to the lung had not actually been carried out. This was, he said, because no such substances had shown up in the blood tests.

It is unclear whether the tests that were carried out on the blood were arranged to check for the presence of any other substances that might have been introduced to the body to cause death, or whether the presence of any such substances would have been revealed by the tests for volatile substances that were undertaken. In addition, Alex Allan, the appointed toxicologist, analysed blood and urine for a range of medications and hard drugs.

In contrast with his leisurely arrival on the scene and approach to establishing the time of death, Dr Hunt's examination of the body at Oxford's John Radcliffe Hospital was a relatively speedy affair. It lasted less than three hours and was over by quarter past midnight.

Unfortunately, the level of detail of these matters revealed at the Hutton inquiry is limited. As James Dingemans himself put it, when questioning Dr Hunt, 'I am not going to trouble you with the details of the toxicology report.'[16] Worryingly, the pathologist was not even subject to any cross-examination, despite the curious aspects of the case. Even when Dr Hunt himself made interesting observations, they were not followed through by Lord Hutton or Mr Dingemans, but instead left hanging in the air. For example, Dr Hunt was asked at the end of giving evidence if he could tell from his examination if there were any signs of a third-party involvement in Dr Kelly's death. His intriguing answer was: 'The features are quite typical, I would say, of self-inflicted injury, if one ignores all the other features of the case.'

Dr Hunt was not asked what these features were. Instead, Mr Dingemans asked him if there was anything further he would like to say on the circumstances leading to Dr Kelly's death. His answer was enigmatic: 'Nothing I could say as a pathologist, no.' Did no-one think to ask him what he meant by this remark?

To be fair to Dr Hunt, even he would later express doubts about the inquiry process that had been adopted, and he subsequently suggested, in a telephone conversation with Channel 4 in March 2004, that the coroner's inquest, which had been suspended when the Hutton inquiry was set up, should be reconvened.

On that point at least, he was exactly right.

3 'Tired, subdued but not depressed'

The village of Kingston Bagpuize lies about seven miles south-west of Oxford, and rather less distance west of Abingdon. The A420, which used to run through the village, has for some time now followed the route of a bypass to the north, leaving the old road relatively light of traffic. Kingston Bagpuize runs west into another village, Southmoor, so that you can't see the join. Together they create a not unpleasant, but hardly distinguished settlement that hugs the old main road like a genteel ribbon development.

At the far end of Southmoor opposite the pub, the Waggon and Horses, was where David and Janice Kelly lived. The house has now been sold and Mrs Kelly has relocated within the village to a less public location. It was from their house that Dr Kelly set off for his last walk that fateful Thursday afternoon, just after 3 p.m. He took regular walks to help his bad back. According to Mrs Kelly, these were normally short affairs lasting between fifteen and twenty-five minutes.

It is not clear what route he took from his house, but he was seen by a villager, Ruth Absalom, shortly afterwards, about three quarters of a mile from his house, at the top of Harris's

Lane. She described him as 'just like his normal self, no different to any other time when I have met him'. They chatted for about five minutes before going their separate ways. His last words to her, she told the Hutton inquiry, were, 'See you again then, Ruth.'

Asked at the Hutton inquiry in which direction Dr Kelly walked off, she said, 'I suppose he went to my right, along the road to Kingston Bagpuize I suppose in the end, if he had gone round that way, but obviously he was going down to the fields down the road or down to the fields down the back.'[1] Admittedly, this statement is not entirely clear, but if he had gone off to the right down the isolated Appleton Road towards Kingston Bagpuize, that would be consistent with a half-hour walk, as part of a circular route back to his house. It would also be in quite the wrong direction to reach Harrowdown Hill.

The only other person who may have seen Dr Kelly that afternoon was a close family friend, local farmer Paul Weaving. He was not close enough to speak to Dr Kelly, but recognised him walking in the fields towards Harrowdown Hill, and they waved to each other.

This recollection appeared in the media only subsequently, and is denied by Mr Weaving, who told Rowena Thursby in an email that 'the early reports were wrong. I did not see David on the day he went missing.' However, Susan Melling, the wife of a local councillor, is quoted as saying that 'Mr Weaving called round and told us what had happened . . . He said he had seen Dr Kelly on his walk on Thursday afternoon, because he was near his farmland at the time.'[2] Nevertheless, it is possible that it may have influenced Ms Absalom's evidence, which seems inherently contradictory in referring both to the road to Kingston Bagpuize and to the fields.

The published list of documentary evidence from Thames Valley Police includes no record of any statement being taken from Mr Weaving. Nor did he give evidence at the Hutton inquiry. That the police did not see fit to pursue the newspaper reports, suggesting that Mr Weaving may have been the last person to see Dr Kelly alive, provides yet another clear example of just how slipshod and unprofessional this inquiry was to be.

When Mrs Kelly came to give evidence to the inquiry, a curious arrangement was agreed upon, doubtless to protect her from unwanted media attention. She sat in a back room and answered questions live. All that could be seen of her, however, was a picture, to accompany her spoken word. The conveyance of meaning through expression and bodily movements, a key part of communication, was therefore lost both to Mrs Kelly and to those listening to her.

In her evidence to the inquiry, Mrs Kelly said that on the Thursday morning when they rose, about 8.30, her husband was 'tired, subdued, but not depressed'. By 12.30, she told Lord Hutton, a 'huge headache' was upon her, and she began to feel sick. 'In fact I was physically sick several times at this stage because he looked so desperate.' Yet nothing in her evidence tells of any startling event in the intervening time that should have changed his mood so dramatically. Indeed, the evidence from Dr Kelly's emails written that morning suggests that his mood was, if anything, upbeat.

A typical email was that sent to Geeta Kingdon, a local Baha'i contact, at 11.18 a.m.: 'Many thanks for your thoughts. It has been difficult. Hopefully will all blow over by the end of the week and I can travel to Baghdad and get on with the real work.'[3] Indeed, so keen was Dr Kelly to get back to Iraq that he discussed a date with Wing Commander John Clark of the Ministry of Defence when he could return. The ministry booked a flight for him the following Friday, 25 July. His diary, recovered by the police, shows that the trip had been entered for that day.[4]

It must be said that none of this fits with the profile of a man about to commit suicide. People about to kill themselves do not generally first book an airline ticket for a flight they have no intention of taking. It seems more logical therefore to conclude that Mrs Kelly's nausea was more to do with her own headache than any portent emanating from her husband.

Mrs Kelly was asked how she would describe him at 12.30 that day. She replied: 'Oh, I just thought he had a broken heart. He really was very, very . . . he had shrunk into himself . . . I had no idea at that stage what he might do later, absolutely no idea at all.'[5] In terms of evidence, this is clearly reinterpreting what was to pass with the benefit of subsequent knowledge of the official explanation for her husband's death. The statement in fact tells us that at the time, nothing had happened to suggest to her that her husband might commit suicide. When he announced that he intended to go for a walk, her response was not one of trepidation for what might happen, but an entirely normal one of simply noting this.

Mrs Kelly went to lie down, on account of her arthritis, she told the inquiry, rather than the nausea or headache she had mentioned earlier. Shortly before 2 p.m., her husband popped upstairs to check how she was feeling.[6]

With a huge headache, being physically sick, and painful arthritis, it seems to be Janice Kelly, rather than her husband, who was well below par. He, on the other hand, appears to have carried on working normally, eaten some lunch, and taken the trouble to go upstairs to check on his wife.

The evidence of Wing Commander Clark to the Hutton inquiry reinforces this view. He was in touch with Dr Kelly a number of times that morning, on the subject of parliamentary questions that had been tabled about the weapons inspector. He told the inquiry, 'When I asked him how he was going, he basically said he was holding up all right but it had all come to a head and his wife had taken it really very badly . . . he did say his wife had been very upset on the morning of the seventeenth.'[7] Dr Kelly, as we have seen, also appeared to be behaving perfectly normally when he meet Ruth Absalom, the last person we know he definitely met before his death.

He therefore seems to have concluded that his wife was having a difficult time, both mentally and physically, and also to have shown concern about her condition. It is hardly likely, then, given that approach, that he would want to exacerbate matters in the worst possible way for his wife by committing suicide that day.

Mrs Kelly told the inquiry that after what seems to have been approaching a couple of hours, she 'began to get rather worried'. She confirmed that his walks would normally last only between fifteen and twenty-five minutes, and that whenever he went for a longer walk, he would tell her, and also where he was going and when he expected to return. He had clearly not done so on this occasion, so Mrs Kelly would doubtless have assumed that his walk was to be a normal short one.

It is perhaps surprising, given how 'shrunk into himself' he had seemed to her at lunchtime, that she did not worry earlier. That again suggests that any thoughts that he might harm himself were far from her mind. It is also odd that she appears not to have tried to contact him on his mobile phone, which was found with his body the following morning. Surely that is the first thing a concerned spouse would do in such circumstances. It is of course possible she tried, and found the phone off, but if so, it is curious that this is not mentioned anywhere in the evidence.

Mrs Kelly did speak to her daughter Rachel on the phone. Rachel had earlier arranged to come across to meet her father to go for a walk and go to see a new foal in one of the fields nearby. After the phone call, she began the twenty-minute journey to her parents' house, arriving some time between 5.30 and 6 p.m., according to Mrs Kelly. On arrival, Rachel said that she would follow her father's normal walk and go out to meet him. She returned at about 6.30 without success. This, incidentally, tends to confirm that his normal walk would have taken something less than half an hour.

One of the Kellys' other daughters, Sian, rang to say that she was coming over with her partner Richard from Fordingbridge in Hampshire, a journey of at least an hour and a half. If either Sian or Rachel attempted to contact their father on his mobile, we are not told about it. Nor is there any suggestion that Dr Kelly himself tried to phone home to explain what had happened.

Throughout the evening, the daughters searched for Dr Kelly around and about, finally returning to the parental home at about 11 p.m. This was now eight hours after Dr Kelly went for a walk that would normally have taken less than thirty minutes, and still the police had not been told. Mrs Kelly explained the delay by saying that they thought that might 'make matters worse'. Dr Kelly had of course been very publicly at the centre of events in the days preceding his disappearance, and it is not unreasonable to think a call to the police would only have added fuel to the flames. Nevertheless, it is still somewhat surprising that the police were not called until twenty to midnight. The family must have had no serious concerns for his health to leave it that late.

A member of the public who contacted me claimed that Dr Kelly's disappearance was featured on Ceefax shortly after midnight on the Friday morning, in other words between thirty minutes and an hour after he had been reported missing.

He maintains that this report, which he says vanished from the screens shortly after, mentioned that Dr Kelly had gone for his walk accompanied by a Special Branch officer, or similar. It seems that no record is kept of such Ceefax entries, so there is no way at this distance of establishing whether there is any basis to this explosive suggestion. If it were true and known to Mrs Kelly, unlikely though this is, it might help explain why she was not more worried that Thursday afternoon and evening.

Even by the Friday morning, Mrs Kelly appeared not to be considering the possibility that her husband might be dead. Journalist Tom Mangold, who writes on matters which would have crossed with Dr Kelly's professional interests, describes himself as a close friend of the family. He told the Hutton inquiry that he received a phone call from Mrs Kelly shortly after 9 a.m. According to him, she 'was still fairly upbeat and felt that [her husband] must have had a heart attack or a stroke and was . . . lying in a field . . . waiting to be found'.[8]

'Upbeat' is perhaps a strange word to use in the circumstances, whether it accurately describes Mrs Kelly's mood or whether Mr Mangold misread it, but it is the word he chose. It also presents a rather different picture of events from that given by Mr Mangold in a long GMTV interview in 2006. On that occasion, referring to the Thursday lunchtime, he told the programme: 'I think Janice realised something awful had happened to David mentally. She went upstairs and was sick a couple of times. She lay down. I think she had already decided she was beginning to lose David.' This version of events is clearly at odds with both his own statement to the Hutton inquiry and indeed that of Mrs Kelly herself.

In fact, Tom Mangold's role overall is a singular one. Even before Dr Kelly's body was officially found on the Friday morning, he was on the phone to Mrs Kelly. His was the voice that filled the media as a 'friend of the family', his was the first analytical piece to appear in the papers, in the Friday afternoon edition of the *Evening Standard*, and his was the first voice to express publicly the definitive view that David Kelly had committed suicide.

Indeed, Mr Mangold seemed strangely keen to declare the death a suicide and to discredit any suggestion to the contrary. In his GMTV interview three years later, he described the idea of murder as 'ludicrous', and suggested for example that for murder to be a possibility, Dr Kelly would have to have been abducted from his house under the eyes of his wife. Clearly this is nonsense. No one bar Mr Mangold has ever suggested that for murder to stand up as an explanation depends on an abduction of the weapons inspector from the family home.

Mr Mangold also went on to say that covering up any murder would have required collusion on a grand scale between law enforcement agencies. 'This case was investigated by the local police, the county police, Scotland Yard, Special Branch, MI5; MI6 had a man present [at the scene where the body was found] and the CIA had a man present because the Americans were interested in this.'[9] But if this was simply a tragic suicide, why were MI5, MI6 and even the CIA so closely involved, if indeed they were? More to the point, how did Mr Mangold know this to be the case, as it was a claim that had been made by no other prior to his GMTV interview?

Curiously, Mr Mangold's evidence to the Hutton inquiry painted a rather different, less intimate relationship with the Kelly family. He was asked how frequently he would speak to the weapons inspector.

'It was not that frequent. I spoke to him whenever I had a query about biological warfare or occasionally chemical warfare subjects. But it was not a frequent relationship.'[10]

When asked how often they met, Mr Mangold suggested 'maybe twice a year'. His relationship with Dr Kelly appears therefore to have been infrequent and professional.

The journalist did turn up for Dr Kelly's funeral at St. Mary's Church in Longworth but it is not clear if he was invited. There is even a story, which Mr Mangold denies, that he was asked to leave the funeral having been caught filming the event. In any case, his contact with Janice Kelly now appears to be much diminished.

We are left wondering, therefore, why Mr Mangold should have been keen to conclude that the death was suicide when the full facts cannot possibly have been known, and why, some three years later, he should have chosen to decry so vehemently any who doubt the suicide explanation.

4 Operation Mason

The police arrived within fifteen minutes of Sian Kelly's call to them. Three officers appeared, equipped with a missing-persons form to fill in.

Initial decision making rested with Sergeant Simon Morris, working the night shift out of Abingdon. He arranged for what the Hutton inquiry was told was 'a reasonably thorough search of Dr Kelly's house and the surrounding grounds to be carried out'.[1] Later, towards five o'clock, as dawn was breaking, a further, more detailed search of their home was undertaken, with a dog being put through the house, while Mrs Kelly was made to wait in the garden.

While the first such search made some sense – Dr Kelly may, for example, have suffered a heart attack while in a little-used part of the house – the second more detailed search, ordered by Assistant Chief Constable Michael Page, is more difficult to understand. Surely if Dr Kelly had been in his house or garden, he would have been found by the initial 'reasonably thorough search'. Would not limited police resources have been more usefully deployed checking out the routes Dr Kelly normally took for his walks?

It is also difficult to understand the purpose of sending a dog through the house. A chief constable with whom I discussed the matter told me that such a procedure would really only be used where it was thought, for example, that a lost child might be hiding somewhere. Nor could he explain why Mrs Kelly might have been asked to leave the house and wait in the garden. In his view, if the objective was to locate Dr Kelly, her knowledge of the house would have been helpful in any search. He described the police actions as 'bizarre'.

Thames Valley Police said that they wanted 'to remove possible distractions from those engaged in the search'. On why a dog was used at all, they replied that 'a dog is used as an aid to search operations as they can detect things beyond human capability'.[2] It is not clear what exactly Thames Valley Police had in mind on this occasion.

We know that David Kelly had his mobile phone on him, and indeed it was found at the scene, although in his coat rather than in the pouch on his belt where he normally kept it. Did the police attempt to call him? If so, was the phone switched off? Furthermore, did the police use the technology which exists, and existed in 2003, to identify the phone's location? Generally, the system will return to the enquirer the last location where the phone registered itself within the network. Even information giving this last identifiable point would have been useful in at least indicating his direction of travel. If the police did attempt to use this technology, and on the face of it this seems an obvious avenue to go down, then we are not told.

Soon after Sgt Morris had taken control, he ordered the police helicopter out to search for Dr Kelly. ACC Page told the Hutton inquiry that this had come from nearby RAF Benson,[3] and Mrs Kelly put the beginning of the aerial search at about 1 a.m.[4] Both of these statements are incorrect. Written answers to parliamentary questions in 2006,[5] provided by the armed forces minister, Adam Ingram, revealed that while the Chiltern Air Support Unit police helicopter based at RAF Benson was on standby that night, it was not used. Instead, a helicopter from Luton was deployed.

Home Office minister Tony McNulty confirmed that the police helicopter at RAF Benson had been 'available for tasking from 17.35 on 17 July until the end of its duty period at 02.30 on 18 July 2003'.[6] It then became available for use again at eight o'clock on the Friday morning. He also revealed that two flights were made in support of the search for Dr Kelly, both using the police helicopter based at Luton.[7] The first lasted from 2.50 a.m. until 4.05 a.m. and the second, following a refuel at RAF Benson, took place between 4.30 a.m. and 5.10 a.m.

There is thus an apparent discrepancy between the ministerial answers and the evidence given to the Hutton inquiry by ACC Page. Given the detail of the parliamentary answers, and the accepted need for accuracy in such answers, this suggests that no helicopter search was begun until a considerable time after it had been requested by Sgt Morris, in which case the question arises why a delay of around three hours occurred in getting a helicopter airborne.

It is surprising, given that the helicopter was equipped with heat-seeking equipment and that this was in use during the searches, that Dr Kelly's body could not be found. The body temperature was still 24 degrees Celsius at 7.15 p.m. the following day, as the pathologist, Dr Nicholas Hunt, belatedly established. It must have been considerably higher when the helicopter was out.

The area of the helicopter search was described by ACC Page, in his evidence to the inquiry, as being 'around the area of the house'. It is not clear how far from the house the helicopter searched, but if ACC Page's phrase is taken literally, it may explain the lack of success of the search. We do not know whether the helicopter used a searchlight. It is also surprising that the helicopter completed its last sortie just as it was getting light. Would not a visual search have been helpful, particularly as heat-seeking equipment had failed to locate the body?

The police told me that 'no information is available on the distance covered or the duration of flight(s)'.[8] This answer implies that the police were not even aware how many flights took place, but that information, and details of their duration, is indeed available, as we have seen above.

The delay in engaging the helicopter seems to have been matched by a delay in marshalling sufficient officers to undertake a search on foot. At the time the helicopter was operational, there were just 'half a dozen' involved in the search, and largely limited in their search area to Dr Kelly's home and immediate surroundings, even though the night would have been a favourable one. July 17 came just four days after a full moon. If Dr Kelly had sustained a serious injury while out walking, or developed a heart condition, say, time would have been of the essence.

To be fair to the police, the numbers they have on duty overnight is obviously limited, but there are significant numbers of army personnel stationed in Oxfordshire at any one time. In July 2004, for instance, there were 2,730 stationed at various locations with the District of Vale of White Horse, where Southmoor is situated.[9] In particular, there is an army site at Abingdon, about seven miles by road from Southmoor. Could army personnel not have been used in this search?

ACC Page was himself first made aware of the incident by a telephone call at 3.09 a.m., three and a half hours after Dr Kelly was first reported missing. The area's chief superintendent had been contacted rather sooner. The ACC then called a meeting at Abingdon police station for 5 a.m., which in fact began at around 5.15. It was attended by, among others, the local head of Special Branch, the detective inspector for the area, Ashley Smith, and Sergeant Paul Wood, a qualified police search adviser.

In his statement to the inquiry, ACC Page revealed his thoughts from that meeting, based on the information he had collated by that time: 'My concerns were that Dr Kelly had gone out for a walk, perhaps become ill, perhaps had an accident befall him, possibly had been abducted against his will, possibly was being detained.'[10] There is no mention of suicide in this reasonably exhaustive list of possibilities, though, interestingly, abduction does feature. Who did ACC Page, in his consideration of possibilities, consider might have abducted Dr Kelly?

ACC Page told Lord Hutton that the decisions from the meeting included one to establish what his favourite walks and haunts were, to inform the search pattern. That information presumably would come from Mrs Kelly and her family, and it is difficult to believe that those questions had not already been asked. Indeed, one would have thought that information would have been established and acted upon within an hour of the police arriving at Mrs Kelly's house. Still, the fact that the overnight searches had thrown up nothing perhaps means that this information had indeed not been sought until this point.

The meeting also apparently decided that the helicopter should be 'brought into play again'. Yet we know from parliamentary answers that no more flights were undertaken by the craft from Luton after the second sortie ended at 5.10 a.m. We also know that the helicopter at RAF Benson had not been used and would be unavailable until 8 a.m. at the earliest.

By about 7.30 am., there were between thirty and forty officers starting to search outwards from the house. Assistance had also been requested from the mounted section, based at Milton Keynes, and from the underwater search unit, but they had yet to arrive. Also by this time, a shortlist of five or six likely locations had been identified for search, with Harrowdown Hill deemed the second most likely, a conclusion that could, and ought to, have been reached about seven hours earlier. Rachel Kelly, in her evidence, mentioned that she had walked up to Harrowdown on the Thursday evening to see if she could see her father coming down the track.[11] She clearly knew where he might have gone. Did the police not know this?

It is worth noting at this point that there is a curious file of evidence submitted to the inquiry by Thames Valley Police, only the cover page of which is publicly available. The page bears the title: 'TVP Tactical Support Major Incident Policy Book' and also the phrase 'not for release – police operational information'. Thames Valley Police have said that this file contains tactical information on their investigation into Dr Kelly's death.[12]

The cover page also reveals that the codename for the investigation was Operation Mason. Chief Inspector, now Superintendent, Alan Young, the senior investigating officer for the case, told me that names for operations are allocated alphabetically, and that 'Mason' was simply the next one due to be used. He said that, given the possible overtones associated with the word 'mason', consideration had been given to adopting a different name, but by the time the matter had been properly considered, the name was out and it was too late. There is nothing to suggest that this is anything other than the truth, and wild rumours of a freemasonry angle to the case are almost certainly without foundation.

What is more concerning, however, is that the start time of Operation Mason is given as 2.30 on the Thursday afternoon, half an hour before Dr Kelly left his house for his last walk and more than nine hours before he was reported missing. The finish time is given as 9.30 a.m., shortly after Dr Kelly's body was officially found.

The police explanation for this curious timing is, according to Supt Young, that once an operation has begun, the start time is fixed not to relate to the moment that the police know of an incident or become involved, but to reflect the period of interest to the police. This sounds superficially plausible, until one reflects that any police investigation worthy of the name would start way before 2.30 on that Thursday afternoon. Whether one believes suicide or murder to be the cause of death, the events of the preceding weeks and the testimony given by Dr Kelly to two parliamentary committees are hardly irrelevant. Any investigation that took 2.30 p.m. on Thursday 17 July as its starting point would be lamentably inadequate.

Indeed, ACC Page told the inquiry that even by the time of his 5.15 a.m. meeting, background information had been sought about what had happened to Dr Kelly over the previous few weeks, and what impact that might have had on him, thus rendering the start time of Operation Mason, if we accept the police explanation for how this time was arrived at, clearly wrong.

Yet what is the explanation, if this is not the case? Premonition and occult powers can be safely discounted, which leaves us with the possibility that at least an element within Thames Valley Police had foreknowledge, to at least some degree, of that afternoon's tragic events. If that were the case, then it would of course clearly point to the involvement of another party in Dr Kelly's death.

Another curiosity of that night's events relates to the communications equipment deployed by Thames Valley

Police. Information about this comes, rather astonishingly, from Mrs Kelly's evidence. It is from her we learn that 'a vehicle arrived with a large communication mast on it and parked in the road, and then during the early hours another mast, [a] 45-foot mast, was put up in our garden'.

The inquiry QC, James Dingemans, asked, 'For police communications?'

'Yes indeed,' replied Mrs Kelly.[13]

This short exchange is all too typical of the unsatisfactory way the Hutton inquiry was conducted. Notwithstanding her reply, Mrs Kelly can have had no direct knowledge of the purpose of these structures, and the question should of course have been put to a senior police officer. It was not. Mrs Kelly was the only witness to be asked about this matter.

Was the presence of such equipment standard? Not according to the chief constable I spoke to. He told me that even in an area of poor reception, he would expect a mast only 15 feet high to be used. Thames Valley Police eventually told me that the mast was in fact even higher, at 110 feet.[14] They say it was 'to assist radio communications in an, at that time, recognised black spot'. They went on to confirm that the force has two such aerials, but that they are rarely used now due to the advent of Airwave, the new police communications system.

The difference in height between what Mrs Kelly told the Hutton inquiry and the actual height underlines the inappropriateness of the inquiry's QC relying on hearsay to establish the facts. She would not have been allowed to give such evidence in a court of law or indeed at a proper coroner's inquest.

What was the purpose of this very high mast? It seems clear that normal police communications would not require such a structure. It might, however, have been required if it were thought necessary to contact an aircraft in the sky a very long way away, such as the one at the time carrying the Prime Minister from Washington to Tokyo.

In the first hours of daylight, the level of police activity to locate Dr Kelly finally increased. This included calling out help from the South East Berkshire Emergency Volunteers, who duly arrived at Abingdon police station by 7.15 a.m. for a briefing. CanTech volunteer search dogs would also be employed to help out.

As far as the police themselves were concerned, Detective Constable Graham Coe was called in from Wantage at around 6 a.m., and, he told the inquiry, sent out to conduct door-to-door enquiries around Longworth. Also at this time, PC Martin Sawyer was called and asked to attend Abingdon police station, where he arrived some two hours later. Shortly after, a similar call went to PC Andrew Franklin, who took just over an hour to arrive from his home in Windsor.

The two volunteers, Louise Holmes (who happened to be the girlfriend of PC Sawyer) and Paul Chapman, and their collie, Brock, arrived at the search area, specifically at the bottom of Common Lane in Longworth, at about 8 a.m., after a car journey of some ten to fifteen minutes. They had been tasked with searching Harrowdown Hill and the track that ran alongside it from Longworth to the river Thames. The pair duly searched the track towards the hill, then the southern edge of the wood until they reached the extensive wire fence that encircles part of the wood along the western edge of the track. They then decided to finish searching the track as far as the Thames before finishing off the wood.

When they reached the river, they came upon a group of three or four people in a boat, who reported having seen the helicopter out the previous night, though whether it was overhead and in the area around the Kelly house was not nailed down. They also reported having seen some police officers earlier that day. Who those police officers were has never been established. Nor do we know who the people in the boat were, or what they were doing there at that hour.

The volunteers then returned back up the track to search the northern end of the wood, entering the wood from the track. Within a few minutes, Brock had picked up a scent and indicated that he had found something by returning, barking, to Ms Holmes. Oddly, although the dog was trained to take his handler towards what he has found, on this occasion he did not do so. He would not even accompany the volunteer, as she made her own way towards the spot in question.

5 Conflicting evidence

Harrowdown Hill is an area just over half a mile north of Longworth village, accessible eventually only on foot, horse or by farm vehicle. Off the main Appleton Road, Cow Lane, with its attractive pub, the Blue Boar, straggles into Tucks Lane, becoming narrower, rougher and eventually petering out within sight of the distinctive raised wood that constitutes the hill. From David Kelly's house to the spot where he was found would have been a walk of two miles or so.

Despite its relative proximity to the nearby villages, the area is particularly quiet and peaceful and feels much as it must have done centuries ago. As you walk along the rough track that borders the wood proper, it is not difficult to imagine others long forgotten, shepherds and farm labourers, doing likewise.

The wood itself, to the west of the track, is surrounded for much of its perimeter by a rudimentary barbed wire fence, though tracks inviting access are not difficult to find. On entering the wood, you are led upwards through undergrowth and trees close enough together so that you know you are in a wood, but not too dense to stop the sunlight breaking through.

On the flat area at the top of the wooded hill can be found one or two small clearings, where trees are sparser. Elsewhere, often behind unexpected runs of barbed wire, spontaneous, chaotic growth has occurred, such that progress can only be made by battling through nettles, bushes and branches.

One day a colleague and I were exploring the wood. When one of these inaccessible areas that we had negotiated suddenly gave way to a clearing we came upon a startling sight. In a corner of the clearing was a fenced pen with a goat in it. The door to the pen was open, and the goat, as startled as we were, bolted through it into the undergrowth. In contrast to much of the rest of the wood, this little area felt dark.

Dr Kelly's body was found in the wood at around half-past eight by Louise Holmes, one of the search volunteers, who shouted to her colleague Paul Chapman to notify the police. Unable to get through on the mobile numbers he had been given, he instead called 999, and asked for someone at Abingdon police station to call him back. The return call came within a couple of minutes, and the two volunteers agreed to return to their car and await the arrival of police officers. On their way back to the car, just a couple of minutes after that call, the volunteers came across three police officers from Thames Valley CID, DC Graham Coe, DC Shields and a third who was never identified.

The officers were walking towards the river. They told the volunteers that they were aware neither that a body had been found, nor that Holmes and Chapman had been out searching that area.[1] Mr Chapman took the officers to the edge of the wood, and then, the police having decided that only one officer was needed, he led DC Coe about 75 yards into the wood to show him where the body lay. Mr Chapman then rejoined his colleague, who had returned to their car, where they had arranged to meet PC Andrew Franklin and PC Martin Sawyer in order to take them to the body. By his own account, DC Coe was left alone with the body for some twenty-five to thirty minutes before other officers arrived to tape off the scene.

Close on ten o'clock, the two PCs arrived at the scene. What they found is described by each in detail to the Hutton inquiry. Descriptions are also given by DC Coe, by the volunteers and by the paramedics who attended. This seemingly comprehensive approach is unfortunately under-mined by the numerous inconsistencies in their statements, and even more so by the failure of either Lord Hutton or James Dingemans QC to reconcile the differences.

The most basic of these relates to the position of the body. The volunteer searchers who first came across Dr Kelly both described him as sitting upright. Mr Chapman, from a distance of some fifteen to twenty metres, told the inquiry that Dr Kelly's body was 'sitting with his back up against a tree'.[2] Ms Holmes concurred, saying that Dr Kelly's head and shoulders were 'just slumped back against the tree'.[3]

DC Coe, however, told Lord Hutton that the body was 'laying [sic] on its back by a large tree, the head towards the trunk of the tree'.[4] PCs Franklin and Sawyer in their evidence endorsed this view, as did the paramedics. Dave Bartlett, the ambulance technician who arrived on the scene after DC Coe, told Rowena Thursby that Dr Kelly's head was at least a foot away from the base of the tree, and Dr Nicholas Hunt, the pathologist, also described the body in the following terms: 'I recall that his head was quite close to branches and so forth, but not actually over the tree.'[5]

Lord Hutton attempted to square this circle in his report. He wrote:

I have seen a photograph of Dr Kelly's body in the wood which shows that most of his body was lying on the ground but that his head was slumped against the base of the tree – therefore a witness could say either that the body was lying on the ground or slumped against the tree.[6]

He told me that he did not know who had taken the photograph, 'but it is likely to have been a police photographer'.[7] In his evidence, PC Sawyer indicated that he had taken photographs of the scene with the digital camera he had on him, so perhaps the photograph Lord Hutton saw was one of those. In any case, it has not, it seems, been seen by persons other than the police and Lord Hutton, perhaps out of understandable consideration for Dr Kelly's family, so we will have to rely on Lord Hutton's description. However, this explanation, rather than clarifying matters, merely muddies them further, contradicting as it does the evidence both of those who maintain the body was sitting up and those who had it flat on its back away from the tree.

To add to the uncertainty, some national papers published the weekend after his death, including Saturday's *Guardian*, and the *Sunday Telegraph* and the *Independent on Sunday*, described his body as having been found 'face down'.[8] The *Scotsman* even described his body as having been discovered 'curled up in a ball on the ground'.[9]

Had the body been moved? Thames Valley Police insist that it had not. In their letter to me earlier this year, Malcolm Hopgood, their Freedom of Information officer, wrote that 'the Senior Investigating Officer [Alan Young] is absolutely satisfied that the body was not moved by anyone engaged in the search operation prior to examination by the paramedics'.[10] Some, such as Rowena Thursby, think that the evidence suggests otherwise, and believe the motivation may have been to produce a position for the body consistent with the vomit stains that were clearly visible on Dr Kelly's face.

In their evidence, both PC Sawyer and Dave Bartlett referred to these stains running from the corners of his mouth to his ears. Clearly, if Dr Kelly had been propped up against a tree as he vomited, the stains would have run downwards, and he must therefore have been flat on his back at the time. Yet what person, intent on cutting their wrists or indeed on swallowing large numbers of tablets, would do so on their back? The natural position, if such a term can be used, is surely sitting, which in a wood does suggest against a tree.

It might be argued that Dr Kelly was in a sitting position for these purposes, but then decided to lie down on the ground, flat on his back. Again, this does not seem very likely. He could not have achieved such a position by accident, and it is a curiously uncomfortable position to choose. It is much more likely, if one follows through the official explanation for his death, that he was sitting against the tree, lost consciousness, and then slumped over. In that scenario, he would have been found curled up near the tree, with the base of his spine near the trunk. The vomit stains of course say something else.

There is also a dispute about the position of Dr Kelly's right arm. Ms Holmes reported the arm as being beside the body, but the two paramedics, Dave Bartlett and Vanessa Hunt, said that they had to move Dr Kelly's right arm off his chest, as they tested for signs of life.

We were told that a water bottle was found beside Dr Kelly's body. PC Sawyer indicated in evidence that when he arrived, the bottle was open, and was propped up, at a slight angle, to the left of his head. The cap was by the side of it. Roy Green, the forensic biologist, confirmed that the bottle was some 10 inches from his left shoulder. The position of the bottle is a curious one, if one considers that Dr Kelly was right-handed, and indeed, if we go by the official version of events, was presumably still drinking from the bottle after cutting his ulnar artery. Water would have been required to aid the digestion of the twenty-nine coproxamol tablets, while a man losing large amounts of blood would also have developed a thirst, as we have seen, and Mr Green confirmed that there were blood smears on the bottle. This, incidentally, makes it even more surprising that there was, according to PC Sawyer, still water in the 500ml bottle when he arrived. Dr Kelly must have used the contents of this small bottle sparingly, if at all.

Under the circumstances, the police might have expected to find the water bottle by his right side, rather than his left, but the configuration is just about possible if Dr Kelly were indeed sitting against the tree. If, however, he were lying flat, we are asked to believe that he placed the water bottle, presumably with his undamaged and natural hand, the right, by his head on the left, and tidily placed the cap next to it. Despite his serious injuries, he even managed to ensure, at this contortionist's angle, that the bottle was propped up.

All in all, it seems clear either that both the volunteers had remembered the position of the body incorrectly (somewhat unlikely, as they gave their statements to police immediately afterwards), or that the body had been moved after their departure from the scene and before the arrival of PCs Franklin and Sawyer. If the latter, then we should recall that DC Coe told the inquiry that he was alone with the body for a full twenty-five minutes between the time the volunteers left and his police colleagues arrived. If the body had indeed been propped against a tree, it would have been interesting to have had the horizontal direction of the vomit stains explained. No such explanation would of course be necessary if the body were flat on the ground.

It is, however, not only in the matter of the position of the body where accounts vary. It is also far from certain what Dr

Kelly was wearing that afternoon. We are told by PC Franklin that when the body was found, he was wearing a blue jacket, a white shirt and blue jeans.[11] DC Coe described him as wearing a Barbour jacket.[12] Nicholas Hunt, the pathologist, described him as wearing 'a green Barbour-type wax jacket'. It seems certain that he was indeed wearing such a coat when the pathologist arrived around noon, not least because Dr Hunt went on to describe what he found in the pockets, namely a mobile phone, a pair of bifocal spectacles, a key fob, and the three blister packs of coproxamol.[13] Yet according to Saturday's *Guardian*, he had been jacketless, a description repeated in the next day's *Observer*. The *Mail on Sunday*, too, had him 'dressed casually in an open-necked shirt and jeans, with no coat'.[14]

The question thus arises at what point Dr Kelly was wearing the blue or green wax coat. Was it when he left the house, despite the reports in the papers? If not, was it put on him before he was found, or, given the statement by PC Franklin, shortly before the pathologist arrived? It is concerning that even a basic matter like this was not cleared up by the inquiry.

Michael Page, then assistant chief constable for Thames Valley Police, also told the Hutton inquiry that a Barbour hat had been found a short distance from Dr Kelly's body. Most significantly, perhaps, the *Sunday Times* of 20 July quotes Acting Superintendent David Purnell of Thames Valley Police as saying that Dr Kelly had left his house 'dressed in jeans and a cotton shirt, despite poor weather'.[15]

The weather in fact had not been that poor. Over Oxfordshire that Thursday afternoon, it was mostly cloudy with a few sunny intervals. RAF Brize Norton, some twelve or so miles from Dr Kelly's home in Southmoor, recorded temperatures in a range from 16.7 to 18.1 degrees Celsius between 3 p.m. and 6 p.m. that day. The wind was a little breezy, at 7 knots, or force 3 on the Beaufort scale. Over the course of the day, just over half an inch of rain fell.[16] Had Dr Kelly intended to undertake his normal short walk, it is quite conceivable that, on a warmish day in July, he would have left the house without a coat. His wife Janice did not actually see him leave so is unable to help us on that point. If, on the other hand, he had set out with the intention of walking to Harrowdown Hill, he may well have taken a coat, given the cloudy skies. Whether he would have donned a heavy wax Barbour in July is more questionable.

What is certain is that he was wearing a coat when found at the scene, so either he took it on his walk, contrary to all the reports in the newspapers, or it was brought there subsequently by another person. If that were the case, unlikely though it may seem, it would imply that a police officer was responsible, given that Dr Kelly's coat was presumably to be found in his house, and only the police had access in that timescale to both his house and the spot where his body lay. It is certainly the case that a good deal of material was removed by the police from the house, and that Mrs Kelly was required to stay in her garden while the search of the house was carried out. Thames Valley Police, when challenged on the matter, would say only that 'we can confirm that the coat found at the scene belonged to the deceased'.[17]

At the scene, as we now know, were found a knife, a water bottle, and three packets which had contained thirty coproxamol tablets. It would have been awkward, though not impossible, to have carried these various items the longish distance from his house to Harrowdown Hill without the benefit of a coat. Logically, therefore, it would seem either that Dr Kelly had indeed brought a coat, which enabled him to transport these items to Harrowdown Hill, or that not just the coat, but the knife, the pills and the water bottle as well were all taken from the Kelly home to Harrowdown Hill by someone other than Dr Kelly, with the express purpose of creating a suicide scene. It is perhaps worth remarking that these three items were not noticed by the volunteers who found the body, but were certainly present when PCs Sawyer and Franklin arrived at the scene after DC Coe's 25-minute vigil. The volunteers must have been truly unobservant to have missed a bloodied knife and a water bottle also smeared with blood.

As was discussed in an earlier chapter, the knife was a singularly inappropriate one to choose to cut one's wrists. But it was presented as the property of Dr Kelly, in a way that, say, a razor blade would not have been. The coproxamol tablets were also presented as Mrs Kelly's, thus linking him firmly both with the weapon used and the tablets.

No mention was made at the Hutton inquiry of fingerprints on the knife. No-one volunteered any information on this matter, and no one was asked. After some delay, Thames Valley Police finally told me earlier this year that 'no fingerprints were recovered from the knife'.[18] None at all. Yet we know from Roy Green that the knife was blood marked.

Try holding a knife tightly, as if you were about to use it to make an incision. Is it not a natural action to use your fingers to apply pressure on the knife to hold it firm and in place? Did Dr Kelly then have a most curious way of holding a knife? Or are we being asked to believe that he tidily wiped his prints off, just as he tidily put the bottle cap next to the water bottle by his left shoulder, and the empty coproxamol blister packs tidily back in his coat?

A key figure in the events of that Friday morning is DC Graham Coe. PC Franklin was asked about DC Coe by James Dingemans. He first volunteered that DC Coe was accompanied by two other officers, a fact supported by the statements made before Lord Hutton by PC Sawyer, Louise Holmes, Paul Chapman and Vanessa Hunt. DC Coe, in his evidence, however, would suggest that there was only one officer, an assertion that went unchallenged.

PC Franklin was then asked if DC Coe was part of his search team, to which he replied in the negative.

'What was he doing?' asked Mr Dingemans.

'He was at the scene. I had no idea what he was doing there or why he was there,' replied PC Franklin.[19]

PC Franklin's response is noteworthy in that it distinguishes between why DC Coe was at the scene and what he was doing there. It may be that his answer was simply tautologous. Or did PC Franklin have reason to suspect that DC Coe's presence was not quite as passive as he would have us believe?

DC Coe appeared before Lord Hutton on 16 September 2003, just less than two months after Dr Kelly died. He recalled that he had reported for duty at Abingdon police station at six o'clock that morning, and was told to go over to Longworth to 'make some house-to-house enquiries in the area where Dr Kelly lived'.[20] By a stroke of enormous good luck, DC Coe quickly came across Ruth Absalom, who in fact lived in Southmoor rather than Longworth. Ms Absalom was the last person known to have spoken to Dr Kelly the afternoon before.

DC Coe told Lord Hutton that Ms Absalom 'lived more or less opposite' the Kellys. Her address at the time was a house named Stanab, in Faringdon Road, Southmoor, which in fact was about 100 yards away. Ms Absalom is no longer there, and a planning application was submitted earlier this year to demolish the house and replace it with four separate dwellings.

DC Coe went on to tell Lord Hutton that, armed with the information Ms Absalom was able to give him concerning Dr Kelly's movements, he and a colleague (singular) decided to go 'to the area where she had last seen him and made a sort of search towards the river'. Whether they sought clearance from a senior officer to abandon the house-to-house enquiries they had been charged with undertaking we are not told. When challenged on this point, Superintendent Alan Young told me that he presumed DC Coe had received a call on his radio unit, redirecting him towards the body. This seems highly unlikely, as it presupposes that someone else, unnamed, knew where to look for the body and coincidentally rang him at exactly the time he had just met Ms Absalom.

On the way towards the river, they met the two volunteers, who told them a body had been found. As we know, DC Coe then repaired to the scene and took charge. According to him, he was alone at the scene for somewhere in the region of twenty-five to thirty minutes. He was asked how close an examination he made of the body. In reply, he stated that he did not go over to the body, but merely 'observed the scene'. Asked how near he got, he answered, 'Seven or eight feet.'[21]

Obviously no police officer will wish to compromise what might be a crime scene, but it is difficult to accept that he really went no nearer than this. Twenty-five minutes is a long time to do nothing. Surely the natural human reaction would have been to approach the body, without touching it, to observe the situation more closely. DC Coe seems almost at pains to tell us he did not go near the body.

Still, with such a long time to pass, we can at least expect that DC Coe would have accurately captured the scene in his notebook, knowing that it was very likely he would have to give evidence at some point. Yet he appears to have done no such thing. He certainly had his notebook on him, because he used it while making his statement to check the time that the ambulance arrived.

Yet he was unable definitively to tell Lord Hutton almost anything else. He did not know if the cap was on Dr Kelly's head or some way from the body. He was not certain if Dr Kelly was wearing walking boots. He thought Dr Kelly's watch was on top of the knife, but was not sure. He thought the water bottle was to the left of Dr Kelly's body. He did not know if there was any water in the bottle.

After a few minutes of this, Lord Hutton asked him, 'Is there anything else you would like to say about the circumstances surrounding the death of Dr Kelly?'

'Nothing whatsoever,' he replied.[22]

Despite his shaky and contradictory evidence and his importance in the case, no attempt was made by Lord Hutton to corroborate anything DC Coe said. We actually only have his word for the whole of his testimony. No senior officer was asked to confirm his statement, and the only colleague we know by name who accompanied him, DC Shields, was not asked to give evidence.

DC Coe did, however, make a private statement to the inquiry in addition to his public comments. All we know of this is the title: 'Witness statement: Graham Peter Coe – not for release – personal witness statement', along with the reference TVP/1/0030-0031. What did DC Coe want to communicate privately that he was not prepared to say in open session?

In his testimony, ACC Michael Page revealed that he had been contacted by a member of the public who had seen 'three men dressed in black wandering around at the time Dr Kelly's body was found'.[23] The sighting was between 8.30 a.m. and 9.30 a.m. And after Dr Kelly's death, the *Daily Mail* received a number of letters and telephone calls reporting that there were men in black clothes on the hill early on in the morning, significantly before Dr Kelly's body was officially found.

ACC Page told Lord Hutton that after plotting the positions of his officers, he was satisfied that the three men in question were police officers, though we are not told their names or what they were doing. It seems clear, in any event, that they were not DC Coe and his two colleagues. PC Sawyer told Lord Hutton that the two officers with DC Coe were uniformed. It was certainly the case, though, that some police officers at least were dressed in black. PC Sawyer, for instance, stated that he and his team were dressed in 'summer search kit: black polo shirt, black trousers and our work boots'. Doubtless others were similarly attired.

Finally, it is worth remarking that Chief Inspector (now Superintendent) Young, who had been appointed that Friday morning by ACC Page to head the investigation into the death, did not give a public statement of any sort to the inquiry, despite his key role in the police action. Is this not rather unsatisfactory? It also meant that the inquiry was not able to explore the 'tactical support operation' that was Operation Mason.

Overall, anyone reading the transcripts of police evidence is left with a feeling of dissatisfaction, even unease. It is aston-ishing that there can be so much conflicting evidence of a crucial nature, even more so that no attempt is made to get to the truth by re-examining witnesses, or indeed drawing attention to contradictions as they first become apparent when evidence is given.

Did Lord Hutton not think it important to establish the facts? Apparently not. Time and again, key questions went begging, interesting asides were not followed up, inconsistencies were blandly brushed off. He wrote in his report:

> Those who try cases relating to a death or injury . . . know that entirely honest witnesses often give evidence as to what they saw at the scene which differs as to details. In the evidence I have heard from those who saw Dr Kelly's body in the wood there were differences as to points of detail, such as the number of police officers at the scene and whether they were all in uniform, the amount of blood at the scene, and whether the body was lying on the ground or slumped against the tree . . . These differences do not cause me to doubt that no third party was involved in Dr Kelly's death.[24]

One wonders how he was able to reach this conclusion without having first established the facts. He appears to be arguing that significant differences in fundamental evidence, such as whether DC Coe was accompanied by one or two other officers, did not need to be cleared up, and that the differences themselves demonstrated that the police officers making these conflicting statements were honest. If they were dishonest, he implies, their stories would have been squared beforehand and been identical.

Yet had they indeed been consistent, could we have expected Lord Hutton to have concluded that this somehow demonstrated prior collusion and that the officers were therefore not revealing all they knew? Clearly not. The consequence of such an approach is that, no matter what the police said, Lord Hutton was going to believe it.

6 The ideal appointment

David Kelly was pronounced dead on the morning of Friday 18 July 2003. Less than twenty-four hours earlier, the House of Commons had broken for its long summer recess, tailing off into nothing at 6.34 p.m. It is quite possible that Dr Kelly was already dead and lying among the trees of Harrowdown Hill as the last of Westminster's MPs were winding up business before returning to their constituencies and thence departing to all points of the compass.

The House would not sit again until 8 September, returning to a political landscape utterly changed from that of 17 July. As so often, Parliament was bypassed when it really mattered, and the government was allowed almost two months' free rein. When news of Dr Kelly's death was announced, the then Conservative opposition leader, Iain Duncan Smith, called for Parliament to be recalled and for the Prime Minister to return from the Far East. He may as well have saved his breath.

Parliament may have been impotent, but the government was in overdrive. Tony Blair was on a long plane journey when he was officially told of the death of Britain's premier weapons inspector. He had left behind him in Washington the adulation of, and seventeen standing ovations from, a political establishment grateful for some overseas cover for the aggressive and almost certainly illegal invasion of Iraq by the United States. Moreover, in Blair they had a man competent and capable of articulating a justification for the invasion in a way that their own President struggled to do.

Now he was on the long journey to Tokyo. He was without Alastair Campbell or Jonathan Powell, his key lieutenants, who were returning direct to London and would arrive at Heathrow around 10 a.m.

Blair had left Washington at around 1 a.m. London time on the Friday for the 14½-hour flight. According to the *Independent on Sunday*, he was told that Dr Kelly was missing some six hours later, and was given confirmation of his death after another two and a half hours, at around 9.30 a.m. By the time the plane touched down in Japan, Lord Hutton had been appointed to head an inquiry into 'the circumstances surrounding the death of Dr David Kelly'. A press statement confirming the appointment was issued by Geoff Hoon, then Defence Secretary, at 3.20 p.m. on Saturday 19 July.[1]

No doubt politically, the announcement of an inquiry was useful in taking the heat out of the situation for the Prime Minister at a difficult juncture. Awkward questions could be batted off with the formula that it was now all a matter for Lord Hutton. The political logic, therefore, in decisively making an early appointment cannot be faulted, but even so, the speed of the appointment startled most. Government wheels normally grind rather slowly.

According to journalists on the plane, Blair turned for

advice to two of his closest allies, Charlie Falconer, the recently appointed Lord Chancellor, and his old Svengali, Peter Mandelson. Both, it seems, recommended Brian Hutton.

That Mr Mandelson had an input into this decision is not doubted by some who accompanied the Prime Minister on his flight that day. It is, for example, stated as fact in *The Survivor*, a book about Blair written by Francis Beckett and the *Guardian* journalist David Hencke.[2] Other journalists say there was no contact between the Prime Minister and themselves on this particular plane. He did not wander down the plane, as sometimes was his wont on such journeys, and no handouts were provided during the flight. They also suggest it would have been difficult to overhear much, given that he was firmly ensconced in first class, with a heavy curtain to separate first from business class, largely occupied by Downing Street staffers but with a few press, and economy, where most of the journalists could be found.

Officially, then, Mr Mandelson had no role at all in this matter. In response to a parliamentary question asking what role he had played, Harriet Harman, minister of state at the Department for Constitutional Affairs, replied simply: 'Mr Peter Mandelson played no part.'[3]

As this answer was completely at odds with the recollections of a number of journalists I had spoken to, I asked for the background material used to draft the parliamentary answer. This was provided, but is in fact extremely short, merely referring to Dr Kelly's death, the setting up of the Hutton inquiry and the subsequent publication of the Hutton report. Noticeably absent is any record of Mr Mandelson having been contacted following the tabling of the original question to ask him for his recollections, so it is unclear how the answer that he 'played no part' could be quite so definitive.

A further letter to Ms Harman elicited the clear statement in response that 'Mr Peter Mandelson was not involved'.[4] It added that the background notes already sent were the only ones that existed. She also confirmed that the reply was 'approved by the Lord Chancellor'. It is certainly the case that Mr Mandelson would have been well acquainted with Lord Hutton in his role as Lord Chief Justice of Northern Ireland, from his stint as secretary of state for the province.

Officially, the process of appointment was set out in a parliamentary answer to the Southend West MP, David Amess. He was told:

> Where a government decides it wishes to invite a senior judge to conduct an inquiry, the Prime Minister invites the Lord Chancellor to recommend a suitable judge. This process was followed on this occasion, and after consulting the senior judiciary, the Lord Chancellor proposed Lord Hutton and he accepted the appointment.[5]

Lord Hutton told me that he had met the Lord Chancellor on the day Dr Kelly's body was found, 18 July, and had agreed his terms of reference at that meeting.[6]

Consultation with 'the senior judiciary' sounds a reasonably thorough process. However, a subsequent parliamentary question[7] revealed that the only one such person was consulted, namely the senior law lord, Lord Bingham, who, in Lord Hutton's words, 'confirmed that he had no objection to my undertaking the inquiry'.[8]

Lord Falconer himself gave further details in his evidence to the House of Commons Public Administration Select Committee. He said:

> I had a conversation with the Prime Minister . . . in which we discussed the possibility of setting up an inquiry . . . I think at the time I had the conversation the position was that Dr Kelly's body had been found in Oxfordshire although I do not think it had been made public that that was the position.[9]

He then told the committee that it was agreed that a senior judge should head the inquiry, and he discussed the matter with his permanent secretary. He went on:

> Lord Hutton was a name that emerged quite quickly as a suitable person to do it. [He was] a senior judge of impeccable standing, he had been a successful Lord Chief Justice of Northern Ireland, he looked completely beyond reproach and he had the right skills to investigate . . . a series of facts leading up to somebody's death.

He had, however, never chaired a public inquiry before, a fact confirmed by Ms Harman, although in his book *Inside Story*, Greg Dyke says that he had in fact chaired one such inquiry, even if only into the diversion of a river in Northern Ireland.

There were perhaps other factors which particularly recommended Lord Hutton to the Prime Minister and his close circle. These include the fact that in his active career, he had always been supportive of, and sympathetic towards, the forces of law and order, especially the security services, whom he would have relied upon to guarantee his safety in Northern Ireland. He had over the years shown himself to be sympathetic towards government and unhelpful towards the media. He had also developed a style that stuck rigidly to a narrow brief. The respected commentator Peter Oborne, writing in the *Spectator* in 2004, highlighted 'the caution of his judgements. He is said to have been habitually chary of making precedents.'[10] The most common adjective used to describe Hutton is 'conservative'.

His specific track record must have been encouraging too, for those looking for a safe pair of hands. In 1973, he represented the Ministry of Defence at the inquests of those killed on Bloody Sunday, when he ripped into the coroner, Major Hubert O'Neill, for venturing to suggest that the soldiers in question had no justification for their shooting of people on the streets of Londonderry.[11] 'It is not for you or the jury to express such wide-ranging views, particularly when a most eminent judge has spent twenty days hearing evidence and come to a very different conclusion,' he lectured him.[12]

This argument is striking, even breathtaking, in its dismissal of any views the coroner, let alone the jury, might hold. Those on the side of law and order must be supported, even when they open fire. It was a pro-establishment view that would be echoed in the Hutton report, when it came to adjudicating between the government and the BBC. It might appear that for him, the purpose of these inquests was to rubberstamp the solitary judge to whom he referred, Lord Chief Justice Widgery, rather than perhaps to discharge the duties properly associated with a coroner's court.

Here too, the investigation into the death of Dr Kelly, such as it was, would also require a judge and a coroner to mark out territory, with the difficulties that ensued.

In 1978 Lord Hutton helped defend Britain in the European Court against Irish government allegations that internees held by the British in Northern Ireland had been tortured. In 1981, he was in charge of a trial where a British soldier had killed two youths after careering at high speed into a group of people in Londonderry. His advice to the jury was 'to consider whether you think that perhaps unconsciously some of the witnesses . . . had a tendency somewhat to strengthen their evidence against the army', and suggested that, while the driving might have been reckless, it might not have been unreasonable given the rioting that had been going on. The jury did indeed 'consider' this and brought in a not-guilty verdict.

Even more controversially, in an American-style verdict, he sentenced ten men in 1984 to a total of 1,001 years' imprisonment, and all on the word of an acknowledged informer, Robert Quigley, who was given immunity from prosecution in return for his evidence. Two years later, he acquitted one Nigel Hegarty, an RUC reservist, who had shot dead a protester, John Downes, at a range of about three yards. Mr Downes had been running towards the RUC officers, carrying a stick. Mr Hegarty did not testify, but Lord Hutton helpfully concluded that he had acted 'probably almost instinctively' and that his actions were not unreasonable given 'the stress of the moment and the obvious determination of the deceased'.

In 1990 Lord Hutton declared two Royal Marines not guilty of the murder of Fergal Caraher. He accepted that the men might be lying when they protested their innocence, but said that he could not trust the evidence given by civilian witnesses, or indeed that of the accused. The next year, he successfully led a public campaign to overturn the 3–2 majority decision taken by the UK's highest court to approve the extradition to Spain of the former Chilean dictator Augusto Pinochet on torture charges. The sole basis of his objection was that one of the five law lords involved, Lord Hoffman, had loose links with the human rights organisation Amnesty International. A reconvened panel of seven law lords overturned the original decision and the Chilean dictator was free to go. Lord Hutton himself sat on this reconvened panel. Nobody accused him of having links with Amnesty International.

In 2002, Lord Hutton was one of four Law Lords who stopped the former MI5 officer David Shayler's attempt to use a public-interest defence in his trial for contravention of the

Official Secrets Act. Mr Shayler, by passing documents to the *Mail on Sunday* in August 1997, alleged that MI5 had been paranoid about 'socialists' and that it had investigated Labour Party ministers Peter Mandelson, Jack Straw and Harriet Harman. This is most certainly a matter of public interest, in layman's if not in legal terms.

Weighed against all that are a few surprising acquittals of suspected IRA terrorists, particularly in the early days of the Diplock courts, which consisted of a single judge. And in 1994, he dismissed Private Lee Clegg's appeal against his controversial conviction for murder, for shooting a joyrider at a Northern Ireland checkpoint – although the appeal was later upheld.

Overall, Lord Hutton is generally regarded as independent and, within the parameters of his own worldview, fair. Nevertheless, it is not difficult to see why he would have seemed the ideal appointment for those looking to help the Prime Minister out of a dangerous spot.

Lord Hutton himself issued a statement on Monday 21 July 2003, through the press office of the short-lived Department for Constitutional Affairs. In it, he noted that the government had promised him 'the fullest co-operation'. And he added, 'I make it clear that it will be for me to decide as I think fit within my terms of reference the matters which will be the subject of my investigation.' He also announced that he had appointed James Dingemans QC to act as counsel to the inquiry, and Lee Hughes from the Department for Constitutional Affairs to be secretary to the inquiry.

The government may have promised Lord Hutton 'the fullest co-operation', but from the outset, there was one striking feature to this inquiry. It had not, as would have been expected, been established as a statutory inquiry under the Tribunals of Inquiries (Evidence) Act 1921. The significance of this is that the inquiry was an informal one, not required to follow normal court procedures. Witnesses could not be subpoenaed if they did not wish to attend. Nor could they be found guilty of perjury if they lied. Nor were the usual protections offered by cross-examination required to be employed. Moreover, Lord Hutton had sole control over who was or was not called as a witness, what documents were or were not produced and, to a large extent, what questions were asked or were left unasked. The Lord Chancellor, Lord Falconer, justified this decision by arguing that 'using a statutory basis for the Inquiry would have led to delays and curtailed the flexibility of form that allowed Lord Hutton to conduct the Inquiry in the manner he felt appropriate'.[13]

It is true that the establishment of a statutory inquiry would have required parliamentary approval, and that could not have been forthcoming until the House reassembled in September or was recalled earlier, as the Conservatives had demanded. The wait before parliamentary approval could be obtained was not, perhaps, the main consideration in the government's mind, though. Such approval would have required a debate in Parliament first, something the government was keen to avoid. As for the 'flexibility of form' the Lord Chancellor refers to, that might better be described as the abandonment of basic procedures and safeguards essential to ensuring the proper examination of facts.

Lord Hutton seemed untroubled by the unusual status of his inquiry. He told me:

> I was not surprised to be asked to conduct the inquiry without formal powers. The reason was that it was very apparent from the outset that I would have to investigate very closely the actions of the government and the actions of the BBC. Because of the intense public interest in the events surrounding Dr Kelly's death I thought it very unlikely that any witness that I required to appear before me from the government or the BBC or from any other organisation or body would decline to do so.[14]

This explanation only underlines that for Lord Hutton, the emphasis of his inquiry appeared to be not David Kelly's death, but the highly political falling out between the BBC and the government. The death was simply the catalyst for the inquiry, rather than the central feature it should have been.

He added that he would not have hesitated to ask for formal powers if that had become necessary as the inquiry progressed, and the fact that he did not do so shows that they were not necessary. This self-fulfilling argument may have some justification in terms of the main focus of his inquiry, though even here we will see that Lord Hutton was given evidence in respect of the famous 'dodgy dossier' which must have been known to be incorrect when it was given. Under an informal inquiry, of course, there can be no offence of perjury. Where the informal approach clearly falls down badly is in respect of the narrower investigation into Dr Kelly's death, where the lack of proper cross-examination, the abundance of conflicting evidence and the failure to secure the attendance of key witnesses are embarrassingly evident.

Lord Hutton would eventually pronounce, despite the flawed process and dubious evidence described in earlier chapters, that Dr Kelly took his own life. If his death had been subject to a normal inquest, the coroner would have had to be satisfied 'beyond reasonable doubt' before bringing in a suicide verdict. I challenge anyone to say that that test was met in this case, based on the evidence presented to the Hutton inquiry. In fact, Lord Hutton seems to have made up his mind about the cause of death even before his inquiry began.

Lord Hutton himself does not accept that criticism. In a letter to me, he asserted, 'You are under the misapprehension that my inquiry was not a rigorous investigation into the cause of Dr Kelly's death and into the question whether it was suicide or murder. The question was fully and thoroughly investigated.'[15] Yet when he set out at length how he intended to interpret his terms of reference before he began his inquiry, there was a great deal about weapons of mass destruction, the BBC broadcasts on that subject and the use of intelligence by the government.[16] There was rather less about Dr Kelly's actual death.

Lord Hutton's assurance that Dr Kelly's death was fully investigated by his inquiry is brought into significant doubt by a hitherto little-noticed piece entitled 'The Conduct of a Public Inquiry', which he produced for the highly specialist publication *The Inner Temple Yearbook 2004/5*. In it, he wrote:

> At the outset of my inquiry . . . it appeared to me that a substantial number of the basic facts of the train of events which led to the tragic death of Dr Kelly were already apparent from reports in the press and other parts of the media. Therefore I thought that there would be little serious dispute as to the background facts . . . I thought that unnecessary time could be taken up by cross-examination on matters which were not directly relevant.

As in controversial cases where he had presided in the past, one could conjecture that Lord Hutton appeared, to a large degree, to have made up his mind in advance.

James Dingemans, the inquiry's counsel, was chosen personally by Lord Hutton. He explained his decision thus: 'Mr Dingemans had often appeared before me as counsel in appeals to the Judicial Committee of the Privy Council. Over a number of years I had formed the highest opinion of his integrity, his ability and his industry . . . My selection of him was entirely justified.'[17] Mr Dingemans is indeed well regarded, though it is perhaps worth pointing out that although he had provided advice in respect of a number of public inquiries conducted in Caribbean jurisdictions, and had appeared in litigation arising out of an inquiry in the Bahamas, this was a new departure for him. Unlike Lord Hutton, who has been prepared to respond to my queries, Mr Dingemans has refused to discuss with me, or enter into correspondence about, his role in this inquiry.

Overall, Lord Hutton, both in his correspondence with me and his public utterances, has refused to accept that there was anything wrong either with the conduct of his inquiry or with the conclusions he reached. Judges, in fact, only rarely comment on cases where they have presided, so Lord Hutton's statements suggest either that he is simply being co-operative or that he has perhaps been stung by criticism of his performance and feels the need to justify his actions.

His most substantial justification appeared in November 2006, over twenty-six pages of closely typed text, in an article he penned for the winter edition of *Public Law*, entitled 'The Media Reaction to the Hutton Report'. Perhaps this can be best summed up in four words: '*Je ne regrette rien.*'

7 Fragmented, non-accountable, variable, ineffective, archaic

It is very unusual for a death to be formally dealt with other than by a coroner at a properly constituted inquest, with all the safeguards and established procedures inherent in such a process. In 1988, however, the government of the day created a power for itself to refer the consideration of deaths instead to a public inquiry. The reason behind this was a sensible one: to eliminate the duplication in inquests that arose when multiple deaths from a single cause occurred.

The power, under Section 17A of the Coroners Act 1988, to bypass the coroner and deal with deaths via a public inquiry has in fact only been invoked on four occasions, according to research conducted by the House of Commons library. It was first used in February 2000 to deal with the thirty-one deaths resulting from the Ladbroke Grove rail crash. Lord Cullen chaired this inquiry, established on a statutory basis under the Health and Safety at Work etc Act 1974. On the second occasion, the 311 deaths associated with Dr Harold Shipman were considered by Dame Janet Smith, with the inquiry again constituted on a statutory basis, this time under the Tribunals of Inquiry (Evidence) Act 1921. And in November 2003, another statutory inquiry, chaired by Mr Justice Steel, was set up under the Merchant Shipping Act 1995 to consider the four deaths associated with the fishing vessel *Gaul*.

In between came the inquiry into the death of Dr David Kelly. This was unique in two respects. Firstly, it is the only occasion to date when the new procedure created by the 1988 Act to replace a coroner's inquest with a public inquiry has been used to investigate not an event involving multiple deaths but a single one. Secondly, it is the only inquiry established since the Act was passed that has not been given a statutory basis. Therefore, far from creating a rigorous process to investigate Dr Kelly's death, the government created one which was less rigorous than a normal coroner's inquest would have been for a routine death.

What did the coroner in whose jurisdiction Dr Kelly's body was found think of this? Not much, the evidence seems to suggest.

Nicholas Gardiner is the long-standing Oxfordshire coroner. He opened and adjourned the inquest into Dr Kelly's death on Monday 21 July 2003. He will doubtless have been aware, not least from the blanket news coverage, that Lord Hutton had by that time already been appointed to head an inquiry into this matter. Indeed, Lord Hutton's first formal statement, setting out how he intended to conduct his inquiry, was made the same day. That statement did not mention the coroner at all.

We can also assume that he will have been familiar with the terms of the Coroners Act 1988, and that his role was effectively being supplanted by Lord Hutton. Under the Act, he was effectively off the case until such time as Lord Hutton would report, at which point he had the jurisdiction to reopen his own inquest, but only if he judged there were exceptional reasons for doing so.

The Lord Chancellor's private secretary, Sarah Albon, formally wrote to Mr Gardiner on the day the Hutton inquiry began its proceedings, to indicate that Section 17A of the Coroners Act 1988 was being invoked. This meant that

> the coroner should, in the absence of any exceptional reason, adjourn the inquest. One of the purposes is to prevent duplication of proceedings . . . He [the Lord Chancellor] has asked if you would kindly signify within 7 days your agreement that there is no exceptional reason why the inquest should not continue to be adjourned.[1]

Mr Gardiner, who replied two days later on 6 August, did not seem very enthusiastic at this development. He replied, 'I had envisaged that it might be possible to conclude the Inquest during September.' He also appeared unhappy with the informal status of the Hutton inquiry, and the marginalisation of his role:

> As you will know, a Coroner has power to compel the attendance of witnesses. There are no such powers attached to a Public Inquiry. If I do adjourn under

Section 17A(1), I would be unable to resume, if at all, until after the Public Inquiry has been concluded and thus would not be in a position to assist Lord Hutton.

That indeed was the position, but it seems not to have worried Lord Hutton, who throughout his inquiry appeared unconcerned about what Mr Gardiner might or might not be doing or thinking.

The coroner's letter of 6 August is also interesting in one other regard. He reveals that the pathologist, Dr Nicholas Hunt, appears to have had a change of heart about the cause of death: 'The preliminary cause of death given at the opening of the Inquest no longer represents the final view of the Pathologist and evidence from him would need to be given to correct and update the evidence already received.' In what way had Dr Hunt's view changed, and what had caused this to happen? We are not told, and Lord Hutton never asks.

Mr Gardiner's letter seems not to have been well received by the Lord Chancellor. Ms Albon wrote back on 12 August in rather blunt terms:

The Lord Chancellor considers that the cause of death of Dr David Kelly is likely to be adequately investigated by the judicial inquiry conducted by Lord Hutton . . . Accordingly, I am instructed by the Lord Chancellor to request (i) that you adjourn the inquest in compliance with Section 17A(1); and (ii) that you resume the inquest only if, pursuant to Section 17A(4), there is in your opinion an exceptional reason to do so.

Section 17A(4) only comes into play at the end of a public inquiry, thereby confirming yet again that the coroner was now expected to relinquish his role.

The Lord Chancellor reluctantly agreed that Mr Gardiner could take evidence from Dr Hunt and the forensic analyst, Alex Allan, on the cause of death, but, Ms Albon wrote, '[he] has asked that you keep the proceedings as short as possible and, so far as the Coroners Rules allow, take the evidence in writing'. The coroner was, it seemed, being bundled off the case. More to the point, he was effectively being asked to cut corners in his procedures. Such pressure from a government minister on an independent coroner is highly unusual.

So it was on 14 August that Mr Gardiner's inquest reopened, in a truncated form, to take evidence from two people only – Dr Hunt and Mr Allan.

Coroners' inquests are public affairs, yet this one seems to have generated little coverage, despite the huge media interest at the time in Dr Kelly's death. Perhaps the reason is that almost nobody knew about it. Not even the Department for Constitutional Affairs had a representative present.[2] Harriet Harman MP, then minister of state at the department, has confirmed that the advance notice of the inquest was limited to the coroner ensuring that interested parties and the press were given 'notification . . . by telephone shortly beforehand'.[3]

The matter was not helped by the official press release issued by the department on 13 August, the day before the resumed inquest, which announced that Lord Falconer had 'directed that the coroner's inquest into the death of Dr David Kelly should be adjourned', but failed to give details of the inquest planned for the next day.

This is at best a rather idiosyncratic approach to a hearing which is required to take place in public. On top of this, the coroner refuses to say who he determined were interested parties, or which media outlets were notified, or when. Nor will he release any notes from the hearing, even though Ms Harman has confirmed that there is a public right of access to written material that is read out in court.[4] His justification for this stance is that any written material read out in court could be accessed by a person attending the court and taking notes, which is perhaps a reasonable answer if you are one of the lucky few who has been telephoned personally to be told when and where the resumed inquest is to take place.

Ironically, an official paper published just weeks earlier, the snappily titled *Death Certification and Investigation in England, Wales and Northern Ireland: The Report of a Fundamental Review 2003*, had drawn attention to the often haphazard arrangements for notifying the press of inquests. The report said, 'Press representatives have told us that many coroners appear to them to have no reliable system for giving public notice of upcoming inquests. They also say that some coroners seem to them to deliberately conceal some inquests from the press and the public.'[5]

At the resumed inquest, which took place after Lord Hutton had begun his inquiry, Mr Gardiner duly took evidence from the pathologist and the forensic toxicologist, and no-one else. On the basis of this limited process, a death certificate was produced, giving itemised reasons for death.

Many will find it troubling that such a conclusion could have been reached on this crucial matter, based on a truncated and rushed process taking evidence from only two witnesses. Moreover, as we have seen, Mr Allan stated in evidence to the Hutton inquiry that Dr Kelly did not have enough coproxamol in his body to enable his death to be attested to it.

So one of the only two witnesses at this peculiar inquest would presumably disagree with the contents of the death certificate that arose from the inquest. And we also now know that the pathologist was uncertain enough of the facts to want to change his evidence from the position he had originally adopted.

It would have been open to the coroner to have issued an interim certificate of death. This would have confirmed that death had occurred, and allowed the family to settle the estate of the deceased, while reserving judgement on the causes. This is expressly referred to in the Coroners Rules 1984, point 30, which reads: 'When an inquest has been adjourned for any reason … the coroner shall on application supply to any person who, in the opinion of the coroner, is a properly interested person an *interim* certificate of the fact of death [emphasis added].'

Harriet Harman argues that a final rather than an interim certificate was issued in this case as there was the possibility the inquest would not be resumed after the public inquiry, and in that eventuality, a final certificate might never have been issued.[6] This is at best a technical nicety, and cannot properly be used to justify the issuing of a full certificate based on incomplete information and following a truncated procedure. It is certainly the case that a final certificate does at some point have to be issued, in order for the death to be registered. Surely it would have been more sensible to resume the inquest after Lord Hutton had reported and to issue a certificate then consistent with his findings. After all, what would have happened if he had reached a different conclusion from the coroner as to the cause of death? The death certificate would then have been seen to be incorrect in its particulars. As it happens, the coroner did, following the Hutton inquiry, send the registrar of deaths a certificate under his hand stating the findings of the public inquiry in relation to the death. This in terms of content is not very far away from a full death certificate, but the latter, had one not been issued previously, would have required a formally reconvened inquest, which all those responsible seemed keen to avoid.

It is, of course, most extraordinary that Mr Gardiner could think it appropriate in August 2003 to allow the causes of death to be formally established when an inquiry had been set up with that effective remit. If the coroner was so confident of his conclusions, what was the point of Lord Hutton? It is hard to argue that Dr Kelly's death was properly investigated, either by the coroner using this peculiar procedure, or by Lord Hutton, distracted as he was by the political issues affecting the BBC and the government. The upshot is that the most sensational death of the year, and one of the most politically sensitive deaths in recent British history, was investigated to a less rigorous standard than would have applied to any sudden or violent death subject to a normal inquest.

It transpires that a meeting had taken place three days before the resumed inquest at the Department of Constitutional Affairs, at Mr Gardiner's request. He had suggested as much in his letter of 6 August referred to above, indicating that he was planning to be in London that day so would be available. Besides Mr Gardiner, the meeting was attended by Victor Round, the Worcestershire coroner, a senior departmental lawyer and the lead policy official. The stated purpose of the meeting was to discuss the mechanics of admitting the evidence from Dr Hunt and Mr Allan. It is not known if the meeting was a convivial one, but it was followed the next day by the rather brusque letter from Sarah Albon referred to above.

I wanted to discuss some of these matters, particularly the resumed inquest, with the coroner himself, but he replied rather sharply that it would be 'quite improper' for him to do so. His assessment did not, however, preclude him from discussing the very same matter in August 2006 with a journalist from the *Sunday Telegraph*, Nina Goswami. In

Ms Goswami's piece, which in fact remained unpublished, Mr Gardiner described the meeting with officials from the Department for Constitutional Affairs as 'impromptu'. He told the reporter that he was planning to be in London anyway, and 'it just seemed convenient to pop down and meet them'. He also confirmed that department officials were reluctant to allow him to reopen the inquest.

It should be put on record that in contrast, the minister responsible for policy in respect of coroners at the time of my investigations, Harriet Harman, was open and helpful throughout. Indeed, at times she was seen by others as perhaps too helpful. On 30 January 2007 in the Commons, for example, she offered me a meeting with relevant officials from her department, but had to rescind that offer less than a week later, 'having taken advice'.[7]

The death of David Kelly is not the only controversial matter to have come the way of the Oxfordshire coroner. Back in 1987 there occurred another death which fell to him to deal with, and one that bore striking similarities to the death of Dr Kelly.

Canon Dr Gareth Vaughan Bennett had that year been given the task of writing the preface to the 1987/8 edition of *Crockford's Clerical Directory*. By convention, these prefaces are anonymous and uncontroversial, but Dr Bennett used his column to argue that the Church of England was in a critical state, and set down a programme to be followed for the Church, as he saw it, to recover its true purpose.

Of the Archbishop of Canterbury, Robert Runcie, he remarked that he 'is usually to be found nailing his colours to the fence' and accused him of 'taking the line of least resistance on each issue'. For good measure, he witheringly added that 'the ineffectiveness of the Synod is shown at every level of its operation'. Many in the Church, though not Dr Runcie himself, were incandescent and determined to uncover the person responsible. Like Dr Kelly, Dr Bennett was a man of serious and sure conviction who did not shrink from the truth. And like Dr Kelly, his anonymous actions would infuriate some in positions of power and lead to a hunt to identify the person responsible.

Dr Bennett returned to his home in Oxfordshire one Saturday morning in December, having been with friends in Cambridge the night before. He dropped a colleague off near his home, saying that he would see him again that evening. He then went to New College to collect his mail. He was found on the Monday morning in his garage. He was lying in the passenger seat of his car, which had been fully reclined, with a hosepipe through the window. There is no doubt that he died from carbon monoxide poisoning.

The inquest, in March 1988, was held by Mr Gardiner. One member of the public who was present was Dr Kitty Little. So concerned was she about the conduct of the inquest that she lodged a complaint with both Lord Denning, the outgoing Master of the Rolls, and Thames Valley Police. In her letter of complaint she wrote:

I was present at the inquest on Dr Bennett this morning, and found the manner in which the Coroner conducted it most unsatisfactory. From the evidence presented I would have thought that the only possible verdict would have been an open one, but the Coroner had obviously made up his mind that it should be suicide. He sat without a jury, and over several points guided his witnesses in that direction.

The case certainly had some strange features, which might explain Dr Little's spirited letter.

The hosepipe was bought about two hours after Dr Bennett could have been expected to have returned home. The shop in question was a branch of the hardware chain Carpenters, but not the nearest one to Dr Bennett's house.

The assistant manager described his customer as 'very pleasant, easy to serve'. He particularly remembered the incident because the customer had known exactly what tap connection he wanted, which he described as most unusual. Moreover, although he rarely sold such hosepipes, he had sold two that day. He was not asked about the other sale. Nor was he able to make a positive identification of Dr Bennett, despite being shown a photograph.

When Dr Bennett's house was entered, his case was found at the bottom of the stairs, where it had presumably been put down when he had returned from Cambridge. A newspaper was still tucked in the strap. His overcoat was thrown over the banister, with his mail, which he had expressly driven to New College to pick up, still unopened in the pocket.

The evidence suggests that Dr Bennett simply dropped off his possessions before going out again. There was no sign of any other activity in the house having occurred, except for the presence of a wine glass with some dregs in it. No suicide note was found, and close colleagues expressed surprise that Canon Bennett would have committed suicide. Like Dr Kelly, he was under some pressure, but those who knew him say suicide was simply not in his make-up, not least for strong religious reasons.

It was very unusual for Dr Bennett's car to be in the garage. This was generally full of junk and it would have required some shifting to be able to get the car in. No forensic evidence was produced to establish whether Dr Bennett himself drove the car into the garage. Nor were the neighbours asked if they heard any noise from the garage, which presumably must have been of a lengthy duration, until the fuel ran out.

The neighbour who found his body stated that the room upstairs where Dr Bennett kept his papers was very disorganised, contrary to its normal appearance. Mr Gardiner's response to this was a leading question: 'But it didn't have the appearance of somebody going through his papers?' It is not clear how the neighbour was meant to be able to distinguish between this scenario and one where Dr Bennett had himself, uncharacteristically, rifled through his papers in a somewhat careless manner.

Most curious of all is that when the police arrived, his cat was found to be dead in the sitting room. It had not starved, for there was dried-up food in its saucer, and several tins of cat food were open. The inquest was told that it 'appeared to have died peacefully'. A question on the matter was quickly ruled out of order, with the coroner making it clear that he was there to deal with the death of a human, not that of a cat. The cat's body was disposed of at an early stage, the coroner having rejected the notion that a post-mortem be carried out on the cat. Nor was the cat's food tested.

Yet surely it would have been relatively easy to establish why the cat had died. It could, of course, have been a coincidence, but given the wider circumstances, potentially a prudent move. But the coroner was in no doubt. 'He [Dr Bennett] decided that he had only the one course of action open to him and he took that course of action.'

Was the evidence sufficient to make the case for suicide 'beyond reasonable doubt'? Dr Little thinks not. She wrote: 'I went to the inquest with that possibility [murder] in mind. By the time the inquest was over "possibility" had been upgraded to "probability".'

Another person present at the inquest was Beverley Pyke, an architect. He wrote that when Dr Bennett's body was found, it was naturally assumed he had taken his own life, given the situation in which he was found. But he went on: 'As the details came out, so many questions arose that the Police who were investigating expected an open verdict. There was nothing conclusive about the circumstances.' Mr Pyke was so concerned that he wrote to Mr Gardiner to ask for a copy of the transcript of the inquest, which of course had been held in public, as the law required. Mr Gardiner brusquely refused this reasonable request, adding: 'If you are dissatisfied with my decision then I can only suggest that you seek legal advice. Yours faithfully.'

But it was another matter that led to the Oxfordshire coroner being much in the news in 2006. To the anguish of the families affected and the embarrassment of the government, a huge backlog of inquests of armed forces personnel had built up in his jurisdiction. Oxfordshire is where RAF Brize Norton is situated, and the bodies of servicemen killed in Iraq are returned to the UK through this base. Under the archaic coroners' rules still in force,[8] that means they all fall to be handled by the Oxfordshire coroner.

Such was the problem, in fact, that ministers made no fewer than five statements to Parliament between June 2006 and June 2007 expressly on the problems with inquests in Oxfordshire.[9] In June 2006, there were fifty-nine inquests into the deaths of service personnel in Iraq outstanding, as well as eleven inquests of civilians who had died abroad and been flown back into the UK via Brize Norton. Some deaths awaiting inquests had occurred as far back as 1998.

It is surprising that such a backlog had been allowed to build up without action being taken earlier. Notwithstanding the archaic rules, there is no absolute requirement that inquests that are the responsibility of one coroner must be undertaken by that coroner. Section 14 of the 1988 Act makes it clear that one coroner may ask another to hold an inquest on his behalf if it is expedient to do so. That Mr Gardiner did not do so, but instead allowed a huge backlog to accumulate, can only have added to the deep distress of the families trying to come to terms with the loss of a loved one in action and seeking closure on a painful episode. Harriet Harman rightly called the delays 'unacceptable'.[10] Furthermore, as the minister confirmed in a parliamentary written answer, a 1983 circular sent to coroners had advised that 'in cases involving a single death from outside England and Wales, the coroner local to where the funeral is to be held should normally deal with the inquest'.[11]

One can perhaps conclude that Mr Gardiner wanted to retain responsibility himself for holding inquests into such deaths, but did not have the capacity or resources to deal with these in anything approaching a reasonable time.

Eventually, ministers appear to have decided that the Oxfordshire coroner had to be bolstered by an influx of support, and we saw the drafting in of three people officially termed 'additional assistant deputy coroners', but who actually comprised Sir Richard Curtis, a High Court Judge, Selena Lynch, a former full-time coroner for Inner South London, and Andrew Walker, a barrister and deputy coroner in London. In addition, three additional coroner's officers were provided to liaise with the bereaved families, the police and so on, together with an additional administrative assistant.

The ministerial statement made on 29 March 2007 listed the then eighty-four inquests long outstanding. Of these, forty-six were allocated to Mr Walker, twenty-eight to Ms Lynch, six to Sir Richard, and only four to Mr Gardiner himself.[12] This list did not include the further sixty-six deaths of service personnel which occurred after 15 May 2006, when the initial action was taken by ministers.

Since the death of David Kelly, the government has announced its intention to reform the coronial system. This has been widely welcomed.[13]

There is undoubtedly considerable public dissatisfaction with the service. A study carried out in 2006 for the Royal College of Pathologists examined 1,691 autopsies, and found that in 310 of them, almost one in five, the cause of death given was questionable.

The study also said that many bereaved families were being 'sold short'.

The foreword to the government's draft Bill on coronial reform, published in June 2006, and written jointly by Lord Falconer and Ms Harman, puts it this way: 'We will address weaknesses that have become increasingly evident over the last 20 years. The coroners' system at present is fragmented, non-accountable, variable in its processes and its quality, ineffective in part, archaic in its statutory basis.'

This is the system that processed the death of David Kelly.

8 '45 mins from doom'

'It is the stickiest, most ill-tempered, most difficult, most exhausting July that I can remember in twenty years of covering politics,' the BBC's political correspondent Andrew Marr said at the time.[1] July 2003 was certainly highly charged, as the government struggled to deal with the aftermath of the invasion of Iraq and the failure to turn up any weapons of mass destruction, even though the stated reason for the military operation was precisely to deal with such weapons.

And in the middle of the month came the sensational death of Dr David Kelly, a man whose name was known to almost nobody at the start of the month, but was on everybody's lips by the end.

The decision of the UK government to join the United States in invading Iraq had been hugely controversial, so much so that between 750,000 and two million people, depending on whether you believe the police or the organisers, had in an almost spontaneous uprising marched on Sunday 16 February through central London to oppose any invasion.

The mood on that Sunday was both determined and peaceful. There was a feel of the 1960s to the event. Placards bearing the slogan 'Make Tea Not War' were much in evidence. This was people power. But would the government listen to such a huge mass of the population?

The Prime Minister, despite being able to use prerogative powers to commit troops, did concede a vote in the House of Commons, and personally turned in a bravura performance, as he generally did when it really mattered. The outcome, though, was never really in doubt, once the Conservatives had decided to support him. The vote, on 18 March, was carried 412-149, an impressive majority of 263, which, however, masked a large revolt by eighty-five Labour MPs (and three Conservatives). The Lib Dems, who had declared themselves steadfastly against invasion, managed a 100 per cent turnout to boost the 'no' vote, achieved at some cost. Menzies Campbell even broke off treatment in Edinburgh to come to London to vote. The Lib Dems and the Labour rebels were joined by the nationalist parties and a few odd others.

Key to the vote, and certainly important in persuading doubtful Labour MPs to support the government, had been the stated nature of the threat posed by Saddam Hussein and specifically his ability to deploy weapons of mass destruction. In an unprecedented move, the government had made publicly available some of the intelligence in a dossier published the previous September.[2] Dr Kelly had been involved in the drafting of this, but, like a number of people connected with the intelligence services, had bridled at the way in which dispassionate and carefully qualified intelligence and assessment had been twisted for political purposes. It was his decision to express his concerns to the BBC journalist Andrew Gilligan that had set off that sticky and ill-tempered July.

The September dossier does not read well today. The picture it paints is one of a belligerent Saddam, with a capability in WMD, likely stockpiles of the same and determined programmes to enhance all this further. In the most dramatic turn of phrase, we were warned that some of these weapons were just forty-five minutes from deployment:

> As a result of the intelligence we judge that Iraq has:
> - continued to produce chemical and biological agents;
> - military plans for the use of chemical and biological weapons, including against its own Shia population. Some of these weapons are deployable within 45 minutes of an order to use them;
> - command and control arrangements in place to use chemical and biological weapons. Authority ultimately resides with Saddam Hussein.[3]

In the event, of course, no chemical or biological weapons were found in Iraq, let alone nuclear ones, despite exhaustive searches. The dossier was, in the mood music it produced, almost entirely wrong. Furthermore, given the determination by Alastair Campbell and others to make the dossier as strong as possible, even if this meant stretching the available intelligence to breaking point (which I shall cover in more detail below), it is very odd that a whole area of concern in respect of Saddam's activities was omitted entirely.

Back in 1998, the *Sunday Times* ran a story which suggested that by 1995, the Iraqi leader had had created a 'dirty bomb' that would, when fired from a supergun, spread a cloud of lethal zirconium dust over nearby Middle Eastern countries. The article quoted Dr Kelly, who appeared to be speaking with government approval, as saying that he and his colleagues were 'surprised, to say the least. Nobody had suspected that Saddam had developed a radiation weapon.'[4]

The newspaper returned to the matter in August 2003, shortly after Dr Kelly's death, quoting extracts from an interview with him in June. In the interview the newspaper asked him why the dirty bomb had not featured in the government's dossier. He said that he did not know, but that perhaps some people in government were sceptical of the potency of such a weapon. In the light of how other intelligence material was treated for the production of the dossier, this hardly seems a likely explanation.

Dr Kelly added in respect of the Iraqi position: 'The threat [from this dirty bomb] was potentially more serious than some other weapons of mass destruction.'[5]

So was the intelligence quoted in the dossier faulty, was the assessment of that intelligence faulty, or was the raw material 'sexed up' to make the case for war? Certainly Dr Kelly believed the last.

It is worth noting that the first draft of a dossier had been produced back in March 2002, but the government had decided not to publish it. Interestingly, this dossier looked at the WMD capabilities of four countries, not just Iraq. The

Prime Minister has refused to confirm the four countries in question, but it would be a reasonable guess that these might be the countries that comprised President Bush's 'axis of evil'.

Perhaps the judgement was that there was not really very much to say. Certainly, when the matter was under further consideration in the summer, Whitehall officials were telling the press that the publication of the dossier would be rather uneventful. This was reflected in newspaper coverage, for instance in pieces by Mike Evans, the defence editor of the *Times*, and Richard Norton-Taylor, the security editor of the *Guardian*, which appeared on the cusp of August and September. Mr Norton-Taylor, quoting a senior Whitehall source, told us that the dossier would no longer have a role, as there was nothing to put in it.[6] Yet when the dossier appeared around three weeks later, it was far from a non-event. The gentle tinkling of wind chimes had given way to the strident ringing of alarm bells.

Contrary to the impression given to the Foreign Affairs Select Committee when it considered the matter in June 2003, activity did not stop after the decision not to publish the March dossier, only to restart in August or September. The Hutton report confirms that a dossier, pulling together three separate papers and entitled 'British Government Briefing Papers on Iraq', was actually produced by 20 June.[7] This was a substantial document of forty-five pages.

What can we learn by examining the history of that most controversial of claims, the 45-minute one? For a start, there was no mention of the claim in either the March or the June dossier. In fact, the raw intelligence for this claim was received only on 29 August, and passed to the assessment staff of the Joint Intelligence Committee the next day for formal consideration at their meeting on Wednesday 11 September.

The Butler review, set up in February 2004 to consider the intelligence that had been available to the government on weapons of mass destruction, raised concerns that the 45-minute claim was 'unsubstantiated' and implied that it had not been correctly reported for assessment. Certainly the haste with which this item of raw intelligence was cascaded through the normal assessment process, to appear in the published dossier less than a month after it was received, does suggest that the normal validation process may have been short-circuited.

Sir Richard Dearlove, then head of MI6, or the Secret Intelligence Service as the government prefers to call it, admitted to Lord Hutton that the 45-minute claim had come from only a single source, an individual of equivalent rank to a senior Iraqi military officer, whom they considered to be a sufficiently reliable source of information.[8] This was a somewhat unsafe assumption, as we shall see.

The 45-minute claim appears in the September dossier four times, including once in the Prime Minister's foreword and once in the executive summary. Despite this prominence at the front end of the document, it appears only twice more in the other forty-nine pages. Both of these are in the eighteen-page chapter entitled 'The Current Position: 1998–2002', including once as a bullet point in the chapter summary at the beginning. This means that, of the four mentions, only one is substantive and three are anticipatory – a big build-up to a damp squib. But then the document itself is divided in multiple ways: bullet points within sub-sections, sub-sections within sections, sections within chapters, and chapters within parts. The opportunities to repeat points and make not very much go a long way are virtually limitless.

By the time the then Foreign Secretary, Jack Straw, gave evidence to the Foreign Affairs Committee in June 2003, the war against Saddam was over, and he was keen to play down the 45-minute claim. He told the committee: 'I do not happen to regard the 45-minute statement having the significance which has been attached to it, neither does anyone else.'[9]

It had all looked rather different the previous September, when the dossier was published. Firstly, the qualifications to the claim had been erased from the dossier. In the first draft, the foreword had the Prime Minister saying: 'The case I make is not that Saddam could launch a nuclear attack on London or another part of the UK (he could not).' This important point, putting the claim in context, was removed from the final version.

The impression was also allowed to be formed, and was not corrected, that British forces, if not Britain itself, were directly in Saddam's firing line. The fact that the 45-minute claim related only to battlefield munitions, rather than missiles, was not spelt out and indeed the Prime Minister himself, somewhat incredibly, claimed he only found this out himself when Lord Butler's inquiry report was published in July 2004.

Yet Robin Cook, Jack Straw's predecessor as Foreign Secretary, revealed in an article he wrote for the *Guardian* that he had been briefed back in February 2003 that the weapons in question were only battlefield ones. The briefing came from John Scarlett, then head of the Joint Intelligence Committee, later to be promoted to head up MI6. Mr Cook wrote:

> When I put to him my conclusion that Saddam had no long-range weapons of mass destruction but may have battlefield chemical weapons, he readily agreed. When I asked him why we believed Saddam would not use these weapons against our troops on the battlefields, he surprised me by claiming that, in order to evade detection by the UN inspectors, Saddam had taken apart the shells and dispersed them – with the result that it would be difficult to deploy them under attack . . . I put these points to the Prime Minister a couple of weeks later. The exchange is recorded in my diary on March 5 2003. Tony Blair gave me the same reply as John Scarlett, that the battlefield weapons had been disassembled and stored separately. I was therefore mystified a year later to hear him say he had never understood that the intelligence agencies did not believe Saddam had long-range weapons of mass destruction.[10]

Just in case the reader had not got the point, he rammed it home:

'Why did Tony Blair himself never ask John Scarlett whether he was talking about long-range or battlefield weapons? Given that the Prime Minister was justifying war to the nation on the grounds that Saddam was a serious threat to British interests, he showed a surprising lack of curiosity as to what that threat actually was. We are asked to accept that from September [2002] to March [2003] the Prime Minister was allowed to think that Saddam had long-range chemical weapons, while the intelligence agencies assessed he had only battlefield weapons . . . This must represent the most extraordinary failure of communication in the history of the British intelligence agencies.

In opposition, Mr Cook was most famous for the analytic demolition he made of the Conservative government for its role as revealed by the Scott inquiry, or 'Inquiry into the Export of Defence Equipment and Dual-Use Goods to Iraq and Related Prosecutions', to give its full title. Little can he have thought that in office, he would be best remembered for a similar demolition job on his own Prime Minister.

Mr Cook died suddenly shortly afterwards, on Saturday 6 August 2005, while out walking in the Scottish highlands.

The implication of Mr Cook's piece, of course, is clear. Both the Prime Minister and John Scarlett did indeed know that Saddam had no long-range WMD capability, but chose deliberately to use language that allowed a contrary impression to be formed.

Lord Butler, in his report, concluded:

The JIC should not have included the '45 minute' report in its assessment and in the government's dossier without stating what it was believed to refer to. The fact that the reference in the classified assessment was repeated in the dossier later led to suspicions that it had been included because of its eye-catching character.[11]

Yet as late as 27 June 2003, Mr Straw was still defending the 45-minute claim. Asked by the Tory MP Sir John Stanley whether the fact that the US administration had not picked up the 45-minute claim meant that there were doubts about its credibility, Mr Straw replied: 'We do not have any doubts about the credibility of the assessment made by the JIC in September reflected in the dossier.'[12]

Less than three weeks later MI6 quietly withdrew the claim, on the basis it could no longer be supported. The day they chose to do so was 17 July, the day David Kelly left his home in Oxfordshire for the last time. Lord Hutton, whose inquiry began shortly afterwards, was never told that the claim had been withdrawn, even though consideration of the issue was a key strand of his work. The Foreign Secretary was told on 8 September 2003, but also did not think it necessary to tell Lord Hutton.

Mr Straw's certainty over the credibility of the assessment does not appear to have been widely shared by his cabinet colleagues. Margaret Beckett, who in 2003 was Environment Secretary, admitted in December 2006, when she was Foreign Secretary, that ministers had realised before the invasion, in other words early in 2003, that the claim that weapons could be deployed within forty-five minutes was probably wrong. The claim was not withdrawn prior to invasion, she implied, because 'nobody thought it was relevant. Nobody thought it was actually a big sweeping statement.'[13]

The 45-minute claim was not the only dubious material masquerading as intelligence in this dossier. We were also told that Saddam had 'sought significant quantities of uranium from Africa, despite having no active civil nuclear programme that could require it'. This suggestion was then repeated by President Bush soon after, in his State of the Union address in January 2003, quoting British intelligence sources. Except that the United States had already investigated this suggestion itself at least twice before the British government's September dossier was published, and concluded that there was no evidence for the claim. But that did not stop Condoleezza Rice clinging onto the September dossier.[14] 'The British continue to stand by their report,' she weakly said, in a somewhat circular justification. She did, however, concede that at least one of the documents underlying the allegation had turned out to be a forgery.

In fact, the CIA had sent a former ambassador, Joseph Wilson, out to Niger in February 2002 to investigate suggestions that Iraq had been trying to obtain yellow cake, a chemical used as a source of weapons-grade uranium, from the country. Mr Wilson spent over a week talking to dozens of people, including former and current government officials and those associated with the country's uranium business. At the end of the process, he concluded that it would be exceedingly difficult for Niger to transfer uranium to Iraq, given the international ownership of the two mines, the scrutiny from the International Atomic Energy Agency and the internal oversight within Niger itself. He shared his thoughts with the US ambassador in the country, Barbro Owens-Kirkpatrick, who had previously researched the allegation herself and reached similar conclusions.

Mr Wilson was unhappy that the President was using what he regarded as unfounded and discredited information to hype up the threat from Saddam, and went public with his concerns in an article for the *New York Times*, which appeared on 6 July 2003. In this, he revealed details of his trip to Niger, and the fact that he had told the CIA on his return that it was 'highly doubtful' that Saddam had been able to buy uranium from that country, indeed that there was no evidence that he had even tried. He also accused the White House of having 'twisted', in other words 'sexed up', the available intelligence on Iraq's weapons programme 'to exaggerate the Iraqi threat'.

The response from the White House was quick, astonishing and brutal. On 14 July, just three days before David Kelly died, another piece appeared, this time written by the conservative journalist Robert Novak, a man closely associated with the White House. The piece revealed that Mr Wilson's wife,

Valerie Plame, was a serving CIA agent dealing with weapons of mass destruction, and alleged that it was she who had suggested that her husband be sent to Niger to investigate the claim.

The reader was presumably supposed to think that a trip to Niger was some sort of junket. The consequence, of course, was to blow Ms Plame's cover – she was officially working for a private sector company – and effectively end her career. Furthermore, naming her in this way is likely to have compromised every relationship and every network she was party to, perhaps running through her entire time with the CIA.

It is a federal offence under the Intelligence Identities Protection Act 1982 to intentionally disclose the name and details of a covert agent. The punishment is a fine of up to $50,000, or ten years' imprisonment. Yet there appears to have been no investigation into this matter, and nobody has been prosecuted for the leak, although Lewis 'Scooter' Libby, Vice-President Dick Cheney's chief of staff, was found to have lied to investigators about conversations where he had mentioned Ms Plame. Subsequently, President Bush commuted his thirty-month prison sentence without Mr Libby ever having had to see the inside of a prison. The reason for the commutation, of course, is that the leaking of Ms Plame's name was unofficially sanctioned, in an act of petty vindictiveness against her and Mr Wilson, and as a clear warning to others what would happen if they dared to blow the whistle on the White House.

So the uranium claim had been discounted by the CIA as long ago as February 2002, yet it still appeared in the British government's dossier published in September to bolster support for an invasion of Iraq. Did the United States not share its assessment with the British? It seems that it did and that there were attempts within the intelligence network to warn the British to back off the claim. That, however, did not stop it appearing in the September dossier, and then in the President's address to the nation. It seems that for both the US and the UK governments, the suggestion that Saddam was attempting to buy yellow cake from Niger was just too eye-catching to drop, evidence or not.

There can surely be no doubt that the dossier was crafted with the shaping of public opinion in mind. Reading it now, it is difficult to escape the conclusion that its primary purpose was to support the case for war, though Lord Butler in his report rejected this conclusion. At the very least, it was surely meant to harden views on Saddam and soften opposition to any actions the government might take, not least by alarming the public unnecessarily.

The evidence shows that the presentational element of the dossier was crucial. We know that Alastair Campbell was heavily involved in this, even to the extent that, despite having no formal intelligence role, he chaired meetings on the progress of the dossier. This practice has since been roundly criticised on all sides. The Foreign Affairs Committee, in its 2003 report, put it baldly: 'We conclude that it was wrong for Alastair Campbell or any Special Adviser to have chaired a meeting on an intelligence matter, and we recommend that this practice cease.'[15]

To be fair to Campbell, it was the Prime Minister who had revived the idea of a dossier and had charged Campbell with overseeing the production and presentation. It was the Prime Minister who should be held responsible for the criticism properly levelled by the Foreign Affairs Committee. There had in fact been controversy over the role of Campbell since day one of New Labour, when Tony Blair used executive powers to allow both Campbell and Jonathan Powell, his chief of staff, each politically appointed special advisers, to issue instructions to civil servants.

The issue was still current in 2007, when Sir Alistair Graham, in a speech to introduce the last annual report under his chairmanship of the Committee of Standards in Public Life, said:

My immediate predecessor, Sir Nigel Wicks, raised concerns in April 2003 about the propriety of special advisers giving direction to civil servants. No. 10's response at the time was that it was unrealistic to expect Alastair Campbell not to be allowed to direct different parts of the government machine, particularly on an issue like Iraq! Unsurprisingly, perhaps, this statement in a lobby note no longer appears on the No. 10 website – but we have a copy.

It is disappointing, though perhaps not unpredictable, that Sir Alistair was not reappointed by the Prime Minister.

Independent scrutineers appointed by Blair had not, it would seem, to be too independent. Encouragingly, just as one of Blair's first acts when he arrived at 10 Downing Street was to invest Campbell and Powell with these powers, so one of the first acts of Gordon Brown as Prime Minister was to strip any successors of these very same powers.

Shortly before the dossier was published, Powell sent Campbell and John Scarlett an email, which contained the following sentences: 'Alastair – what will be the headline in the *Standard* on day of publication? What do we want it to be?'[16] The *Evening Standard* is important because it is London based and can set the agenda for both that day's broadcast media and the following day's papers. In the event, the second edition on the day in question will not have disappointed Messrs Campbell, Powell and Scarlett. It read: '45 minutes from attack – dossier reveals Saddam is ready to launch chemical war strikes.' And the story opened: 'Saddam Hussein's armoury of chemical weapons is on standby for use within 45 minutes, the government's dossier on Iraq revealed today. He is developing missiles that could reach British military bases in Cyprus.'

Other papers followed suit the next day. The *Sun*, for example, offered us 'Brits 45 mins from doom'. None of this was remotely true. Moreover, even at the time, as we have seen from the testimony from Robin Cook, nobody in the intelligence services or at the top of government believed that Saddam was developing a WMD missile capability.

One might have thought that the government would want to correct these very misleading stories, but in fact, they seemed happy for this alarmist picture to be painted. Geoff Hoon, then Defence Secretary, appeared supremely indifferent. The following exchange took place at the Hutton inquiry when the BBC's counsel, Andrew Caldecott QC, cross-examined Hoon:

Caldecott: Are you aware that on 25 September [2002] a number of newspapers had banner headlines suggested that this [the 45-minute claim] related to strategic missiles or bombs?

Hoon: I can recall, yes.

Caldecott: Why was no corrective statement issued for the benefit of the public in relation to those media reports?

Hoon: I do not know.

Caldecott: It must have been considered by someone, must it not?

Hoon: I have spent many years trying to persuade newspapers and journalists to correct their stories. I have to say it is an extraordinarily time-consuming and generally frustrating process.

Caldecott: I am sorry, are you saying that the press would not report a corrective statement that the dossier was meant to refer, in this context, to battlefield munitions and not to strategic weapons?

Hoon: What I am suggesting is that I am not aware of whether any consideration was given to such a correction. All that I do know is that, generally speaking, newspapers are resistant to corrections. That judgement may have been made by others as well.

Caldecott: But Mr Hoon, you must have been horrified that the dossier had been misrepresented in this way. It was a complete distortion of what it actually was intended to convey, was it not?

Hoon: Well, I was not horrified.[17]

After a few more such exchanges, the BBC's counsel pointedly asked: 'Do you accept that on this topic at least you had an absolute duty to try to correct it?'

'No, I do not,' replied Hoon.[18]

Actually, it was worse than indifference. It was contempt. Contempt for the inquiry process, for the questioner and, most of all, for the public.

The reason, of course, that there was no enthusiasm to correct the stories is because they were exactly what the government wanted to see. We do not know what answer Jonathan Powell received to his question but it is a fair bet that the ideal headline this cabal wanted would not have been very different from the one that finally appeared in the *Evening Standard*.

There is in fact evidence that the papers were led in the direction of such a sensationalist headline. For the first edition of the *Standard* that day did not have such a dramatic headline linked to the 45-minute claim. A journalist then working in the lobby for the regional press told me that a mysterious fax arrived with them at about 8 a.m., after the first edition had gone to press. The significance of the fact that it was the regional press that received this is that they traditionally benefit from early release of embargoed material to help them meet their deadlines. The fax was the cover note of a briefing related to the dossier, with the 45-minute claim highlighted. Just in case they missed the point.

At the Hutton inquiry, Alastair Campbell was asked whether he had any hand in the *Standard* headline. He replied, 'I did not. I do not write headlines for the *Evening Standard*.'[19]

Apart from the now notorious claim, there is a good deal of further evidence that suggests the raw intelligence in the dossier was firmed up for presentational purposes. The Hutton report includes a memorandum sent by Campbell to John Scarlett, suggesting sixteen changes to the wording of the dossier as it stood on 16 September. Of these, only three dealt with purely presentational matters, such as the correction of a date or the number of bullet points. The other thirteen all called for a strengthening of the language used, implicitly therefore making judgements on intelligence matters. Around half of these suggestions were accepted by Mr Scarlett, who was officially in charge of the document.

One crucial such suggestion accepted by Mr Scarlett was in the following sentence: 'The Iraqi military may be able to deploy chemical and biological weapons within 45 minutes of an order to do so.' As a result, the final version replaced the cautious 'may be' with the definitive 'are'. Yet subsequently, the Prime Minister told the House of Commons:

There was no attempt, at any time, by any official, or minister, or member of No. 10 Downing Street staff, to override the intelligence judgements of the Joint Intelligence Committee. That includes the judgement about the so-called forty-five minutes. It was a judgement made by the Joint Intelligence Committee and them alone.[20]

This is Tony Blair in typically robust form, shoring up not only his doubtful backbenchers but also wider opinion in the House. Unfortunately, as we have seen, the assurance is, as the quaint language of the Commons might put it, at variance with the facts. A terminological inexactitude, even.

Campbell, when asked at the Hutton inquiry if he had had any influence on the inclusion of the 45-minute claim in the dossier, replied, 'None whatever . . . I had no input, output, influence upon them [the words in the dossier] whatsoever at any stage in the process.'[21] Perhaps he had forgotten the significant textual change he had put forward. Happily, as mentioned earlier, the Hutton inquiry was not established on a statutory basis, so nobody was required to give evidence under oath.

The general case Campbell made was that the text in the main body of the dossier was inconsistent with the language in the executive summary, and it could be argued that to point this out was indeed a presentational matter. However, he did not just point it out. He called, in virtually every case where he believed there were differences in emphasis, for the language of the weaker version to be strengthened. That reveals both an interference in intelligence judgements and a desire to have the dossier as strong as possible. Neither practice is acceptable.

In respect of the sixteen textual alterations suggested by Mr Campbell, Mr Scarlett was to write back to him reassuringly, 'We have been able to amend the text in most cases as you proposed.' Lord Hutton would later suggest, in his inquiry report, that Mr Scarlett may have been 'subconsciously influenced' by political considerations.[22]

Subsequently, Mr Scarlett was to become head of MI6, in which role he appeared to be rather more robust in resisting political pressure. In January 2007 he refused Blair's request that MI6 endorse a dossier in which the government claimed that a major corruption inquiry into Saudi Arabian arms deals with British Aerospace was threatening national security. Contrary to Lord Goldsmith's statement to the House of Lords that the intelligence agencies 'agreed with the assessment' in the dossier, the agencies went out of their way to make it quite clear to the press that this statement was incorrect and that there were in fact significant differences between themselves and the government over the language used by Lord Goldsmith, which sources said 'contained quite a degree of conjecture'.[23]

Campbell's involvement would be examined in considerable detail by the Foreign Affairs Committee some months later, when an interesting and confidential analysis was carried out to compare what he had said to the committee about the dossier with what he subsequently told Lord Hutton.

A 'discrepancies' paper was produced for the committee, running to some fourteen pages. The document was never released and withheld even from MPs not on the committee – an official request I submitted for a copy was refused. I was, however, able to obtain a copy, thanks to help of unlikely origin.

The detailed analysis shows that there are in fact notable differences between what Campbell told the committee and what he told Lord Hutton just a matter of weeks later. For example, Campbell told the committee that the draft dossier had said that Iraq had sought to secure uranium, and that he had asked if any had been secured. Yet the memorandum from Mr Campbell to Mr Scarlett, produced at the Hutton inquiry, revealed that, as one of the suggested drafting changes proposed by Campbell, he had written: 'Can we say he has secured uranium from Africa.'

Crucially, Campbell, when asked to identify the textual changes to the dossier he had suggested, did not tell the committee of his proposal to change 'may be' to 'are' in respect of the 45-minute claim.

At the same time as I managed to procure a copy of the paper, I discovered that on 9 March 2004 a proposal by opposition MPs to haul Campbell and Jack Straw back before the committee to discuss the discrepancies was blocked by a straight vote of all the Labour MPs on the committee, who formed a controlling majority, with the exception of Andrew Mackinlay, who abstained. A second proposal, that Campbell alone be recalled specifically to explain why he had not informed the committee of his proposed change in wording in respect of the 45-minute claim, was also defeated, with voting along identical lines.

One might have thought that a probing and resolute committee of the House would have wanted to hold the government to account on such important matters, but it seems not.

The Prime Minister's foreword, written by Mr Campbell and signed off by Mr Scarlett, has some of the most assertive and hence most unjustified language in the dossier. It included the following: 'In recent months, I have been increasingly alarmed by the evidence from inside Iraq that . . . Saddam Hussein is continuing to develop WMD, and with them the ability to inflict real damage upon the region, and the stability of the world.'

The phrase 'increasingly alarmed' suggests either that the threat from Saddam had been growing 'in recent months', or that more and more evidence was being uncovered to reinforce the already held perceptions of a serious threat. Neither is true. If this paragraph is true at all, it must be in the sense that the Prime Minister had become 'increasingly alarmed' himself as he considered and reconsidered the same flimsy evidence. The use of that phrase also chimes in with an email written to Campbell and other colleagues on 11 September by Daniel Pruce, a member of the Downing Street press office. He wrote, 'Our aim should also be to convey the impression that things have not been static in Iraq but that over the past decade he [Saddam] has been aggressively and relentlessly pursuing WMD while brutally repressing his own people.'[24]

Robin Cook, in his evidence to the Foreign Affairs Committee the following June, put the matter in context: 'If you read the September dossier very carefully there is a striking absence of any recent and alarming and confirmed intelligence. The great majority of the paper is derivative . . . It is also a highly suggestible [sic] document.'[25] Campbell would later suggest that Mr Pruce was offering comments above his pay-grade.

Yet on the same day, less than two weeks before publication, an email was sent to the intelligence agencies by a Cabinet Office official. It included the following: 'No. 10, through the Chairman, want the document to be as strong as possible within the bounds of available intelligence. This is therefore a last call for any items of intelligence that the agencies think can and should be included.'

This email was condemned by Sir Rodric Braithwaite, himself a former chairman of the Joint Intelligence Committee from 1992 to 1993. He told the BBC's *Panorama* in January 2004: 'It is not their job to fiddle with documents to make them more presentable to the public. If they start doing that, they get involved, instead of [in] analysis, which is their job, in presentation. It is ceasing to be objective, it's becoming an advocate.' And in a swipe at Mr Scarlett he added, 'If your job is simply to analyse things . . . you have to avoid getting into the magic circle that surrounds any Prime Minister.'

By and large, each draft of the dossier became stronger and more certain in its language, despite the absence of new intelligence to justify such upgrading. Tony Blair in his foreword summed up the position in a way that was consistent with the kind of narrative Mr Pruce had identified, and certainly could be described as 'as strong as possible': 'What I believe the assessed intelligence has established beyond doubt is that Saddam has continued to produce chemical and biological weapons, that he continues in his efforts to develop nuclear weapons, and that he has been able to extend the range of his ballistic missile programme.'

You get the drift. Take intensified WMD production, add in a threat of nuclear weapons, season with missiles with an extended range – how far? – and garnish with a 45-minute claim. It did not matter that none of it was true. It was sufficient to mobilise enough MPs and public opinion onto the Prime Minister's war footing.

And even then came the caveat: 'I also believe that, as stated in the document, Saddam will now do his utmost to try to conceal his weapons from UN inspectors . . . I am quite clear that Saddam will go to extreme lengths, indeed has already done so, to hide these weapons and avoid giving them up.' In other words, if we find them, that proves we were right to invade. If we do not, then obviously they are still there, but he has hidden them. You might as well argue that a woman tied to a ducking stool was guilty of witchcraft if she survived the plunge but innocent if she drowned.

Incidentally, if Saddam had gone to such great lengths to hide his weapons, how was he going to be able to deploy them within forty-five minutes?

The dossier was written to whip up the public mood against Saddam and to justify the case for military action against him. If the intelligence could be found to make that case, then well and good. If it could not, and it transpired that it could not, then what was available would have to be written up in such a way that the central objective of the dossier – the justification for invasion – was still met. We were indeed, as the then Lib Dem shadow Foreign Secretary, Sir Menzies Campbell, said, being taken to war 'on a flawed prospectus'.

The Prime Minister told the House of Commons that the dossier was 'extensive, detailed and authoritative'.[26] It was later described by Lord Butler in his report as 'vague and ambiguous'.

You would be hard pressed, of course, to find such criticism of the government in Lord Hutton's report.

9 Dodgy dossiers

Those who are inclined to give the government the benefit of the doubt over the September document should perhaps consider the next dossier, issued in February 2003. This one, entitled *Iraq: Its Infrastructure of Concealment, Deception and Intimidation*, was to earn the sobriquet 'the dodgy dossier' (although the September publication was also dodgy in its own way), when it was discovered by Cambridge academic Glen Rangwala and revealed by Channel 4 News that large parts of it had been lifted straight from an article published by the *Middle East Review of International Affairs* available online. Even the grammatical mistakes were copied.

The author was Ibrahim al-Marashi, in 2003 a research associate at the Center for Nonproliferation Studies at the Monterey Institute of International Studies in California. He was never contacted by anyone involved in the preparation of the dodgy dossier and was given no credit on the publication itself. It also transpired that the article in question largely comprised material relating to the 1991 Gulf War.

Mr al-Marashi was tracked down by the House of Commons Foreign Affairs Committee and appeared before them on 19 June 2003. He told them: 'I was quite shocked to see it end up in this dossier. That was not my intent, to have it support such an argument to provide evidence necessary to go to war.'[1]

The dossier was the work of the Coalition Information Centre, a unit established by Alastair Campbell in October 2001. Although technically based in the Foreign Office, it was staffed by eager young Turks who answered directly to Campbell. Not even the Foreign Secretary knew what the unit was up to. At its height, the unit contained twenty-eight staff. It was finally wound up in May 2003. The member of staff responsible for the lifting of Mr al-Marashi's material from the internet, Paul Hamill, rather appropriately had as his official title Head of Story Development.

Campbell admitted to the committee that the idea for this dossier had come from his personal spin unit, that neither the intelligence agencies nor ministers, not even the Foreign Secretary, had been consulted. Nor, he conceded, had the final document even been seen by John Scarlett. Yet on 3 February the Prime Minister had told the House:

> We issued further intelligence over the weekend about the infrastructure of concealment. It is obviously difficult when we publish intelligence reports, but I hope that people have some sense of the integrity of our security services. They are not publishing this, or giving us this information, and making it up. It is the intelligence that they are receiving, and we are passing it on to people.[2]

The vast majority of MPs will have concluded from this statement that this latest publication represented yet more up-to-date intelligence, and that the concerns apparently felt within the security services had been ratcheted up further. They will also have taken for granted, especially given the words used by the Prime Minister, that the document was one produced by the intelligence agencies in a thorough and rigorous way.

Nothing could be further from the truth.

Jack Straw, in his evidence to the committee, had little option but to come clean: 'The way in which this document was produced was unsatisfactory and it should not have happened in this way, and it should have been subject to proper procedures. It is an episode which has been a very great embarrassment to the government.'[3] He termed the document 'a complete Horlicks'.[4] Campbell preferred to call it 'a storm in a teacup'.[5]

In fact, in his evidence to the committee, Campbell was prepared to admit to only one mistake, namely that the author of the material had not been credited. He was nevertheless also keen to play down the significance of the February dossier, and distance it from the September one. The later one, with the cat out of the bag, was now pretty much indefensible, notwithstanding his best efforts, so distance between the two dossiers had to be established to protect the reputation of the September one.

But there were clear and worrying similarities between the two publications. Just as MPs were misled by the contents of the September dossier, so they were misled by the February one. On both occasions, they were allowed to think that what they were receiving was a document prepared by the intelligence services in a sober fashion without involvement from No. 10, save perhaps for the foreword in the Prime Minister's name. And on both occasions, sensationalist and inaccurate content was used, with scant regard to the facts. The function of each was to strengthen the case for war.

In the 'dodgy dossier', there was pure invention. The online article may have been copied verbatim, grammatical errors and all, but in a couple of crucial aspects, it was indeed changed. Most outrageously, the phrase 'opposition groups' was removed and replaced by 'terrorist organisations'. There was no basis whatsoever for this alteration.

Mr al-Marashi, questioned on this point, told the committee:

> For example, the Iraqi government was helping a rival wing of the Ba'ath party in Syria. That rival wing . . . is not a terrorist organisation. It is an opposition group to the regime of Hafez al-Assad . . . Any links between terrorist organisations – I just could not find evidence to include them in this article and for that reason I refrained from stating it like that.[6]

Once again, as with the 45-minute claim, the need to make a political case was allowed to trump the available intelligence.

One dodgy dossier may have been a mistake. Two looked like premeditation. Incredibly, there was even an attempt at a third, this time with the fingerprints of John Scarlett all over it.

The occasion was the preparation in January 2004 of a report by the Iraq Survey Group, the body sent in by the United States and the UK after the invasion to find weapons of mass destruction and evidence of programmes to produce such. One of the weapons inspectors charged with the task was the Australian Rod Barton, chosen by the CIA to be the special adviser to the group. He and his colleagues were preparing to conclude not only that there were no weapons of mass destruction to be found in Iraq, but that Saddam had not even had a programme to manufacture such weapons since 1991. Clearly this was potentially hugely embarrassing to the UK and the USA.

The response by senior figures in British intelligence was to prevent the Iraqi Study Group's interim report, a far from dodgy dossier, from being published. Those who had been so keen to rush out questionable material before the war were now curiously coy about releasing this particular document.

Mr Barton says that Martin Howard, the deputy chief of defence intelligence at the Ministry of Defence, wanted publication delayed until something 'substantive' had been found. He left Mr Barton in no doubt that the UK, for whom he purported to speak, would prefer the report not to be published. When it became clear that publication could not be stopped, Mr Barton alleges that Mr Scarlett tried to repeat the trick that had worked with the September dossier – the insertion of questionable material to make the position look stronger than it actually was.

According to a report in the *Observer* by Antony Barnett, Charles Duelfer, the CIA-appointed head of the Iraqi Study Group, called Mr Barton into his office on 8 March to show him an email received from Mr Scarlett. It suggested the inclusion of nine 'nuggets' of information to make the case that Saddam's WMD programmes were still active and a threat, the exact opposite of what the group had concluded.[7] It is believed that these nuggets included allegations that Saddam was working on a smallpox weapon, that he possessed mobile laboratories, and that he had been developing research equipment for use in nuclear weapons. None of this was true.

Mr Barton told the paper:

> I couldn't believe it. He was suggesting dragging things from a previous report to use them to, well, sex it up. It was an attempt to make our report appear to imply that maybe there were still WMD out there. I knew that he had been responsible for your dossier [the September one] and I realised he was trying to do the same thing.[8]

I put these allegations to Foreign Office minister Kim Howells in a parliamentary debate on 19 July 2006, and in subsequent correspondence. He described them as 'old and false allegations', adding: 'Mr Duelfer has already made it clear that he initiated a request to Mr Scarlett to set out items from an earlier classified report which might usefully be included in the report then being prepared by Mr Duelfer.'[9]

Rod Barton, who was Mr Duelfer's special adviser and was personally responsible for the preparation of the interim report, totally rejects this. He told me: 'This is incorrect…Mr Duelfer did *not* request anyone to suggest nuggets for insertion [emphasis in original].'[10]

Kim Howells is generally a well-regarded minister. It would be interesting to know whether he took the trouble to establish the accuracy of his letter, doubtless with some contribution from officials in MI6, now run by one John Scarlett, before signing it.

Taking the three dossiers together, including the Iraqi Study Group interim report referred to above, it is breathtaking how far not just government ministers, but their advisers and officials and even key intelligence personnel such as Mr Scarlett were prepared to pervert raw intelligence to fit in with the established political direction of travel. The 45-minute claim in the first dossier, the hyped-up internet article in the second, and the attempted insertion of nine so-called nuggets in the third – these were no accidents, but a determined and concerted effort to 'sex up' material for political purposes.

This is, as far as we are aware, completely unprecedented and certainly alien to good government. As Lord Butler concluded in his report, in respect of the September dossier, 'The government wanted an unclassified document on which it could draw in its advocacy of its policy.'[11] He added: 'Judgements in the dossier went to (although not beyond) the outer limits of the intelligence available . . . The publication of

134

such a document in the name and with the authority of the JIC had the result that more weight was placed on the intelligence than it could bear.'[12]

It is welcome that Gordon Brown, in June 2007, announced that he would as Prime Minister take steps to reassert the independence of the intelligence agencies. But why was this unprecedented corruption of intelligence undertaken? To understand that, we need to look across the water to Washington, and to the determination of the Bush administration to take military action against Iraq.

There is no doubt that the hawks in the Republican Party had long wanted to attack Iraq. While Bill Clinton was President, the Republican Congress had pushed through the Iraq Liberation Act, which was duly ignored by President Clinton but not forgotten by the Republicans when George W. Bush came to office.

We can speculate as to when President Bush and his inner circle first decided upon military action. Some date it to the publication of *Rebuilding America's Defenses*, the work of a powerful group called the Project for the New American Century, which included among its membership people who would become centre stage in the Bush administration, including the Vice-President, Dick Cheney; the Defense Secretary, Donald Rumsfeld; his deputy, Paul Wolfowitz; and the President's brother Jeb. The document, which first appeared in September 2000, talked about military action in the Gulf and contained the passage: 'While the unresolved conflict with Iraq provides the immediate justification, the need for a substantial American force presence in the Gulf transcends the issue of the regime of Saddam Hussein'.

Others simply believe that President Bush came to office determined to finish the job his father had not completed in the first Gulf War, by deposing Saddam Hussein. A third explanation is that, while Iraq was a constant irritant to Washington, there was really no intention to take action until the attacks of 11 September 2001 occurred, which caused a furious United States to lash out rather wildly. Whatever the reason, the intentions were certainly clear shortly after the attacks, indeed even on the day itself.

A CBS News report from 4 September 2002 quoted notes taken by Mr Rumsfeld's aides. These notes record that at 2.40 p.m. the same day Rumsfeld ordered the military to begin working on plans to strike at Osama bin Laden (UBL). Crucially he added: 'Judge whether good enough hit SH [Saddam Hussein, of course] at same time. Not only UBL . . . Go massive. Sweep it all up. Things related and not.'

President Bush himself, in his first State of the Union address after the attacks, devoted a significant section of his speech to Iraq. He said:

Iraq continues to flaunt its hostility toward America and to support terror. The Iraqi regime has plotted to develop anthrax and nerve gas and nuclear weapons for over a decade . . . This is a regime that has something to hide from the civilised world. States like these, and their terrorist allies, constitute an axis of evil.[13]

Saddam Hussein was firmly, in the sights of the US administration, Public Enemy Number One.

Iraq, of course, had no connection with the events of 11 September, and, however barbaric Saddam Hussein was to those inside his country, and he certainly was pathologically so, he was no fool and had shown no interest in actively threatening others since the Gulf War of 1991, when his invasion of Kuwait had left his fingers badly burnt. In addition, the weapons inspection process, where David Kelly played a leading part, had been very successful in locating and destroying his stocks of biological and chemical weapons, and his capacity to rearm.

Over the next couple of years, a great deal of effort would be put in to try to find some links between Saddam's regime and al-Qaeda, yet the evidence that was discovered suggested, if anything, hostility between the two camps. That would not stop Vice-President Cheney asserting, as late as 14 September 2003, that 'Saddam had long-established ties with al-Qaeda'.

Paul R. Pillar served with the CIA for twenty-eight years until his retirement in 2005. He latterly worked as the national intelligence officer for the Middle East, in which role he was in charge of co-ordinating all of the intelligence community's assessments regarding Iraq. Following his retirement, in an article for the journal *Foreign Affairs*, he wrote:

The greatest discrepancy [between intelligence and policy] concerned not WMD but the relationship between Saddam and Al Qaeda. The enormous attention devoted to this subject did not reflect any judgement by intelligence officials that there was or was likely to be anything like 'the alliance' the administration said existed.

The administration's rejection of the intelligence community's judgements became especially clear with the formation of a special Pentagon unit, the Policy Counterterrorism Evaluation Group. The unit . . . was dedicated to finding every possible link between Saddam and Al Qaeda, and its briefings accused the intelligence community of faulty analysis for failing to see the supposed alliance.[14]

You could be forgiven for concluding that Bush was more interested in dealing with Saddam, for whatever reason, than with those responsible for the 11 September attacks. In which case it was hardly surprising that a poll in February 2003 showed that 72 per cent of US citizens believed that Saddam was personally involved in the attacks.[15]

On 8 July 2002, President Bush asserted publicly that, in respect of Iraq, 'it's the stated policy of this government to have a regime change. And it hasn't changed . . . And we'll use all tools at our disposal to do so.'[16]

Regime change. Here lies the explanation for the stance

taken by the British government, certainly from the summer of 2002 until the invasion. President Bush was going to invade, and Tony Blair's determination to stay as close as possible to him meant he decided that the UK would have to follow suit.

Except a desire for regime change is an illegal basis in international law for invading a country. So we had the hyped-up dossiers and the pretence that, if only Saddam would co-operate with the UN and its inspectors, invasion could be avoided.

Ironically, then, the deception that occurred in the stated intentions of the US and the UK can be laid firmly at the door of Blair's government. The US administration, as seen above, was quite happy to flout international law and talk brazenly of regime change. It was in order to satisfy British sensitivities that the convoluted, complicated and essentially dishonest talk of weapons of mass destruction and Security Council resolutions was generated. It has to be said that using British influence in this way was a fruitless and self-defeating expenditure of effort and capital. The US approach, Wild West though it may have been, at least had the benefit of honesty.

That Blair certainly knew by July 2002 that a US-led invasion of Iraq to secure regime change was inevitable cannot be doubted. Nor can his determination to stick close by the Americans, wherever that led him. This view was confirmed by Mr Pillar. In an email to me he wrote: 'I believe that what was most important to Prime Minister Blair was to preserve the closeness of the relationship with Washington. If the Bush administration had not been out in front on this issue [Iraq], then Mr Blair's government certainly would not have been either.'[17]

There is some evidence, in fact, that Blair knew of US intentions shortly after the attacks of 11 September. Up to that point, it had been the practice for transcripts of telephone conversations between Prime Minister and President to be available to senior British figures in Washington and New York. After the attacks, that practice petered out. The Prime Minister had begun to run his own special foreign policy, and the experts within the Foreign Office were no longer to be in the loop, perhaps even could not be trusted, on this most sensitive of issues. Britain offered no real constructive alternative to military action, and the UK's policy drift to war was allowed to go unchallenged and uncorrected.

It is worth remarking that, as far as the United States is concerned, the decision to deceive and mislead Congress with false claims about WMD and Saddam's alleged links with the events of 11 September is an impeachable offence.

If there was a doubt in the public mind, it was ended by the publication in the *Sunday Times* on 1 May 2005 of a highly secret memorandum dated 23 July 2002.[18] This recorded a meeting involving Blair; the Defence Secretary, Geoff Hoon; the Foreign Secretary, Jack Straw; the Attorney General, Lord Goldsmith; the head of MI6, Sir Richard Dearlove; John Scarlett; and of course Alastair Campbell. Admiral Sir Michael

Boyce, Chief of the Defence Staff, and David Manning, foreign policy adviser to the Prime Minister, were also present, along with Jonathan Powell and Sally Morgan from the Prime Minister's office.

The minute was taken by Matthew Rycroft, then the Prime Minister's private secretary, and bore the warning in bold, and underlined: '**This record is extremely sensitive. No further copies should be made**.'

At that meeting, Sir Richard or 'C', as the head of MI6 is quaintly known, gave his assessment of the US position. The memo reads:

C reported on his recent talks in Washington. There was a perceptible shift in attitude. Military action was now seen as inevitable. Bush wanted to remove Saddam, through military action, justified by the conjunction of terrorism and WMD. But the intelligence and facts were being fixed around the policy. The NSC [National Security Council] had no patience with the UN route, and no enthusiasm for publishing material on the Iraqi regime's record.

It went on with a statement that would sadly be all too fully vindicated: 'There was little discussion in Washington of the aftermath of military action.'

According to the minute, Hoon added that 'the most likely timing in US minds for military action to begin was January, with the timeline beginning thirty days before the US Congressional elections.' The Foreign Secretary seemed concerned, not to stop an illegal war, but to find a justification for it:

It seemed clear that Bush had made up his mind to take military action, even if the timing was not yet decided. But the case was thin. Saddam was not threatening his neighbours, and his WMD capability was less than that of Libya, North Korea or Iran. We should work up a plan for an ultimatum for Saddam to allow back in the UN weapons inspectors. This would also help with the legal justification for the use of force.

The Prime Minister said: 'If the political context were right, people would support regime change. The two key issues were whether the military plan worked and whether we had the political strategy to give the military plan the space to work.' Meanwhile, the Attorney General warned that regime change was not a legal basis for invasion.

The central conclusion of the memo was that 'we should work on the assumption that the UK would take part in any military action'.

There is also evidence that Tony Blair was considering war on the illegal basis of regime change even earlier. Campbell's diary entry for 2 April 2002 reads: 'We discussed whether the central aim was WMD or regime change . . . TB felt it was regime change in part because of WMD but more broadly because of the threat to the region and the world.'*

None of this of course was reflected in what Parliament was told. MPs were assured that the government was working for a peaceful outcome, when it was preparing for war; that Iraq was a major world threat, when the assessment was that it was not; and that the government wanted the weapons inspectors back in, when they actually wanted Saddam to refuse to allow them back in.

Even after the war, the Prime Minister was maintaining the pretence that war had not been inevitable. On 8 July 2003, he was asked by the House of Commons Liaison Committee, the senior committee made up of chairs of all the House's other select committees, when he had decided to go to war. He replied:

> I decided that we could not avoid conflict in the few days before the vote on 18 March because it was then that it was obvious that we could not get a second UN resolution that delivered an ultimatum to Saddam . . . Up until that point I was still working to avoid the conflict.

---

* It is perhaps unwise to put too much store on Campbell's diaries. Like many diaries, they have a propensity to show the author in an almost unfailingly good light, where each judgement he makes is sound while others around him all too often show human frailty. In addition, Campbell admits in his preface to *The Blair Years* that some of the entries are rewritten, but fails to specify which these are. As *Private Eye* pointed out (20 July 2007), some entries refer to individuals such as Robin Cook in the past tense when they were in fact still alive on the day of the relevant diary entry. Perhaps it is not surprising that the satirical magazine labelled them *The Dodgy Diaries*.

For good measure, he had earlier said: 'I should tell you that I have absolutely no doubt at all that we will find evidence of weapons of mass destruction programmes, no doubt at all.'[19] The certainty had moved from WMD themselves onto programmes connected with them, but even that was to prove optimistic.

The leaked memo of 23 July 2002, appearing as it did less than a week before the 2005 general election, was clearly timed to cause shockwaves in the run-up to that election. Yet perhaps because it was so close to polling day, it actually got somewhat lost in the pre-election melee.

At the Hutton inquiry, the Prime Minister was asked what had changed between the decision taken in March 2002 to mothball any dossier, and the reversal of that decision formally taken in early September that year. He replied:

> What changed was really two things which came together. First of all, there was a tremendous amount of information and evidence coming across my desk as to the weapons of mass destruction and the programmes associated with it that Saddam had. There was also a renewed sense of urgency, again, in the way that this was being publicly debated. I recall throughout the August break that literally every day there were stories appearing saying we were about to go and invade Iraq.

This was less than honest. What had really changed was the realisation that the United States had decided that war would occur, resulting in the knock-on British decision to join the US in this endeavour, as set out clearly in the Downing Street minutes of the meeting that took place on 23 July.

The Prime Minister implied in his evidence to Lord Hutton that the dossier was somehow forced on the government, an inevitable riposte to the continual drip of press stories. In reality, those press stories were all too accurate, and the dossier's function was to further the case for war. The speculation about an invasion of Iraq, far from being an inconvenience for the Prime Minister, was useful in advancing the case he wanted to see made.

There is really only one realistic construction that can be put on the Prime Minister's actions during this period. He and his senior ministers had already decided to join George Bush in his illegal invasion, but wanted to secure UN authorisation for this course of action, hence the exaggerated threat from WMD as a way to pressurise the rest of the international community into adopting a resolution which would explicitly authorise military action. Unfortunately for the Prime Minister, this neat little stratagem fell apart when the rest of the UN Security Council refused to go along with it. Tony Blair was left exposed, committed to military action but without any legal cover. So suddenly we were told that there was already explicit authorisation for invasion under an old UN resolution, 1441. That interpretation is at the very least debatable.

On 12 September 2002, President Bush addressed the UN General Assembly: 'Right now, Iraq is expanding and improving facilities that were used for the production of biological weapons.' In his book *The Weapons Detective*,[20] Rod Barton picked up on this speech. He wrote that this statement 'came as a complete surprise to us: we had no intelligence to support this and wondered what he could possibly be referring to, since all the capable facilities had been destroyed under UNSCOM supervision in 1996'. The President's speech, which both referred to non-existent weapons and suggested that the threat was increasing, was made just two weeks before the publication of the UK's September dossier, which was faulty in the same two ways.

Paul R. Pillar, in his article for *Foreign Affairs*, spelt out what he had himself personally witnessed. He wrote:

> It has become clear that official intelligence analysis was not relied on in making even the most significant national security decisions, that intelligence was misused publicly to justify decisions already made, that damaging ill will developed between policymakers and intelligence officers, and that the intelligence community's own work was politicized . . . The Bush administration used intelligence not to inform decision-making but to justify a decision already made.[21]

On 16 October 2002, Congress formally authorised the

President to go to war with Iraq. But force would only be used 'as a last resort', Bush assured the American people. 'I hope the use of force will not become necessary.'

In the light of what we now know, that assurance rings very hollow. On 20 March 2003 the invasion began, and less than six weeks later President Bush stood on the deck of a US aircraft carrier to announce to cheering troops: 'In the battle of Iraq, the United States and our allies have prevailed.' In the background hung a banner proclaiming: 'Mission accomplished.'

But four years on the Americans, and the British, are still there in large numbers. Civil society is barely functioning and life-claiming terrorist incidents occur daily. The *Lancet* estimates that by spring 2007, up to 650,000 Iraqis had lost their lives as a result of the invasion, along with more than 3,000 US and 150 British soldiers. In addition, 50,000 US soldiers have been wounded. Over the same period, an estimated 1.7 million Iraqis have fled the country, taking refuge in nearby Syria or Kuwait.

And according to a reliable estimate based on Congressional appropriations, the war had cost the United States more than $400 billion. By contrast the US budget for tackling AIDS between 2003 and May 2007 was just $15 billion.

For the UK the cost of the war was reckoned at over £5 billion. But it has perhaps suffered an even greater deficit, and that is to its international reputation, which has been immensely damaged by the decision to position itself as the back wheel on George Bush's penny-farthing. This catastrophic failure of British foreign policy has been so enormous that it has led to unprecedented criticism from those who would normally remain silent, and criticism voiced in decidedly undiplomatic terms.

In April 2004, the *Independent* published on its front page an unprecedented, public letter to Blair from more than fifty diplomats, amongst them former British ambassadors, high commissioners, governors and senior international officials, which bluntly expressed their 'deepening concern [over] the policies which you have followed on the Arab–Israel problem and Iraq, in close co-operation with the United States'. In damning prose, the letter went on to accuse Blair of

abandoning the principles which for nearly four decades have guided international efforts to restore peace in the Holy Land and which have been the basis for such successes as those efforts have produced . . . at a time when, rightly or wrongly, we are portrayed throughout the Arab and Muslim world as partners in an illegal and brutal occupation in Iraq.

The letter ended by stating bluntly that, if the Prime Minister was unable to exert any influence over the United States to right the wrongs of the way in which the war in Iraq was being conducted, then there was 'no case for supporting policies which are doomed to failure'.[22]

But the most damning verdict of all must go to Sir Rodric Braithwaite, the former chair of the Joint Intelligence Committee, in a piece he produced for the *Financial Times* in August 2006. He wrote:

A spectre is stalking British television, a frayed and waxy zombie straight from Madame Tussaud's. This one, unusually, seems to live and breathe. Perhaps it comes from the Central Intelligence Agency's box of technical tricks, programmed to spout the language of the White House in an artificial English accent.

There is another possible explanation. Perhaps what we see on television is the real Tony Blair, the man who believes that he and his friend have the key to the horrifying problems of the Middle East.

… Mr Blair's prime responsibility is to defend the interests of his own country. This he has signally failed to do. Stiff in opinions, but often in the wrong, he has manipulated public opinion, sent our soldiers into distant lands for ill-conceived purposes, misused the intelligence agencies to serve his ends and reduced the Foreign Office to a demoralised cipher because it keeps reminding him of inconvenient facts. He keeps the dog, but barely notices if it barks or not. He prefers to construct his 'foreign policy' out of self-righteous soundbites and expensive foreign travel.[23]

For a distinguished former civil servant, himself renowned for his expertise in foreign affairs and security issues, to lambast a serving Prime Minister thus is unprecedented.

Is Tony Blair so arrogant that he could simply dismiss these astonishingly damning interventions from key insiders? Did he alone in Britain not cringe when the off-microphone conversation between himself and President Bush was inadvertently broadcast, in which he was addressed with the demeaning 'Yo, Blair' and was heard having his Uriah Heep offer to go to the Middle East swept aside by that intellectual colossus George W. Bush? So consistently craven has his approach been to the US President and his administration that one has to ask: if the White House held information on Blair so incriminating that its release would have caused his immediate resignation, in what way would the British Prime Minister have behaved differently from the way he did?

Perhaps we should be grateful that it was not worse than it was. There was, after all, a secret telephone conversation between Bush and Blair in January 2003, even before the war on Iraq was launched, in which the US President said that he 'wanted to go beyond Iraq'. The telephone call was transcribed on Downing Street paper by Michael Rycroft, and in that form a copy found its way to the press in October 2005.

According to the transcription, Bush indicated that after Iraq, Saudi Arabia, Pakistan, Iran and North Korea might have to be tackled. Does anyone seriously think that Blair would suddenly have developed some independence and unhitched his wagon from the madly careering one of the President? One can only speculate what might have happened if Iraq had not proved to be a quagmire for the United States.

And still, to the very end, Blair and Bush paraded before the cameras for their photo-opportunities, relaxed and smiling.

10 Changing question marks to exclamation marks

It was a routine meeting, the sort that occurs every day. A journalist was meeting a contact and getting the inside track on a current issue. Certainly when David Kelly met Andrew Gilligan to discuss Iraq, neither could have known that the touch paper had been lit for a political explosion, let alone that less than two months later Dr Kelly would be dead.

The now famous meeting took place in the less than salubrious surroundings of the Charing Cross Hotel, an old British Rail establishment and still very much a railway hotel. It was a venue conveniently close to Whitehall, yet anonymous.

Mr Gilligan had graduated from defence correspondent on the *Sunday Telegraph*, when I first met him, to becoming a key reporter for the prestigious *Today* programme on Radio 4. Over the years, ploughing his own furrow and without help from the government machine, he had produced some top-class stories. His contacts book would certainly make interesting reading.

Naturally, such a talent did not endear him to Alastair Campbell and others in government who wanted to control the news rather than react to unwelcome and difficult stories.

Over the next month, Mr Campbell's dislike of Mr Gilligan would become obsessive. For a short time it even seemed as though this dislike became the focal point of the government's activities.

A slightly odd character, Mr Gilligan, then aged thirty-five, looks somewhat older than he is and when he arrives for a meeting, always gives the impression of having rushed from somewhere else and expended considerable energy in doing so. Drops of perspiration will glisten on his forehead.

So it was that on 22 May 2003 he sat down with Dr Kelly to discuss Iraq. The meeting had been requested by the journalist, but Dr Kelly was happy to accede. The weapons inspector had a good number of journalists with whom he kept in contact and discussed matters related to his work. This was far from unusual. The Foreign Office, though less so the Ministry of Defence, recognised that there was a need for journalists to be informed on technical matters, and Dr Kelly had for some years implicitly had licence to engage with the media on this basis. He had even attended a Ministry of Defence senior officers TV course at Wilton Park in Sussex.

Dr Kelly told the Intelligence and Security Committee that he had 'interacted with the media extensively since 1991'.[1] On many of these occasions, he had gone on the record, without, it seems, anyone batting an eyelid. His own annual reports highlighted the dealings he had with the media over that year. James Bone, who reported from New York for the *Times* and who was one of Dr Kelly's regular contacts, told the *Observer* that Dr Kelly 'was sophisticated with the press, but he wasn't slavishly party line. In my experience, he didn't initiate leaks, but he gave candid answers to honest questions.'[2]

The Ministry of Defence would call the meeting with Mr Gilligan 'unauthorised', which is true in so far as nobody had been asked for, or given, specific permission for the meeting to take place, but then this frequently did not happen. Dr Kelly was in fact keen to meet Mr Gilligan again as the reporter had recently returned from Iraq and Dr Kelly was interested to know how the land lay. They had discussed the journalist's plan to visit Iraq when the two had last met, some three months earlier in February, also at the Charing Cross Hotel. Prior to that, they had met only once, at the International Institute for Strategic Studies the previous September.

The contents, even the length, of the conversation are in some dispute, depending on which version of events you believe, but it is common ground that the 45-minute claim did feature. The reporter made contemporaneous notes on his personal organiser, which included the following: 'Transformed week before publication to make it sexier . . . The classic was the 45 minutes . . . Most people in intelligence weren't happy with it because it didn't reflect the considered view they were putting forward.'[3]

Ironically, given how matters would turn out, Dr Kelly was supportive of the government's general position in respect of Iraq. He did believe that Iraq was a threat, and might well still have had weapons of mass destruction. For example, he put the likelihood of there being a store of chemical weapons at 30 per cent, both when talking to the reporter and subsequently to the ISC. He was also supportive of the concept of a dossier, but parted company when it came to the weight placed on the intelligence in the publication.

That Dr Kelly was unhappy with the 45-minute claim in particular is not disputed. He expressed his doubts both to colleagues and to friends in the Baha'i movement, to which he belonged. 'He broadly endorsed the intelligence in the dossier, but objected to the spin put on it,' one local Baha'i member in Abingdon told me.

Interestingly, Dr Kelly, in his evidence to the Intelligence and Security Committee, answered in the affirmative when asked if he thought Mr Gilligan was a reliable witness. That was a view that would not be shared by the Foreign Affairs Committee, whose chairman termed him 'an unsatisfactory witness'.

A week later after their meeting, at 6.07 a.m. on 29 May 2003, *Today* broadcast a live report from Mr Gilligan, in which he quoted a source alleging that the September dossier had been sexed up: 'What this person says is that a week before the publication date of the dossier, it was actually rather a bland production. Downing Street . . . ordered it to be sexed up, to be made more exciting and ordered more facts to be "discovered".'

Reading the transcript of the live broadcast today, the most striking aspect is just how accurate were the allegations Mr Gilligan was reporting. He reported his source, Dr Kelly, as saying the document had been rewritten shortly before publication to make it sexier. We now know that it was indeed strengthened and many of the ambiguities normally found in intelligence assessments had been replaced with certainties. Mr Gilligan reported that the 45-minute claim had been added late, that the intelligence services were dubious about the weight placed on it, and that the information came only from a single source. All of that was proved right.

In his enthusiasm for the story, his language in places was not as tight as it might have been, and did go further than what he had been told would justify. Given the importance of the story, this is unfortunate. Nevertheless, the story was essentially correct, and the BBC did not deserve to have its world fall in on its head, as happened when the Hutton report was published in 2004.

It was particularly ironic, and galling, to see Alastair Campbell haranguing the BBC mercilessly because Mr Gilligan had in his view broken the corporation's producer guidelines by relying on just one source for his story, when the same criticism was being levelled behind the scenes at Campbell and his colleagues over the single-sourced 45-minute claim.

Following the item on *Today*, No. 10 issued an immediate and categorical denial, saying: 'Not one word of the dossier was not entirely the work of the intelligence agencies.' This denial looks threadbare today, to put it charitably. We now know, thanks to the Hutton inquiry, of the detailed involvement of Campbell and his suggested changes, which included the text redrafted to read that the Iraqi military 'are able to deploy' chemical and biological weapons within 45 minutes, as opposed to 'may be able to deploy'. We also know belatedly that there was a mysterious first draft of the dossier, the existence of which only became publicly known in November 2006. Lord Hutton was not told about it.

The government has steadfastly refused to release this document, despite a ruling from the Information Commissioner, Richard Thomas, that it should.[4] We know, however, that it was written not by a member of the intelligence agencies, but by a senior Foreign Office press officer, John Williams. Mr Williams, like his colleague Campbell, is a former *Daily Mirror* political journalist. His involvement, and the government's desperation not to have to make the draft public, leave open the very real possibility that the bulk of the final dossier was not the work of the intelligence services at all, contrary to the firm assurances given by everyone from the Prime Minister down.

Other elements of the BBC picked up the Andrew Gilligan Radio 4 story. Presumably coincidentally, the BBC News correspondent Gavin Hewitt also rang Dr Kelly, following which the main television news bulletin that evening quoted the weapons inspector, anonymously of course, as saying: 'In the final week before publication, some material was taken out and some put in . . . some spin from No. 10 did come into play.'[5] And Susan Watts broadcast a similar piece on BBC2's *Newsnight* on 2 June, again after talking to Dr Kelly, except this time she taped the conversation. We later learned that Dr Kelly had told the reporter that 'it was very difficult to get comments in because people at the top of the ladder didn't want to hear some of the things'.

Dr Kelly was not alone in having doubts about the dossier. This was a period when others connected with the intelligence services, some very senior indeed, were giving similar messages to journalists over a series of lunches. Later John Morrison, the former Deputy Chief of Defence Intelligence, told the BBC's *Panorama* that he could 'almost hear the collective raspberry going up around Whitehall' when the Prime Minister, quoting from the September dossier, told the Commons that the threat from Iraq was serious and current.[6] And at the Hutton inquiry, we had the testimony of Dr Brian Jones, then the long-experienced head of the Scientific and Technical Directorate of the Defence Intelligence Staff. He was responsible for analysing all intelligence on chemical, biological and nuclear weapons.

It seems obvious that Dr Jones's views would have been important and useful as part of the production process for the dossier. Not so. He told Lord Hutton that he and a colleague had written to the Deputy Chief of Defence Intelligence to voice their reservations about the wording in the dossier, an almost unprecedented step for someone in Dr Jones's position. His comments changed nothing in the dossier, which only got stronger as publication approached.

Brian Jones had known David Kelly since 1986 and they were reasonably close colleagues. Dr Kelly's comments quoted above may well have been referring to Dr Jones and his team. It is certainly the case that, as late as 19 September 2002, Dr Kelly sat down with Dr Jones and around seven or eight other colleagues in the Defence Intelligence Staff to consider the dossier in its draft form at that date, and a number of comments, many emanating from Dr Kelly, were passed up the line, but to no avail.

Dr Jones was particularly concerned about the claims in relation to the alleged stockpiles of chemical and biological weapons in Iraq, and the supposed ability to deploy such weapons within forty-five minutes. He avoided the phrase 'sexed up', preferring instead the more prosaic 'over-egged'. And he added: 'I think there was an impression that there was an influence from outside the intelligence community.'[7]

The evidence to Lord Hutton was followed up by an article in the *Independent* in 2004 in which he wrote: 'At no point did we suggest that our knowledge was sufficient to justify, in any quasi-legalistic sense, an invasion to eliminate a threat, because we did not know that such a threat currently existed.'[8] The article was published in time for his comments to be taken into account by Lord Butler in his report on the use of intelligence in connection with the Iraq war.

Lord Butler took a dim view of the way Dr Jones's department had been sidelined. He wrote: 'The exclusion of Dr Jones and his staff from readership of the original report meant that this intelligence was not seen by the few people in the UK intelligence community able to form all-round,

professional technical judgements on its reliability and significance.'[9] But then the government did not appear to set great
store in all-round professional judgements, particularly if they
interfered with a helpful propaganda line.

Later, in June 2004, more support came from Carne Ross,
who occupied the important post of first secretary to the UK
mission at the United Nations in New York from December
1997 to June 2002. He was responsible for Iraq policy in the
mission, including matters to do with weapons inspections. In
a submission to the Butler review, he wrote:

I read the available UK and US intelligence every
working day for the four and a half years of my posting.
This daily briefing would comprise a thick folder of
material, both humint and sigint [from human and
interception sources]. I also talked often and at length
about Iraq's WMD to the international experts who
comprised the inspectors of UNSCOM/UNMOVIC.

Having established his top-notch credentials, Mr Ross then
contributed the following unambiguous paragraph:

During my posting, at no time did HMG [Her Majesty's
Government] assess that Iraq's WMD (or any other
capability) posed a threat to the UK or its interests. On
the contrary, it was the commonly held view among the
officials dealing with Iraq that any threat had been

effectively contained. I remember on several occasions the UK team stating this view in terms during our discussions with the US (who agreed). (At the same time, we would frequently argue, when the US raised the subject, that 'regime change' was inadvisable, primarily on the grounds that Iraq would collapse into chaos.)

He went on:

Iraq's ability to launch a WMD or any form of attack was very limited . . . Iraq's airforce was depleted to the point of total ineffectiveness . . . there was no evidence of any connection between Iraq and any terrorist organisation that might have planned an attack using Iraqi WMD . . . There was moreover no intelligence or assessment during my time in the job that Iraq had any intention to launch an attack against its neighbours or the UK or US.[10]

This is powerful stuff from one of a handful of key people working for the government on this issue.

Curiously, Geoff Hoon's version of events is rather different, typified by what he told the *Guardian* in an exclusive interview in May 2007: 'I saw the intelligence from the first time I came into the office in May 1999 – week in, week out – that said Saddam Hussein had weapons of mass destruction.'[11] This would suggest both that Hoon was receiving a steady stream of incorrect intelligence, week in, week out, and that it was different material from that being shown to Mr Ross, which turned out to be much more reliable. Perhaps the passage of time has played tricks on Hoon's memory.

Although he left his role in June 2002, Mr Ross told Lord Butler that he kept in touch with senior colleagues at the Ministry of Defence and the Foreign Office. They told him no new material had come in to change the assessment in place when he left and which is referred to above. He also said that he discussed the matter at length with Dr Kelly, who agreed that the September dossier was overstated.

We might never have seen this important submission had it not been for the persistence of the Labour MP Andrew Mackinlay, who effectively forced its release by his line of questioning when Mr Ross was examined by the Foreign Affairs Committee in November 2006. At the public evidence session, Mr Ross called UK policy in Iraq 'a rank disaster' and asserted that the 'invasion has been a much greater disaster even than Suez'.[12] Interestingly, he also noted, in his written submission to the committee, that while he had been in Kabul in April 2002, he had been told even at that early stage that UK troop numbers were limited, because 'forces were being held back for Iraq'.

Internationally, support for Dr Kelly's views came from Hans Blix, the former United Nations chief weapons inspector, who told me when we briefly met in London in June 2006 that Dr Kelly had informed him that there were most likely no weapons of mass destruction in Iraq, but there probably were programmes. He was also scathing about the war in general. 'When you sentence someone to death, you must have very good evidence. Can you sentence a country to death with flimsy evidence?' he asked.

And in a shrewd and neat comment on the September dossier, he lent weight to the view that the document had been sexed up. The government 'exercised spin', he said in a broadcast on 12 March 2007. 'There were question marks but they changed them to exclamation marks.' He added that the occupation of Iraq had been 'a complete failure'.

It is necessary to quote these experts at length, given that Tony Blair, even up to his swansong performance before the Liaison Committee in June 2007, shortly before he left office, was showing no regrets, let alone remorse, for his role in the invasion. The world was a better place without Saddam (and also the Taliban in Afghanistan), he told the committee. Here again is Blair rewriting history. Regime change was not the reason for invasion, he had told Parliament at the time. Indeed, he made it clear that if Saddam complied with the demands put upon him then he could remain in office. Yet now, with no weapons of mass destruction anywhere to be found, Blair had convinced himself that the removal of Saddam was, if not the objective of the invasion, certainly a retrospective justification. His capacity to believe sincerely what he needs at any moment to believe is remarkable.

The same logic, of course, has not been applied to Zimbabwe, for example, whose President, Robert Mugabe, must be a strong contender for the world's worst leader, or Saudi Arabia, which has one of the world's most repressive regimes. But then the latter at least has oil and is our friend. Morality is indeed a branch of geography.

Back with the BBC, the government seemed unfazed by the television reports featuring Susan Watts and Gavin Hewitt, but rankled by Andrew Gilligan, who had upped the stakes in a piece he wrote for the 1 June edition of the *Mail on Sunday*, in which he alleged that Dr Kelly, when asked who was responsible for the transformation of the dossier in the final week, had responded with the one word 'Campbell'.

It was only on 25 June, however, that the smouldering wood caught fire. Alastair Campbell, giving evidence to the Foreign Affairs Committee, went on the offensive, accusing the BBC of 'lies' and demanding an apology. His diary recorded his satisfaction that he felt a lot better and had 'opened a flank on the BBC'. The pressure was now firmly on David Kelly.

11 The leak of Dr Kelly's name

By Monday 30 June, David Kelly had decided that he needed to alert Bryan Wells, his line manager at the Ministry of Defence, to the conversation he had had with Andrew Gilligan. It may be that he was dutifully reporting something which circumstances dictated now needed to be known, or perhaps he was concerned that the intense media interest in the conversation might lead to his identity being revealed, and he wanted to pre-empt that.

In a long and detailed letter, Dr Kelly admitted that the 45-minute claim was discussed, and he recorded that he told Mr Gilligan that he did not know to what it referred, and that it was probably there for 'impact'. He accepted that the name Campbell had come up, but maintained that this had been generated by Mr Gilligan in an aside.

In any case, by 3 July, the letter was in the hands of Sir Kevin Tebbit, the most senior civil servant at the ministry, who decided that Dr Kelly should be interviewed by Dr Wells and Richard Hatfield, the MoD's personnel director.

At the interview, which lasted almost two hours, Dr Kelly was warned at the outset that he might face disciplinary action for having talked to the media without explicit clearance. The mood among the Ministry of Defence senior staff will not have been improved by Dr Kelly's revelation that he generally sought clearance from the Foreign Office rather than Defence. When pressed on this, he said that the reason was that the Foreign Office paid his salary, which is true, though in reality it was more likely to be because the Foreign Office was more 'hands off'.

The meeting appears to have been handled in a proper structured way, and the points raised with Dr Kelly were not unreasonable. For instance, it was pointed out to him that one of the journalists with whom he had been in contact, Jane Corbin, was married to a member of the Foreign Affairs Committee, John Maples. Dr Kelly conceded that he had not known this.

At the end of the interview, Mr Hatfield said he accepted Dr Kelly's account 'in good faith' and that disciplinary action would not be instigated, but that the matter could be reopened if further information came to light.

The Defence Secretary and the Prime Minister were each told that day, 3 July, that an official had come forward who had admitted speaking to Mr Gilligan, but not at this stage the name of that official. Others, however, including John Scarlett, did know the official's identity, so there can be no certainty that ministers were not informally made aware of it.

On 5 July an article appeared in the *Times* under the byline of Tom Baldwin, a journalist widely known to have had a close relationship with Alastair Campbell. Indeed, other journalists have described his relationship with Campbell as 'one of the great love stories of our age'[1] and Mr Baldwin himself as one of the most 'prominent cheerleaders' for New Labour.[2] The article gave further hints as to the identity of Mr Gilligan's source, which made it seem more likely to those who were aware of Dr Kelly's involvement that his cover might be blown, a fact drawn to the attention of No. 10 by Sir Kevin.

By Monday 7 July, Mr Scarlett was recommending that Dr Kelly be required to undergo 'a proper security-style interview' to help establish if he was in fact Mr Gilligan's source.[3] Part of the purpose of that interview, according to a minute written later that day by Dominic Wilson, Sir Kevin's private secretary, would be to establish 'Kelly's readiness to be associated with a public statement that names him and carries a clear and sustainable refutation of the core allegation [Gilligan's] on the "45 minute" intelligence'.[4] It is clear Dr Kelly had become a potentially useful tool in the government's battle with the BBC.

The whole matter was discussed at the highest level, with meetings on 7 and 8 July in Downing Street, chaired by the Prime Minister. What started as an internal Ministry of Defence disciplinary issue was being rapidly escalated into a highly political event. This included discussion of Dr Kelly's view on the threat or otherwise from Iraq; Sir Kevin warned that if Dr Kelly was summoned to give evidence, he might 'be uncomfortable on specifics such as the likelihood of there being weapons systems being ready for use within 45 minutes'.[5]

On the 7th, Dr Kelly was indeed reinterviewed. Mr Scarlett's own aide-memoire, which was reproduced in the Hutton report, noted that Sir Kevin had been asked to arrange for Dr Kelly to return for London for this,[6] and Mr Wilson's minute, referred to above, noted that arrangements had been made for the interview to take place at 4 p.m.

Subsequently, a suggestion arose that at some point following his letter to Bryan Wells, Dr Kelly was taken to a safe house in Hockley, Essex, for debriefing. The story appeared on page 2 of the *Southend Echo* on Monday 28 July, under the heading 'Safe house quiz for "mole" Kelly'. Billed as coming from MoD sources, it alleged he had spent a day in a two-bedroom bungalow with two civil servants including Mr Hatfield. Amongst other details, we learn that Dr Kelly dined on a microwave ready-to-eat Indian meal before planning to fly from Southend to Jersey to meet his wife. However, he later phoned her, we are told, to say that he would be staying in Essex a bit longer, and would afterwards return to the family home in Southmoor.

It is not clear if this story is referring to the interview which had been decided upon by Mr Scarlett and others, or whether this was a subsequent one, details of which have never been released. The proposition that the two interviews are one and the same is supported by the presence of Mr Hatfield and the purported purpose of the Hockley event. On the other hand, Mr Scarlett's aide-memoire talked of an interview in London. Furthermore, we know that Dr Kelly was at RAF Honington, in Suffolk, by 8.30 the following morning to finish a training course so it seems difficult to square that with the suggestion that he was in Hockley for a whole day. It is also not clear why it would have been necessary to remove him from London. It would certainly have been more inconvenient for all concerned. Nor has there ever been any other suggestion that Mrs Kelly was that month visiting, or intended to visit, Jersey.

Could there have been a further debrief later on, about which we were not told? Certainly a window could have been found between his flight from his home on the Wednesday evening and his appearance the following Tuesday before the Foreign Affairs Committee, but it seems unlikely.

For its part, the Ministry of Defence has categorically denied that Dr Kelly was at a safe house in Hockley at any time in July 2003. In a parliamentary written answer, the Defence Secretary Des Browne stated: 'Both meetings between Dr Kelly and Mr Hatfield on 4 and 7 July 2003 took place in Mr Hatfield's office in London. Neither Dr Kelly nor Mr Hatfield stayed at any accommodation in Hockley.'[7]

The main conclusion drawn by the senior Defence officials from the interview on the 7th was that Dr Kelly might well have been Andrew Gilligan's single source, but that the reporter might have heavily embellished what he had been told. Dr Kelly was also warned, for the first time, that while there was no intention to reveal his name, the press interest was such that it may come out.

Alastair Campbell, in particular, was keen that it should indeed come out. As early as 4 July, his diary records that he was told by Geoff Hoon that a possible source had come forward. The entry continues: 'GH said his initial instinct was to throw the book at him, but in fact there was a case for trying to get some kind of plea bargain . . . It was double-edged but GH and I agreed it would fuck Gilligan if that was his source.'[8] From this it is clear that Campbell saw the potential propaganda value in using Dr Kelly in his battle with the BBC. Though he tried to spin it in his evidence to the Hutton inquiry, it seems clear from the use of the phrase 'plea bargain' that Campbell had in mind an arrangement whereby Dr Kelly would not have the book thrown at him, provided he was able to make a public contribution helpful to Campbell's case.

His diary entry for 6 July talked of the need to get 'a clear win not a messy draw'. The same diary entry recorded that 'GH and I both wanted to get the source up but TB was nervous about it. Felt that we should not push K. Tebbitt [sic]/Omand too hard, and could maybe bring it out tomorrow if we needed to.'[9] The tomorrow in question was, of course, the day Dr Kelly was reinterviewed, and at 6pm that day, Campbell spoke to Hoon on the telephone and suggested that Dr Kelly's name be given to a friendly journalist.

The Hutton inquiry heard that the idea was rejected at that stage by Hoon, and by the Prime Minister's official spokesmen, Godric Smith and Tom Kelly. By this time, however, Dr Kelly himself was in no doubt his name would emerge, a view he relayed that evening to a friend, Dr Olivia Bosch, an ex-weapons inspector, formerly of the International Institute for

Strategic Studies and today working on international security at Chatham House.

On the morning of 8 July, a second article appeared in the *Times* under the byline of Tom Baldwin, which gives further significant clues to Dr Kelly's identity. Had Campbell, in his obsession to nail the BBC, ignored the Defence Secretary and contacted Mr Baldwin with sufficient details to hope that Dr Kelly could be identified? Campbell in his evidence to Lord Hutton denied doing so.

Later that day a draft press release was produced in the Ministry of Defence which confirmed that an individual had come forward, but which did not name him. The statement was cleared with Dr Kelly and released shortly afterwards, at 5.45 p.m.

As part of the preparation within the Ministry of Defence press office for the calls they rightly expected would come in from journalists following the release of this statement, a basic question and answer guide was produced. The first draft of this document had, as the suggested reply to a direct question asking the identity of the person who had come forward the following construction: 'We are not prepared to name the individual involved.' But by the time the document had reached its final draft, that had been changed to an instruction to ministry press officers to confirm Dr Kelly's name if it was suggested by a journalist, each of whom was allowed an unlimited number of guesses. That was tantamount to revealing it.

Just in case this was not sufficient, the question-and-answer sheet provided for press officers included some easy clues for journalists. In response to a question asking how long the source had been in the Ministry of Defence, the suggested answer was: 'He has been in his current position for three to four years. Before that he was a member of UNSCOM.' Eventually, at around 5.30 p.m. the next day, Wednesday 9th, James Blitz from the *Financial Times* correctly guessed the name. Another journalist from the *Times* hit the bull's eye on his twentieth attempt. The anonymity had lasted less than twenty-four hours from the issuing of the first release.

What had happened to lead to this crucial change in tactics? The answer lay in a meeting held in Downing Street and chaired by Tony Blair. It was held without Sir Kevin Tebbit, who throughout the whole period sought to apply proper procedures and protect Dr Kelly from the political circus. Sir Kevin had been in Portsmouth during the morning, and due to a misunderstanding over the time of the meeting, only arrived at No. 10 as it was finishing, so having little option but to accept this decision as a fait accompli. Speaking afterwards, he said drily: 'I was not actually invited to challenge the judgement of a meeting that had been chaired by the Prime Minister.'[10]

The decision to force Dr Kelly to appear in public before the Foreign Affairs Committee was taken by Hoon, overruling Sir Kevin, who, again attempting to stick by the rules, felt it would be inappropriate. According to a report in the *Mail on*

Sunday, Hoon, pulling rank in a rather unpleasant way, indicated to Sir Kevin that he would have to 'consider his future' if he refused to allow Dr Kelly to appear. The paper also alleged that Pam Teare, the MoD's director of news, who confirmed Dr Kelly's name to the press, was unhappy with the decision to out the scientist.[11]

After his death, the circumstances surrounding the release of Dr Kelly's name inevitably came under some scrutiny. Blair was defiant. The government had 'acted properly throughout'. It was 'completely untrue' that he had authorised the leak of Dr Kelly's name. When asked why the Ministry of Defence had confirmed the name, he said: 'That's a completely different matter once the name is out there.'[12] Of course the name was not out there at all until the ministry released its series of clues.

This spirited, if illogical, defence from Tony Blair mirrored the evidence he gave at the Hutton inquiry. In an unusually hesitant and uncertain performance, the Prime Minister, cornered on the issue, ended up arguing that because the name was likely to come out anyway, it made sense for the Ministry of Defence to hurry that process along.

Julia Quenzler, the freelance court artist who covered the Hutton inquiry from start to finish for the BBC, told me that the Prime Minister, normally such a polished performer, was the most nervous of all those who gave evidence before Lord Hutton. He was clearly very uncomfortable for some reason.

Hoon, for his part, insisted that his department had 'made great efforts to ensure Dr Kelly's anonymity'.[13] Presumably this included 'getting the source up' and the instruction to confirm his name to journalists if it was offered.

Dr Kelly was not told that his name had been released, through the farcical confirmation process that had been adopted, until after 7 p.m. Shortly afterwards, Nick Rufford, a journalist from the *Sunday Times*, arrived at Dr Kelly's house, having driven down from London.

I have known Mr Rufford for many years. A tall angular man with a finely developed sense of humour, he has always played it straight in his dealings with me. Over the years he had produced a number of well-sourced stories relating to the world of intelligence, and had known the weapons inspector for some time. When he reached Southmoor, he warned Dr Kelly that his name was out, and that the media would shortly be descending on him. The *Sunday Times* could find a hotel for them, he offered. Janice Kelly described the offer as coming with the expectation of an exclusive, which Mr Rufford denied. In any case, it was not accepted.

Mrs Kelly indicated in her evidence that the meeting, which had taken place at the end of the family garden abutting the pavement, was a fractious one, but Mr Rufford, when we spoke, insisted it had been perfectly friendly.

After Mr Rufford left, various phone calls between Dr Kelly and the Ministry of Defence ensued, during which he was given clear advice to leave their house without delay. He and his wife quickly packed some clothes and within a quarter of an hour had gone.

Meanwhile, the Foreign Affairs Committee was publishing its report, which cleared Alastair Campbell of playing a role related to the insertion of the 45-minute claim into the September dossier. The BBC, however, still refused to apologise, on the basis that Campbell had not been cleared unanimously. Indeed, it even pointed out provocatively that he had only been cleared on the casting vote of the Labour chairman, Donald Anderson.

In her evidence, Mrs Kelly indicated that the couple had departed for Cornwall, staying overnight in a hotel in Weston-super-Mare, which they reached between 9.30 and 9.45 p.m. Given the long distance to Cornwall and the time of day, it doubtless made sense to break the journey. What does not make sense, however, is what is supposed to have happened the following morning, Thursday 10th. According to Mrs Kelly's evidence, she and her husband left Weston-super-Mare at about 8.45 a.m. They headed for the Swindon area, so that Dr Kelly could drop off some paludrine, an anti-malarial medication, to one of his colleagues who was planning to return to Iraq with him, the man known to the Hutton inquiry as 'Mr A'. He was in fact Rod Godfrey, a UK chemical weapons expert, whose knowledge in this area matched David Kelly's in biological weapons.

The trip to the Swindon area would have required the Kellys to head back in the direction of Oxfordshire, rather than onward to Cornwall. If there really was a need for Dr Kelly to drop this medication off personally, particularly given all the other distractions at the time, would it not have made more sense to have dropped it off on the way to Weston-super-Mare the night before? Did he forget to do so and only realise in the morning?

But there are other problems with the version of events we are asked to accept. Mr Godfrey, in his evidence to the inquiry, said he received a phone call from Dr Kelly on the morning of the 10th, which he described as 'slightly odd'. He recalled: 'He rang to say he had the medication and was quite happy to drop it off. This was quite odd. I was quite happy to travel the short distance to his home to pick it up. But he almost insisted he drop it off. Within about half an hour he arrived at my house.'[14]

Swindon is 62 miles from Weston-super-Mare and the AA Route Planner estimates that the journey time by road would be one hour and eight minutes. It seems therefore that Dr Kelly cannot have been in Weston-super-Mare when he called. Nor does he appear to have advised Mr Godfrey that he was not at home, when the latter offered to come round. Surely the most natural thing would have been to explain where he was and then his insistence that he come round would perhaps not have seemed so odd.

Mr Godfrey said Dr Kelly seemed distracted and wanted, uncharacteristically, not to talk about work. Instead, they talked of other matters as they drank coffee and walked through the garden.

Where was Mrs Kelly? Certainly not in the garden. Mr Godfrey suggested, when asked, that 'she could have been in

1. Lord Hutton.
(©Julia Quenzler/Photonews Service Ltd)

2. Geoff Hoon, the Defence Secretary, being questioned at
the Hutton inquiry.
(©Julia Quenzler/Photonews Service Ltd)

3. Prime Minister Tony Blair leaving the High Court
after giving evidence at the Hutton inquiry.
(©Steve Maisey/Photonews Service Ltd)

4. John Scarlett, head of the Joint Intelligence Committee,
giving evidence at the Hutton inquiry.
(©Priscilla Coleman/Photonews Service Ltd)

5/6. Alastair Campbell, Tony Blair's director of communications *above*, and Andrew Gilligan, journalist on Radio 4's *Today* programme *below*, giving evidence at the Hutton inquiry.
(©Priscilla Coleman/Julia Quenzler/Photonews Service Ltd)

7. ACC Michael Page of Thames Valley Police leaving the High Court after giving evidence at the Hutton inquiry. (©Reuters/Matt Dunham)

8. DC Graham Coe of Thames Valley Police giving evidence at the Hutton inquiry. (©Priscilla Coleman/ Photonews Service Ltd)

9. Mai Pederson.
(*Mail on Sunday*)

10. James Dingemans QC
questioning Mrs Janice Kelly
by video link at the Hutton
inquiry.
(©Julia Quenzler/
Photonews Service Ltd)

RESTRICTED - STAFF

MINISTRY OF DEFENCE

CERTIFICATE OF: DEVELOPED VETTING CLEARANCE

To   Personnel Dept, Rm G8, 401 Bldg   Copy(s) attached for: Security Office
      DERA Pyestock, Farnborough, Hants

Name   David Chnstoper KELLY   Ref PS12946

CLEARANCE FOR THE ABOVE NAMED IS RE-AFFIRMED ON REVIEW FOR ACCESS, ON THE "NEED TO KNOW" PRINCIPLE, UP TO AND INCLUDING

- *a   Regular and constant access to TOP SECRET information of UK origin

- *b   Any access to TOP SECRET information of US origin.

- *c   Any access to TOP SECRET Atomic information SUBJECT TO INDOCTRINATION

- *d   Any access to TOP SECRET International Defence Organisation information SUBJECT TO INDOCTRINATION

- *e   Access to sensitive intelligence material (eg Codeword) SUBJECT TO INDOCTRINATION

THIS CLEARANCE EXPIRES ON **23 FEBRUARY 2007**

- •   This person is deemed suitable to occupy those posts formally attracting an EPV clearance requirement without further reference to DVA(MOD)AS2a3.

BSOs· If this person transfers to another Directorate or Establishment, this certificate should be forwarded to the receiving BSO or Security Office

Signed ~~~~~~~~~ DVA(MOD)AS2a3   Date 24 February 2000
      MRS J C EDWARDS

*delete as appropriate

DVA(MOD) Form 83   RESTRICTED - STAFF

11. David Kelly's Ministry of Defence security clearance
(see p. 257).

the car', though this seemed to be based on speculation rather than any evidence that would have led to that conclusion. It is difficult to imagine that Dr Kelly would have left his wife in the car for a prolonged period while he wandered round Mr Godfrey's garden drinking coffee. But if she was not there, then where was she?

Mr Godfrey then added: 'I myself did not understand how the whole Weston-super-Mare/Cornwall trip works in the chronology.'[15]

He had every reason to be perplexed. Apart from the inconsistencies already identified, Mrs Kelly also told the inquiry that they were in Mevagissey in Cornwall by just after midday. Yet Mevagissey is 201 miles from Swindon, a road journey the AA estimates would take very nearly four hours. We are thus asked to believe that the Kellys covered 263 miles, a round trip that should take over five hours, in just over three, and that is without adding in the time that Dr Kelly spent drinking coffee with Mr Godfrey. Needless to say, neither Lord Hutton nor James Dingemans felt it necessary to unravel all this, despite Mr Godfrey's prompting.

I spoke to Mr Godfrey but he was unable to shed any more light on matters. He confirmed that he lived about half an hour's drive from Southmoor. He also told me that on the occasions when Dr Kelly did come to see him, he would come without his wife.

One possible explanation might be that Mrs Kelly went alone to Weston-super-Mare. If she had left there for

Cornwall at the time she specified, then an arrival just after noon in Mevagissey would accord with the times she offered. It would also explain how Dr Kelly was able to get to Mr Godfrey within half an hour, if he had not been in Weston-super-Mare overnight. But if he had not been there, then where had he been? And why would Mrs Kelly suggest otherwise?

In his evidence to the Hutton inquiry, Dr Richard Scott, Dr Kelly's line manager at Porton Down, the British centre for work related to chemical and biological weapons, revealed that he had received a phone call from Dr Kelly on the morning of the 10th, at around nine, cancelling a meeting which Dr Kelly had been due to have at that time. Dr Scott, who incidentally told Dr Kelly in the phone call that he would not be facing disciplinary action, told the Hutton inquiry that he believed Dr Kelly was speaking from his home, though he could not be certain.

It seems, in the light of Mrs Kelly's evidence, far-fetched to suggest that Dr Kelly did not stay overnight in Weston-super-Mare, and even more so that Mrs Kelly, perhaps under some external pressure, would have told Lord Hutton he did. But unless we accept that both Mrs Kelly and Rod Godfrey were hopelessly wrong about the timings they gave, that Dr Kelly would have double-backed to Swindon on the way to Cornwall, and that he would have left his wife alone in their car for an extended period while he drank coffee with Mr Godfrey, it is difficult to construct an alternative explanation to fit the facts.

Mrs Kelly added in her evidence that Dr Kelly drove back on his own from Cornwall on the 13th, and that she returned alone by train on the 16th.

This must have been a highly charged period for Dr Kelly, coming as it did between his public outing and his appearance before the Foreign Affairs Committee, yet we know nothing of his movements for this key period over the weekend before his death, the period between the departure of Nick Rufford from his house on the evening of the 9th and Dr Kelly's arrival at his daughter Rachel's house in Oxford on the 13th (bar the one meeting with Mr Godfrey on the morning of the 10th), other than what Mrs Kelly has told us.

The hearing of the Foreign Affairs Committee on Tuesday 15 July, televised and taking place in the full glare of publicity, conjured up images of a Soviet Union-style show trial. Here was a witness, clearly intimidated and ill at ease, with his ministry minders sitting behind, who appeared to have been schooled in what he should say.

This was actually Dr Kelly's second appearance before the committee, the first having been on 25 September 2002, when he had appeared in a supporting role to the Foreign Secretary, Jack Straw. On that occasion, Dr Kelly's contribution was limited to seven words. Invited by the Foreign Secretary to agree with him, Dr Kelly said: 'You are absolutely right in that analysis.' Mr Straw was later to complain that he had been accompanied by only a middle-ranking official, which doubtless reflected the confusion that existed, given Dr Kelly's complicated employment position, but nevertheless hurt him.

On this second occasion, Dr Kelly would be required to contribute far more than seven words as he underwent a grilling for more than an hour. Throughout the session, he spoke so softly that, even with the room fans turned off, he repeatedly had to be asked to speak up. Every word was weighed carefully and some painful circumlocutions resulted.

'It is not one that I recognise as being conversations I had with him,' he said at one point. At another: 'I do realise that in the conversation that I had there was reinforcement of some of the ideas he has put forward.' And the ultimate backstop: 'I cannot recall that. I find it very difficult to think back to a conversation I had six weeks ago. I cannot recall but that does not mean to say, of course, that such a statement was not made but I cannot recall it. It does not sound like the sort of thing I would say.'

Later, many would point to this uncomfortable session and conclude that herein lay the seeds of Dr Kelly's suicide. It is, however, far from certain that Dr Kelly was severely shaken by his testimony before the Foreign Affairs Committee, contrary to the now accepted wisdom. Simon Hoggart, the *Guardian* columnist who was present when Dr Kelly faced the committee, described as a 'worrying myth' the suggestion that Dr Kelly was 'sent to his grave' by a 'fierce and harsh interrogation'. Referring to Dr Kelly's departure from the Commons committee room, he recorded at the time that 'as he pushed past me at the end to leave . . . he was smiling'.[16]

It should also be noted that when he gave evidence at the Intelligence and Security Committee the next day, Dr Kelly's normal good mood had certainly returned, and the transcript of that session shows that he even managed to crack a joke or two.

Before the Foreign Affairs Committee, Dr Kelly sought to give the impression that his involvement with the dossier was a limited one, related to the historical context only, which is true in terms of what he contributed directly. It did not of course rule out the possibility that he had discussed with colleagues the content of the final dossier before publication, as indeed we now know he did.

On one matter, however, he was absolutely clear. Asked by the Labour MP Greg Pope if he believed that the September dossier had been transformed by Alastair Campbell, he replied crisply: 'I do not believe that at all.' He had backtracked significantly from the position he had taken both with colleagues and indeed with BBC journalists, and seemed desperate not to be identified as the source for Andrew Gilligan's broadcast on 29 May. He had also backtracked from what he told Susan Watts. Then, when he was asked if he could confirm that Campbell was responsible for the 45-minute claim, he had replied: 'All I can say is the No. 10 press office. I've never met Alastair Campbell. But I think that Alastair Campbell is synonymous with that press office, because he is responsible for it.'[17]

It would have suited both Dr Kelly and the government if he were not thought to be the main source. For the former, this had the potential to get him out of hot water. For the latter, it could give the impression that, if there had been any sexing up going on, then it was Mr Gilligan that had been engaged in it.

Given his testimony, it is perhaps not surprising that the committee concluded, incorrectly, that Dr Kelly had not been Mr Gilligan's main source. Dr Kelly himself put this view forward: 'I do not believe I am the source,' he told the Tory MP Richard Ottaway. The committee's belief that Dr Kelly was not the source also explains the exchange between the Labour MP Andrew Mackinlay and him, which was much replayed on television following Dr Kelly's death:

Andrew Mackinlay: I reckon you are chaff; you have been thrown up to divert our probing. Have you ever felt like a fall guy? You have been set up, have you not?
Dr Kelly: That is not a question I can answer.[13]

This was seen by many as an attack on Dr Kelly, the haranguing of a good man by a bully-boy MP. Dr Kelly himself is said to have felt stung by it.

Certainly the papers the next day were not impressed. Writing in the *Daily Mail*, Quentin Letts described Dr Kelly as having 'the bearded, grey-shoed manner of a geography teacher . . . These MPs, many of whom had been cowards when faced with Alastair Campbell, really had a go at the quivering boffin.'[19] This is, of course, exaggerated for effect, but the underlying perception is one that most who watched the session will have shared. Other journalists were less elegant with language, the *Guardian* reaching rock bottom: 'With his receding hairline, silver beard and gold-frame glasses Dr Kelly resembled a retired doctor, or to put it another way, Harold Shipman, though probably less popular with the government today.'[20] The comparison with Britain's most prolific mass murderer was, even then, in appallingly bad taste.

In reality, Mr Mackinlay was trying to express sympathy for the position that Dr Kelly had found himself in, and anger with those, perhaps in the Ministry of Defence, who had pushed him forward, though few saw it that way at the time, particularly when the clip was taken out of context. Mr Mackinlay, who is an honest and principled politician, nevertheless felt remorse for his remarks, and after the weapons inspector's death, apologised for them. It was a noble gesture, not matched, it has to be said, by any of the principal players in government who had rather more to apologise for.

Geoff Hoon, in particular, seemed relatively unbothered by Dr Kelly's death. With the body barely cold, the Defence Secretary was photographed enjoying VIP treatment at Silverstone. The story subsequently appeared in the *Daily Mail* on Monday 21 July, under the headline 'Nice day out Mister Hoon?' In it, a spokesman for the minister tried to explain away the visit by claiming that he was investigating plans to adapt motor-racing quick-fuelling systems for use with military helicopters.[21]

For Campbell, the priority on the weekend following Dr Kelly's death was closer to home – Alastair Campbell, in fact, and especially his battle with the BBC. According to the same article, he was 'working the phones with friendly Fleet Street editors to shore up his position'. Certainly his diaries do not convey any sense of compassion for Dr Kelly. His entry for 6 July 2003 reads: 'TB . . . backed off after speaking to Omand, who felt the guy had to be treated properly and interviewed again. GH and I felt we were missing a trick.'[22] He also variously describes him as 'a nobody re the dossier', 'an ex-inspector' and 'a bit of a show-off'.[23]

Shortly afterwards, it was the turn of the Blairs, still on their visit to China, to try to put all this unpleasant business behind them, as Cherie Blair sportingly took the microphone for a public rendition of the Beatles' 'When I'm 64'. Perhaps her husband attempting P. J. Proby's 'I Apologise' might have been more appropriate.

For the government, the need to survive and the desire to enjoy both came well ahead of any remorse for the death of one of Britain's most distinguished scientists.

There was one further insult in this charged period after Dr Kelly's death. Downing Street shockingly decided that its own survival prospects would be strengthened if Dr Kelly's character could be brought into question. They had already downplayed his importance, so as to lessen the significance of the remarks attributed to him. Now, in an unattributable briefing at the turn of the month, a handful of journalists were advised by the Prime

Minister's press spokesman, Tom Kelly (definitely no relation), that Dr Kelly was a Walter Mitty character who may have contributed to his own downfall. He had told Andrew Gilligan more than he knew and then failed to tell his employers the whole truth about his contacts with journalists.

The use of an off-the-record briefing, shortly before Dr Kelly's funeral, was a disgraceful and cowardly attempt to tip the wink to journalists and get them to run a story helpful to the government but without No. 10's fingerprints anywhere near it. The ruse only failed when the *Independent*'s Paul Waugh broke the unofficial rules and ran the story.[24] Other journalists who were told respected the unattributable nature of the briefing.

Walter Mitty is a fictional character, created in 1941 by James Thurber. He is a meek and mild man with a vivid fantasy life, imagining himself alternately as a wartime pilot, a surgeon and a swaggering killer. Mr Waugh is quite clear that the Walter Mitty remark was not an off-the-cuff comment, but a calculated phrase. When the story appeared, Ann Chivas, who was standing in that day for Tom Kelly at the normal lobby briefing, denied the remark had been made, but Mr Waugh flatly contradicted her in front of the assembled journalists.

John Prescott, who was standing in for the Prime Minister, hit the roof and read the Riot Act to Tom Kelly. He issued instructions via the Cabinet Secretary that more respect must be shown to the dead microbiologist. He is the only minister who comes out of this period with any credit to his name. Mr

Kelly was forced to apologise, but happily for him, his job prospects were not damaged. He was promoted to chief spokesman after Godric Smith became head of strategic communications in 2004, but lost his job in June 2007 when Gordon Brown became Prime Minister.

12 Convinced beyond reasonable doubt

So how did David Kelly die?

The official verdict, of course, delivered by Lord Hutton, was suicide. This, however, was delivered at the end of an inquiry which concentrated for the most part on the battle between the BBC and the government, with consideration of the circumstances of Dr Kelly's death a poor second.

In so far as Lord Hutton did consider the death, it was dealt with under a non-statutory process that meant no witnesses could be compelled to attend, none was required to give evidence under oath, and the normal rules and safeguards of court process, including cross-examination, simply were not applied.

The non-statutory nature of the inquiry also meant that Lord Hutton was able to conclude that Dr Kelly had committed suicide on what is tantamount to an informal basis, whereas under normal coroners' rules such a verdict can only be reached if the coroner or his or her jury is satisfied 'beyond reasonable doubt' that this is the explanation. Lord Hutton was not required to apply that test to his proceedings.

The coroner also appeared to conclude that this was a case of suicide, and we have seen how, on the basis of a truncated inquest held just as Lord Hutton was starting his deliberations, he felt able to determine the cause of death and have issued a death certificate, based on evidence from only two people, one of whom, the forensic toxicologist, appeared to question the matter when he gave evidence to Lord Hutton. Mrs Kelly has also been clear in her limited statements subsequent to the death of her husband that she believes that he committed suicide, though as we have seen, she appeared to think otherwise all the time he was missing, even on the Friday morning before his body was found.

Her view of the certainty of suicide as an explanation for the death of her husband is not one shared by all members of the family. Dr Kelly's adopted brother, Tim, contacted me to say that he had done considerable research himself. 'He didn't commit suicide,' he told me. The death was 'unfinished business'. Another relative felt she had to contact me but did not want her identity revealed. She told me: 'David was the most unlikely person to commit suicide. Anyway, he was a biochemist and would have known how to kill himself much more easily.' She herself had been told by another family member to be sceptical of the official explanation: 'Don't believe everything you hear. That's not what happened.'

None of this is very satisfactory. There has not been a proper process, equivalent to a proper hearing in a coroner's court, to test the evidence, about which a considerable number of unanswered questions remain. This does not of course in itself mean that Dr Kelly did not commit suicide, merely that the case has not been proven.

If it were suicide, what would be the rationale?

Evidence at the inquiry came from Keith Hawton, Professor of Psychiatry at Oxford University. Lord Hutton described him to me as 'one of the most eminent experts on suicide in this country'.[1] Professor Hawton was in no doubt that Dr Kelly had taken his own life. He reached this conclusion based on the fact that Harrowdown Hill is a pleasant place to choose to end one's days, that the injuries to his wrist were indicative of self-harm, and that there were no signs of violence on the body.

Now, these may well be features one expects to associate with a suicide, but they hardly constitute proof. Presumably murders also take place in pleasant locations, wrist injuries can be generated if an external agent wishes to suggest suicide, and individuals can be overpowered with drugs without signs of violence showing on the body. Of course on the basis of limited evidence, it is not possible to assert that the above sentence represents what happened. But nor is it possible for Professor Hawton to be so sure in his analysis.

A better argument is put by Tom Mangold and others. We have seen how Dr Kelly's mood had improved after the ordeal of the televised hearing of the Foreign Affairs Committee, so much so that he told friends that he was looking forward to returning and on the morning of his disappearance had even had a plane booked for his next trip. Those, such as Mr Mangold, who believe that the weapons inspector committed suicide suggest that there must have been a violent swing in mood, and that may have been occasioned by one of the phone calls he received from the Ministry of Defence that morning.

It is certainly the case that there was unfinished business between Dr Kelly and the department. At his initial interview with senior officials back on 7 July, he had been told no action would be taken against him, but that might change if further information came to light. Since then, Dr Kelly had painfully given evidence to the Foreign Affairs Committee, trying to balance honesty on the one hand with an attempt not to incriminate himself on the other. It was a juggling act that proved too difficult.

In particular, he seemed to have been thrown by the reference to BBC *Newsnight* journalist Susan Watts. At the committee meeting, Lib Dem MP David Chidgey read out what he termed 'notes that were made' by Ms Watts following a meeting with Dr Kelly. These were batted away by Dr Kelly with the answer that he had only met the reporter once, and that had been the previous year. This was dissembling, because of course a number of telephone conversations had indeed taken place, but no meetings face to face.

But Tory MP Richard Ottaway returned to the issue. He read out the notes again and asked Dr Kelly if they were his words, to which Dr Kelly gave the evasive reply: 'It does not sound like my expression of words. It does not sound like a quote from me.'

He was then asked point blank if he denied that those were his words, to which he responded with the one word 'yes'.

This was untrue. And Ms Watts, it transpired, had made a tape recording of the telephone conversation.

So it is possible that Dr Kelly received a phone call from the MoD on the Thursday morning, telling him that the tape existed, that he had, on the face of it, misled a parliamentary committee – a serious matter – and that his position was being reconsidered by the department. Under this scenario, Dr Kelly, having thought that the worst was over, suddenly realised that his careful attempt to pick his way through the minefield had blown up in his face. He then realised that the game was up, that he would not be able to work again, and that his career was over. Moreover, he would be exposed as having been less than truthful, something that went strongly against his personal ethic. He thus took a sudden decision to end it all.

This is certainly a plausible explanation for his suicide, if that is what it was. Indeed, it is the most plausible. But even this sequence has a number of objections to it.

First, the Hutton inquiry was given no proof that such a phone call to Dr Kelly from the Ministry of Defence actually occurred. Indeed, it seems unlikely, as Ms Watts maintained that, despite pressure from her line managers, she did not reveal her source to anyone but *Newsnight* editor George Entwistle until 18 July. Furthermore, no testimony was produced at the Hutton inquiry to suggest that Dr Kelly's future was in question following his evidence to the Foreign Affairs Committee, though it is certainly possible that, if such a threat had been made, the government would not have been keen to incriminate itself by revealing details of it.

Second, Dr Kelly was fifty-nine and had for some months, according to friends and colleagues, been thinking of retiring and emigrating to the United States.[2] There is no question but that his unmatched knowledge in this area would have commanded a high price. He had confided to colleagues that he disliked being under the yoke of the Ministry of Defence, preferring either his previous berth at Porton Down or the more relaxed environment the Foreign Office provided. In addition, he confided to colleagues, such as Professor Julian Perry Robinson, that becoming a consultant in the United States would allow him to pay for the treatment that his wife Janice needed. She had suffered from lengthy bouts of ill health. Given his clear concern for his wife, it would be strange if he were to take his own life and so lose the chance to improve matters for her.

Third, Dr Kelly was an adherent and relatively recent convert to the Baha'i faith, which strongly outlaws suicide. The Baha'i publication *Lights of Guidance* states: 'Suicide is forbidden in the Cause. God who is the Author of all life can alone take it away, and dispose of it in the way He deems best. Whoever commits suicide endangers his soul, and will suffer spiritually as a result in the Other Worlds Beyond.'[3]

Fourth, Dr Kelly was, almost universally in the eyes of those who knew him well, just about the last person that might be expected to commit suicide. Even Alastair Campbell recognised this. He told the Hutton inquiry that 'the way that he [Dr Kelly] was being described was actually of a very strong, resolute character, clearly of deep conviction and who had been in many difficult, stressful circumstances'.[4] Professor Sergei Rybakov, who acted as Dr Kelly's deputy in a weapons inspection team in Iraq, put it bluntly: 'He was not capable of killing himself.'[5]

Ron Imms, who regularly played cribbage with Dr Kelly at their local pub, told Rowena Thursby: 'Knowing him as I did, I would say he was the last person to commit suicide.' Another cribbage player, David Heavens, told her: 'I don't think any of us believe he committed suicide.'

Rod Barton, the Australian weapons inspector, wrote in his book: 'It was said that he had committed suicide, but I found this hard to believe or understand. He was the most sane, level-headed and rational person that I had known, and suicide seemed totally inconsistent with this.'[6]

The *Times* journalist James Bone, who broke the story of Dr Kelly's involvement with Mai Pederson, said, 'This was a man who reduced Dr Germ, the Iraqi anthrax expert, to tears in interrogation. He was not someone to buckle under media pressure, unless there was something else going on. There must be some other explanation.'[7]

Fifth, Dr Kelly left no suicide note and made no special effort even to bid farewell to his wife as he left his house for the last time. While suicide notes are not an invariable feature, they are very common and one might have been expected in this case.

Sixth, and crucially, this explanation provides only a motive, without in any way satisfying the many objections, medical and others, which argue against a suicide. This last point seems to have been ignored by those who appear to feel that it is only necessary to construct a mindset for Dr Kelly that covers his death without the need to consider the evidence connected to the actual death.

For instance, shortly after I had a longish piece published in the *Mail on Sunday* questioning the assumption that this was a suicide, Andrew Gilligan ran a piece in the *Evening Standard*, under the banner headline 'Those who say David was murdered are so wrong'.[8] I was very surprised to see this piece appear. For one thing, Mr Gilligan had agreed to meet me a month or so earlier to discuss my concerns, but only on condition that the meeting between us remained confidential. Yet in the *Standard* piece, he refers to the conversation we had. In his article, he does not counter the serious medical evidence that challenges the conclusion that Dr Kelly's death was suicide, but does make much of the fact that the article I wrote did not, quite deliberately in fact, identify a motive, and that ergo it must have been suicide.

This is curious logic. If a man is found in the street with a knife in his back, the fact that nobody can be found who might have wanted to stab him does not disprove the view that this is murder. Rather, the logical way to approach matters relating to a death must surely be to examine the available evidence and draw a conclusion from that, if possible. In Dr Kelly's case, both natural causes and an accident can clearly be completely ruled out, which leaves suicide or murder as the possible explanations.

In order to decide which of these two explanations is the correct one, it is necessary to examine the medical evidence in particular. Those who maintain that Dr Kelly's death was suicide need to provide convincing counter-arguments to the numerous objections raised in particular by a significant number of highly qualified medical experts. To date, they have not done so.

But if it was suicide, then there can be no doubt what the primary cause of this was: the disgraceful way in which Dr Kelly was used as a pawn in a political game by Tony Blair, Alastair Campbell and Geoff Hoon. It is they who plotted how to force Dr Kelly into the public glare. It is they who overruled the permanent secretary at the Ministry of Defence, Sir Kevin Tebbit, who it seems wanted to stop Dr Kelly being offered up as raw meat for the Foreign Affairs Committee. And it is they who spun against Dr Kelly, downplaying his role so as to make his concerns seem less important than they were. And all simply to score a victory over Mr Gilligan and the BBC. For this, if it was suicide, a good man died.

All three apparently do maintain it was suicide, yet none of the triumvirate has ever apologised for being instrumental in Dr Kelly's death. Politicians weigh their words carefully, and there is a world of difference between an expression of regret and an apology.

Perhaps, however, the matter did play on Blair's conscience. At the press conference which he held, in the Japanese spa resort of Hakone, after the news of Dr Kelly's death had come through, the usual careful management of questions was even tighter than ever. Only two questions were allowed, neither from journalists likely to rock the boat. That, however, did not stop the intrepid *Mail on Sunday* journalist Jonathan Oliver from shouting out: 'Have you got blood on your hands, Prime Minister? Are you going to resign over this?'

For a few moments, time stopped. Blair stared forward into the air, saying nothing, caught like a rabbit in headlights. It was electric. The reporter never did get an answer.

Perhaps his conscience also came into play in his decision, never publicised but confirmed to me by a friend of hers, to invite Mrs Kelly to visit him at Chequers, or was it also a political calculation on his part? Certainly Mrs Kelly left having been subject to a full gamma ray blast of the Blair charm, telling friends what a nice man he was, a result Hoon had painfully failed to achieve when he visited her at her home shortly after her husband's death.

For my part, and for the reasons set out in some detail in earlier chapters, having examined the available evidence, I am personally convinced beyond reasonable doubt, to apply that test, that it is nigh-on clinically impossible for Dr Kelly to have died by his own hand in the manner described, and further, that both his personality and the other circumstantial evidence strongly militates against suicide.

That leaves only one alternative – that Dr Kelly was murdered, by person or persons unknown.

There were certainly some odd incidents which suggest that all was not quite as it seemed. Two of these regard statements Dr Kelly himself made, satisfactory explanations for which have never really been provided.

The first statement relates to a conversation he had some months before his death with David Broucher, then a permanent representative to the Conference on Disarmament in Geneva on behalf of the UK government. As part of that conversation, Mr Broucher told the Hutton inquiry, he asked Dr Kelly what would happen if Iraq were invaded. Dr Kelly replied that he 'would probably be found dead in the woods' – as indeed he was. At the inquiry, this was construed as meaning that he had already had suicidal thoughts. That, of course, is patently absurd, and an interpretation designed in retrospect to lend support to a conclusion reached before the evidence had been heard. Nobody can seriously suggest that Dr Kelly was suicidal at the time the meeting took place.

Mr Broucher told Lord Hutton that he himself interpreted it at the time, rather more logically in fact, to mean that 'he was at risk of being attacked by the Iraqis in some way'.[9] Even so, if it was some understanding that Dr Kelly had that invasion might make him personally vulnerable, it is uncanny that he should have alighted on that very phrase.

One strange aspect to this conversation between the two men is the uncertainty over the date of the meeting. Mr

Broucher himself in his evidence first put the date of the meeting at 27 September 2002, but shortly afterwards corrected this to 27 February 2003. Certainly the contents of the conversation as relayed by Mr Broucher, with talk of the dossier and other current matters, suggests the February date is more likely. Mr Broucher, who those in diplomatic circles tell me is an entirely honest and principled person, also told Lord Hutton that he had a clear recollection of the meeting. Yet an entry in one of Dr Kelly's diaries, discovered subsequently by his daughter Rachel, recorded the meeting as having taken place not in February 2003 but a year earlier.

Could this have been a transcription error by Dr Kelly? Rachel told the inquiry that her father's habit was to record painstakingly events in his diary after they had happened, and she gave examples of where plans made by her father had changed, leading to corrected entries being made after the event. The one entry in Dr Kelly's diary relating to Mr Broucher reads as follows: 'Monday 18th February 2002, 9.30, David Broucher, US mis.' Rachel goes on to say that this entry gives details of her father's flights both into Geneva on 17 February, and out again on the 20th.

To further complicate matters, Sarah Pape, Dr Kelly's half-sister, told the inquiry that another of Dr Kelly's daughters, Ellen, got married five days before Mr Broucher said he met Dr Kelly in Geneva. She recalled him flying out afterwards, not to Geneva, but to New York. Moreover, Dr Kelly's diary for this period showed that on 27 February, the day Mr

Broucher said he met him, he was still in New York on UNMOVIC business, was on leave on the 28th, when Mr Broucher alleges Dr Kelly had a meeting in Baltimore that he had cancelled to be in Geneva, and that he flew back to London on 2 March.

What are we to make of this? Mr Broucher told Lord Hutton that he had only met Dr Kelly once, that they discussed matters such as the dossier that could not have been discussed in 2002, and that he had a clear recollection of the meeting. Yet if he is correct, then why should there be false entries, and missing entries, in Dr Kelly's diary?

Naturally, no attempt was made by Lord Hutton or James Dingemans to resolve these discrepancies. In his report, Lord Hutton would conclude: 'It appears to be clear that Dr Kelly's one meeting with Mr Broucher was in February 2002 and not in February 2003.' But that is tantamount to saying that Mr Broucher either had a very poor memory or told the inquiry a pack of lies. Was that really Lord Hutton's view?

It is certainly his conclusion that Mr Broucher's version of events is wrong, judging by the contents of his letter to me, responding to my queries on the matter. In essence, he pointed out, not unreasonably, that there was documentary evidence for the meeting having taken place in 2002, and more such evidence making a meeting in Geneva on 27 February 2003 an impossibility.

One further strange aspect is that Mr Broucher apparently had no record of the meeting in his diary, itself unusual for a senior diplomat whose time would need to be carefully managed. Mr Broucher himself explained this to the inquiry by saying that the meeting took place 'at very short notice. I remember that Dr Kelly rang to say that he was in Geneva and he was going to pop in and see me.'[10] But this explanation actually raises further questions, rather than putting the existing ones to bed. Would Dr Kelly really just ring up and expect Mr Broucher to be there and be able to see him at no notice? Why would Dr Kelly not ring him before he left England to see if a meeting would be possible, rather than relying on luck when he reached Geneva?

I contacted Mr Broucher, who is now EU policy adviser to the presidential administration in Romania, to try to make sense of the various inconsistencies. He refused to be drawn, however, mysteriously remarking only that he had written a paper on the matter and deposited it with the Foreign Office. Just before publication of this book, the Foreign Office released his letter to me, extracts of which appear in the Epilogue on page 354.

The second statement came in an email Dr Kelly wrote on the morning of his disappearance to Judith Miller, a controversial American journalist on the *New York Times*. Ms Miller was jailed in 2005 for contempt of court for refusing to testify before a federal grand jury which was investigating the outing of Valerie Plame as a CIA agent. As referred to in Chapter 8, this had actually occurred less than a fortnight before Dr Kelly's death. She maintained that her journalistic ethics would not allow her to reveal what she knew of the matter, but finally told the grand jury, after having spent eighty-five days in prison, that her source had been Lewis 'Scooter' Libby, chief of staff to Vice-President Dick Cheney. She subsequently testified against him and he was sentenced to thirty months' imprisonment. It could have been twenty-five years. In the event, even this was too long for President Bush, who quickly intervened, using presidential powers, to secure his release before he even got to prison.

Ms Miller had emailed Dr Kelly on Wednesday 16 July with the following: 'David, I heard from another member of your fan club that things went well for you today. Hope it's true. J.' In this email, Ms Miller must almost certainly have been referring to Dr Kelly's testimony to the Intelligence and Security Committee, which had indeed gone well. It is interesting, if this is the case, that she was able to get feedback, and so quickly, on a session that had been held in private. She did of course have good connections in the intelligence world.

Dr Kelly's reply was pregnantly cryptic: 'I will wait until the end of the week before judging – many dark actors playing games. Thanks for your support. I appreciate your friendship at this time.'[11] This email was sent at 11.18 on the Thursday morning, less than four hours before Dr Kelly left his home for the last time. It contains one of the most striking phrases of the Hutton inquiry, and one that was left hanging in the air.

Given the likely context of Ms Miller's email, it is reasonable to speculate that Dr Kelly's 'dark actors' were those seeking to use him for their own purposes, including possibly Messrs Blair, Campbell and Hoon. Using him to discredit the BBC could certainly be seen as 'playing games'. The other interesting aspect of his reply is his rational assessment that he would 'wait until the end of the week before judging'. This measured approach does not suggest the emotional churning that might be associated with someone about to commit suicide just a few hours later.

There were also a number of odd occurrences after Dr Kelly's death. One of these concerns his dental records. His dentist was aware that he was shortly due for an appointment, and on hearing of his death, she went to the filing cabinet where his notes were kept, with the intention of preventing any communication being sent out, which might cause distress to his family. She found the notes missing, and one window unsecured. The dentist reported this to Thames Valley Police, who carried out a full examination of the surgery. Nothing was found.

Then two days after his death, on the Sunday, the dentist again called the police to report that the notes had reappeared, in their correct place in the filing cabinet. The police again attended and forensically examined the notes. According to Assistant Chief Constable Michael Page, no evidence of extraneous fingerprints was found.

Now it is of course possible that the notes had been in the filing cabinet all the time, though the dentist appeared to be a methodical, thoughtful woman, and doubtless carried out a full search before calling the police. The police also appeared to take the matter seriously, and ACC Page went so far as to have DNA checks carried out on the body found on Harrowdown Hill to ensure it was indeed Dr Kelly's. Had the body been that of someone else, that of course could have been revealed by comparing the teeth of the body with Dr Kelly's dental records, the theft of which would obviously have prevented this basic check from being carried out. Of course, the fact that the dentist raised the alarm with the police meant that DNA checks were indeed carried out, which would have rendered any theft of the dental records redundant.

It is difficult to envisage what other purpose the theft of the dental records could have had. Was the objective to alter them in some way, before returning them to the dentist's cabinet? But if so, why? In the absence of any credible theory, we have to assume that the records were indeed present in the cabinet all the time, and were for some reason overlooked by both the dentist and the police, though such a conclusion seems almost as unlikely.

What is certain, though, is that if the notes were indeed removed and replaced within a couple of days, whoever did so can reasonably have expected that their actions would have gone undiscovered, and with most dentists, they surely would have been.

Another curious incident occurred in London, also on the Sunday after Dr Kelly's death. According to a report which appeared in the *Daily Telegraph* on 1 August, and the *Mail on*

Sunday two days later, a 'mystery blonde' was discovered that day in possession of confidential documents in Dr Kelly's office in a secure part of the Ministry of Defence. The woman, in her late thirties, was allegedly spotted by a member of the Ministry of Defence Guard Force as she left the office on the fourth floor of the Metropole building in Northumberland Avenue. She was holding a large paper bag containing documents to be shredded, which she placed in the corridor before leaving the building. It is also reported that she was not recognised as a staff member, but was apparently not challenged. This is rather odd. It cannot be easy to gain access to high security areas of Ministry of Defence buildings, and if she was not a ministry employee, then the implication is that she must have been working for the security services. Who else would be able to gain access in this way? Even if that were true, of course, it does not explain why she was not asked to prove her identity or show her authority when spotted.

At the Hutton inquiry, the presence of a 'mystery blonde' was denied by Stephen Macdonald, assistant director on the central budget for security and safety at the Ministry of Defence. He admitted, however, that, contrary to established procedure, a burn bag of confidential material awaiting disposal had that day been found by a security guard in an unlocked and unsecured office on the third (as opposed to the fourth) floor of the Metropole building, and that that bag had been found to contain a crumpled piece of paper with the handwritten words 'David Kelly' visible on it. Mr Macdonald reported that the piece of paper in question set out military and political developments in Iraq to be considered by the Information, Campaign and Co-ordination Group. It was not made available publicly through the Hutton inquiry.

An internal inquiry followed which, according to Mr Macdonald, concluded that there had been no shredding of documents 'which were relevant to the inquiry', that there had been no unauthorised access to Ministry of Defence property, and that he had received no other reports of any documents relating to Dr Kelly being destroyed. These assurances, of course, do not rule out the shredding of documents deemed not to be relevant to the inquiry or the disposal of relevant documents by means other than shredding. Nor does it rule out the removal, as opposed to destruction, of documents relating to Dr Kelly. Lastly, it does not rule out the presence in the building of a stranger who nevertheless had authority to be there.

I have spoken to the two journalists who ran the stories in their papers, Chris Leake for the *Telegraph* and Neil Tweedie for the *Mail*, and while, naturally, neither would reveal their sources, it is clear from what they did tell me that their tip-offs did not originate from the same person. Simply put, one source is still working in Whitehall, whereas the other is now dead. The fact that the story originated from two different people but was essentially the same does not of course prove that it was correct, but it certainly lends it more weight.

What the original stories did not report was that the mystery blonde is said to have found what she was looking for. This included a tape cassette she is alleged to have removed from a hand-held recorder as well as written material. While neither the 'mystery blonde' incident nor the dental records one can be definitively stood up, it is interesting that both are said to have occurred in the forty-eight hours following Dr Kelly's death, and both allege the removal of material relating to the weapons inspector.

Meanwhile in Dr Kelly's own village of Southmoor, shortly after the death of the weapons inspector, a local reporter, Robert Wilkinson, who had been present at Wantage police station when the discovery of the body was announced and who attended the scene of the death, was making enquiries around the village.

While he was interviewing neighbours, he noticed a car conspicuously parked at the Waggon and Horses, the pub nearly opposite Dr Kelly's home. Its two occupants were also talking to local residents, including Ruth Absalom, the last person known definitely to have seen Dr Kelly alive.

Curious to discover the identity of these men, Mr Wilkinson himself spoke to Ms Absalom and asked who the two men were. She told him that they had asked her many questions, but she was not able to reveal what these were, as the two men had impressed upon her that she was not even to reveal on whose behalf they were purportedly carrying out their questioning. She was most insistent that she could not tell. Mr Wilkinson then tapped on the car window to ask the two men who they were working for. They laughed and one of them answered: 'Thames Valley Police.' The reporter told me that this struck him as most unlikely, as they were not in uniform and to him they were clearly not members of Special Branch either.

The same day, he rang Thames Valley Police in his capacity as a journalist and asked if any officers were that day interviewing neighbours. He was told no officers were, and then explained why he had asked. Two days later, he received a call out of the blue from Thames Valley Police, telling him that they had made a mistake and that the occupants of the car, and the car itself, were indeed from the constabulary.

It was remarkably helpful of the police to come back to a journalist in this way. Someone somewhere will have decided that it was not helpful for a journalist to conclude that arms of the state other than the police were looking into this matter, and that a suggestion that the car and occupants in question had indeed come from Thames Valley Police was a way of shutting this down.

Who would want to do this, and who would be able to persuade Thames Valley Police to make this phone call? Perhaps some element of the intelligence services, whose presence in Southmoor a few days after Dr Kelly's death suggests that some at least suspected the explanation for his death was not quite so straightforward as public statements would have us believe.

13 Who was responsible?

I had concluded in my mind, after analysing the facts and available information as carefully and objectively as I could, that David Kelly's death could not have been suicide, and that therefore it must have been murder. It was a sober moment when I realised that this was where my investigations had taken me.

I was now in uncharted waters. If it really was murder, then who was responsible, and why?

A good starting point seemed to be the interesting responses I had had to my *Mail on Sunday* article, particularly those which suggested some inside knowledge. So it was that in late August 2006, I found myself speeding westwards on a Great Western train to Exeter to see a man, recently retired, with connections to both the police and the security services. Like others I would meet, he would only agree to do so on condition of anonymity and after rather circuitous arrangements had been followed. I do, however, know his name, and subsequent careful checks have confirmed that he is who he says he is. These were carried out by journalists at the BBC, with my contact's full knowledge. He wanted to leave no doubt about the genuine nature of his credentials.

We had finally agreed to meet at Exeter St David's station. It had taken some weeks to organise, and had at his request involved the complicated use of public telephone boxes to try to minimise the likelihood that his contact with me would be discovered. We adjourned to a rather nondescript club, and over a glass of wine he told me his story. He had had nagging doubts about Dr Kelly's death for some time, and, like many, was appalled by the contents of the Hutton report when it was published. He began to make his own surreptitious enquiries around Southmoor, and spoke to locals in the three pubs in the area. Then he went up to Harrowdown Hill, where, to his surprise, he came across two people in a car parked as close as the road allows to the wood where Dr Kelly was found. They confronted him and coldly told him to 'piss off'.

His curiosity driven, he next phoned Thames Valley Police headquarters, posing as a freelance journalist, and asked to speak to either Detective Constable Coe or Assistant Chief Constable Page, key players in the aftermath of the death, as we have seen. The attempt was unsuccessful, but within the hour he received an unexpected return call. The person on the other end of the line did not bother with formalities, but instead cut to the quick. How would my contact welcome a full tax inspection of his business, VAT, national insurance, the lot? Life could be made very difficult. How did he fancy having no money?

Naturally, this prospect did not appeal, and there he left matters until on the occasion of a wedding he chanced upon an old friend whom he described to me initially as a very senior civil servant, but later as a 'spook' from MI6. He told him of his interest in the Kelly affair and also of the threatening phone call he had received. His friend's reply was a serious one: he should be careful, particularly when using his phone or his computer. Moreover, he should let the Kelly matter drop.

But my contact did not, and when he saw his friend again a couple of weeks later, this time in a pub, he again pressed him on the matter. His friend took him outside the pub, and as they stood in the cool air, told him Dr Kelly's death had been 'a wet operation, a wet disposal'. He also warned him in very strong terms to leave the matter well alone. At that point, my contact did indeed decide that he had taken his enquiries as far as he dared.

I asked my contact to explain what he understood by the terms his friend had used. Essentially, it seems to refer to an assassination, perhaps carried out in a hurry.

A few months after we had met, I called my contact to check on one or two points to ensure my understanding of events was accurate. He told me that three weeks after our meeting in Exeter, his house had been broken into and his laptop stolen. The laptop, where he had stored his material relating to his own limited inquiries into the death of Dr Kelly, had been hidden on a top shelf of a filing unit not visible from the road. Other valuable goods, including a camera and an LCD television, had been left untouched. Nothing else was taken. He also told me that since our meeting, his friend had failed to return any of his calls and had effectively cut him out of his life.

My mind went back to a couple of strange incidents that had occurred as I had begun my own investigations in earnest, in the spring of 2006. Early on, I had decided to visit Harrowdown Hill and the village where Dr Kelly lived. A friend of mine in Lewes who was helping me at this stage offered to accompany me so I picked her up from her house.

When we returned later that afternoon, however, as I pulled up outside, we saw that her front door was wide open. The door is one which it is required to lock on the way out, so it could not have been left open by accident. Indeed, I remember seeing her lock it. Furthermore, it transpired that the back door was also wide open. Yet, so far as my friend could tell, nothing had been taken from the house. Nor had any of her family been back home during her absence.

Also around that time, she began receiving strange silent phone calls, exactly on the hour. Eventually, I registered a complaint with Sussex Police, immediately after which the calls ceased. They have not recurred.

A few weeks after that, it was my turn to be on the receiving end of a curious incident. Towards six o'clock one late afternoon, my office manager was sitting at her computer in my constituency office when the screen went blank for a split second before a heart-sinking message appeared briefly on the screen – ERASING HARD DRIVE. And so it was. Within a matter of seconds, the computer was wrecked, with no sign of life whatsoever. A local expert I brought in the next day professed himself astonished and could only scratch his head when I asked him what might have caused this. He doubted it could be a virus.

I mentioned this incident in passing to a BBC journalist in London, which was rather naïve of me, and before long there was a television camera outside my Lewes office and a reporter wanting an interview. I agreed to give a comment, but refused to say that the computer had been sabotaged because of my investigations, by now public knowledge, into the death of Dr Kelly, for I had no way of knowing what had happened. That did not, of course, prevent the connection being made in the papers the next day, which also seem to have concluded that I had lost some or all of my research material. As it happens, I had lost none, as I had not used that computer at all for research purposes.

I reported the matter to the police, and they removed the computer for analysis. Some weeks later they returned it to me, telling me that a virus had in fact been responsible.

These incidents, the ones involving my friend and the damage to my computer, of course prove nothing. They may well indeed be entirely unconnected with the matter in hand. Nevertheless, it did occur to me that if I was right in my conclusion that Dr Kelly had been murdered, then it might be prudent to consider whether this should affect how I would proceed.

I had also been contacted by an individual who had served in Northern Ireland, whose professed reason for writing to me was to make me aware of interception and surveillance techniques and how to counter them. He produced nine pages of detailed information, based on his experience in the collection, collation and analysis of intelligence. He did not claim to know anything of the specific circumstances around the death of Dr Kelly but, perhaps because of his experience in Northern Ireland, seemed to regard the possibility of assassination as almost mundane.

We corresponded slowly by mail, he using an accommodation address. His return letters would be posted by hand through the letterbox of my constituency office. Eventually we met up in a back room in Seaford, the largest town in my constituency. He was an interesting man, and I am grateful that he got in touch. He will hopefully not be offended if I say that I noted what he told me with interest without automatically believing or indeed disbelieving it. Nevertheless, his advice to me on certain practical matters, such as the storage of information, seemed eminently sensible, and I adopted much of it.

If I was going to make progress in discovering what had happened, I now needed to consider what the motive for murder might be, and who would stand to benefit. It seemed to me that a sensible approach would be to identify every possible motive, and every possible perpetrator, no matter how unlikely, and then seek to eliminate each possibility one by one.

As far as motive was concerned, it seemed a safe conclusion that Dr Kelly's death was connected with his professional employment. There has been no suggestion of anything in his private life that could possibly have led to his killing.

Three distinct possibilities occurred to me. The most obvious was that Dr Kelly had in his head information which might be highly damaging to an individual or individuals if it came out. The fact that Dr Kelly was under pressure might have been thought to have made that possibility rather greater. A second possibility was that this was an act of revenge, for something he had done, perhaps as part of his weapons inspection activities. A third, and it seemed to me less likely, explanation might be that his murder was carried out *pour encourager les autres*.

It is worth recording at this point that Dr Kelly had in fact had discussions with a book publisher, so clearly had in mind the idea of writing something about his work and experiences. The publisher in question was Oneworld Publications, an outfit with Baha'i connections. The *Daily Mail* implied that the idea had come from the publishers, and quoted Victoria Roddam, their commissioning editor, as having written to him a week before his death with a politically explosive suggestion: 'I think the time is ripe now more than ever for a title which addresses the relationship between government policy and war.'[1] Unsurprisingly, Ms Roddam was much in demand in the aftermath of Dr Kelly's death and went to ground.

Oneworld Publications was located in the middle of a bustling shopping street in Summertown, Oxford, yet hidden away so that it required a deal of searching to find the entrance down the side of a building. Certainly I had had no idea that it was there, although I am an occasional user of the shops in the straggling parade – my wife's mother lives literally around the corner.

When I visited their offices in the summer of 2006, Ms Roddam was still nowhere to be found, but I was able to speak with Novin Doostdar, one of Oneworld's co-founders, who said he was in charge of Ms Roddam and knew as much about the connections with Dr Kelly as she did. Mr Doostdar, who is also a Baha'i follower, told me that he had only met Dr Kelly once, a few months before his death. They had talked about a book which Dr Kelly wanted to write after his retirement, but that the discussion had not been a detailed one. There had, for example, been no identification of a synopsis or even of chapter headings. As far as he was aware, there the matter lay.

There also occurred a bizarre incident when I was walking along a street in Lewes one day in January 2007. A rather battered white pick-up truck screeched to a halt, and the driver leaned over to speak to me. He was about fifty-five, with gold front teeth, suggesting he might have played too much rugby in his life, and introduced himself as Archie. He said that he supported my investigations into the death of Dr Kelly and that there was something I should know.

He had apparently visited a printer in Croydon not long after Dr Kelly's death – he was chasing early editions of Billy Bunter books – and the printer had told him that Dr Kelly had personally arrived, armed with a manuscript, asking if he would publish this. He allegedly told the printer that he would be dead in two weeks.

I gave Archie my card and asked him to get the printer to ring me, but have heard nothing since. Unfortunately, I was in something of a rush when stopped and did not secure all the information I should have to enable me to pursue this sensibly. However, it sounds very much as if this printer was fantasising in a rather sensational way. Herein, of course, lies one of the problems with cases such as this: separating the facts from the fantasy.

Having identified three possible motives, I turned now to the possible party responsible. It seemed to me that any list should include consideration of those countries, and individuals within those countries, with which Dr Kelly had had dealings in his professional work. That would have included the UK and the United States obviously, Iraq and Russia, in both of which Dr Kelly had spent time on official business, but also South Africa and Israel, with which he had had professional connections.

This was a pretty wide list of possibilities from which to begin, but I was reasonably satisfied that it was comprehensive. I was wrong.

A mysterious message led me to a Little Chef café somewhere off the M11 near Harlow. My enquiries were certainly taking me to parts of Britain I would not normally have cause to visit. When I arrived mid-morning, the café, which looked just the same as the last Little Chef I had visited some twenty years earlier, was close to empty, so I had no trouble identifying the author of the email. He was in his mid-forties, thin on top, wearing glasses and a blue T-shirt.

I awaited with interest for my correspondent to elaborate on his email. I could not have anticipated what I was about to hear. According to him, the area surrounding the place where Dr Kelly's body was found has historically been used for what he described as 'unconventional purposes'. Harrowdown Hill, he went on, is a place where 'certain esoteric practices' have taken place. He also suggested to me that the hill sits on a ley line which connects certain Oxford colleges and also, as it happens, traverses the village of Cumnor, where the Oxfordshire coroner's office can be found.

Expanding further, he told me that there was a tree circle in the wood on Harrowdown Hill, at the centre of which hawthorn can be found. In his view, Dr Kelly's phrase 'many dark actors playing games' suggested a negative ritual carried out in this tree circle by persons dressed in black.

Where did Dr Kelly come into all this, I asked. Perhaps, I was told, he had, on one of his normal walks, come across a ritual taking place, and had, moreover, recognised one of the circle as a man of standing in the community. He had done nothing about this, but when in July 2003 he was suddenly thrust into the public eye and seemed to be under pressure, those whom he had witnessed could not be sure he would continue to keep his counsel and took action accordingly. The fact that the method used to kill Dr Kelly was rather amateurish only reinforced the view that the act was not carried out by professionals.

I should say, for the avoidance of doubt, that my interlocutor appeared perfectly normal and rational, and indeed fully recognised that his theory was 'difficult to get a handle on'.

While what he suggested was not impossible, it struck me as highly improbable, particularly the bizarre explanation for the 'dark actors' email. In the absence of any supporting evidence, I decided to discount it as an explanation.

If this was highly improbable, other so-called explanations were absurd. One correspondent wrote this:

He died under mysterious circumstances on a remote Marian Hill near the River Isis on that goddess's birthday. But Mary is clearly code for the Goddess of the blood-red planet Mars, and Mars rules the Hawthorn tree, otherwise known as May; and this is May country with its St Mary's at Longworth, and the ancient Maybush Inn and Rose Revived on Newbridge nearby. Hawthorns will abound on Harrowdown. As most everyone knows by now, the planet Mars is closer to Earth than it has been for 73,000 years. Mars the god of war, a weapons inspector with a name that means war and he dies at the site of a civil war battle. We may be talking of a blood-sacrifice here.

There were several pages of this, which I confess I did not manage to plough through. For those interested, the book *Atlantis, Alien Visitation and Genetic Manipulation* is apparently recommended for further reading.

Another weird explanation can be found in a document

included in the material made available on the Hutton inquiry website. This document, dated 31 July 2003, written in a curious typeface with selected letters in bold for no obvious reason, alleged there was a connection between the death and what it termed 'The World's Worst Paedophile Ring', members of which, it said, were present at the murder of Dr Kelly – although the document stated that he was not a member of the ring. Those wishing to take the matter forward are advised by the document to 'consult the Federal Bureau of Investigation in China, Asia' for further information. There is, of course, no evidence whatsoever of any paedophile connection, and not even a suggestion of any beyond this rather bizarre document.[2]

The interesting aspect here is why anyone would bother including such a document on the Hutton inquiry website. Specifically, there must have been a good number of wacky communications coming in to either Thames Valley Police or Lord Hutton following Dr Kelly's death. Why select uniquely this one for inclusion?

Naturally, documents like this, aided perhaps by the internet, produce all sorts of wild rumours. One, actually repeated to me in all seriousness by a very senior BBC executive, was that a leading figure in the Hutton inquiry process was known by the government to have had a paedophile past in a part of the United Kingdom well away from London. Was the inclusion of this particular document a way of reminding him to 'do his duty'?

All these various offbeat suggestions made me more determined than ever to stick to the facts and only assert that which could be stood up.

14 Dead scientists

When a series of events occurs, apparently unconnected but with a common theme, the question inevitably arises: is there some greater scheme at work, a hidden hand directing events?

For some who have contacted me, the death of David Kelly is indeed part of a wider pattern of unexplained deaths of microbiologists and other scientists across the world which happened within a short space of time. On the face of it, such an explanation seemed rather unlikely. Who would be this Mr Big, whose reach stretched across the globe? What on earth would the motive be? Furthermore, could these deaths not just be coincidences? After all, coincidences do occur. I recall reading of the death of two twins in Australia. They had been separated soon after birth, yet both ended up in the same town, both were working as taxi drivers, both had wives of the same name, and neither knew the other was in town. The only time they met was when the taxis they were driving crashed head on, killing them both.

It is very tempting to read into this some profound explanation – divine providence, or perhaps the hidden ties that bind and direct the actions of twins. But the mundane explanation of a coincidence, while emotionally less satisfying, is almost certainly correct.

Sometimes, what appears to be an extraordinary coincidence may simply be a function of statistics. How many people, for instance, would you need in a room to create a 50 per cent chance that two of the occupants have the same birthday? Many people would guess 182 or 183, half the number of days in a year. The actual answer, surprisingly, is a low twenty-three. If you widen the conundrum to two people who were born either on the same day or within a day of each other, the number required drops to just fourteen. This instinctively feels counter-intuitive, but is statistically true.

By the time I had assembled a list of those scientists alleged to have died in mysterious or violent circumstances, it contained ninety-six names and I could detect a wild goose chase in the offing. It seemed to me therefore that the best way to test this theory was to select the cases based on the greatest professional overlap with Dr Kelly, and the most suspicious circumstances of death. The final list looked like this:

- Benito Que, 52, an expert in infectious diseases, found comatose on 12 November 2001, died on 6 December 2001.

- Don Wiley, 58, a professor of biochemistry, who supposedly fell from a bridge in Memphis and was reported missing on 16 November 2001.

- Vladimir Pasechnik, 64, a leading microbiologist, who allegedly had a stroke. Died on 21 November 2001.

- Dr Robert M. Schwartz, 57, found murdered in his Virginia home on 8 December 2001.[1]

- Set Van Nguyen, 44, found dead in an airlock in an Australian laboratory on 14 December 2001.[2]
- Ian Langford, 40, an expert on environmental risk, who was found half-naked under a chair at his Norfolk home on 11 February 2002.[3]
- Paul Norman, 52, Dr Kelly's successor at Porton Down, who died in a plane crash on 27 June 2004.[4]

It can be seen that there was a cluster of deaths at the tail end of 2001.

This is not the first time a suggestion has been made that multiple individual deaths were a sign of a deep conspiracy. Back in 1988, there were rumblings about events involving British employees of Marconi. Seven leading defence scientists employed the company, and at least half a dozen others working for other companies in the field, had died in apparent suicides in the space of a couple of years.

- Marconi's grisly sequence of events began on 4 August 1986, when the body of Vimal Dajibhai, a software engineer who tested computer control systems for torpedoes, was found under Clifton suspension bridge, having apparently fallen 240 feet from the deck of the bridge. A needle-sized puncture wound on the left buttock was explained away as being a result of the fall. He was in his last week of employment with Marconi and had told friends that he was looking forward to beginning a new job in the City of London the following week.

- Two months later, Ashad Sharif, a computer analyst who had been working on systems to enable the detection of submarines by satellite, tied one end of a rope round his neck, the other around a tree, and put his car into gear and slammed the accelerator pedal down. Like Mr Dajibhai, he lived near Stanmore, on the outskirts of north London, and, like his colleague, he was found dead in Bristol. He had spent the last night of his life in a bed-and-breakfast, and was seen to have a bundle of high-denomination banknotes in his possession, though these were neither found nor referred to at the inquest.

- In March 1987, David Sands, who was working on a secret satellite radar system, drove up a slip road and into a cafe at 80 miles per hour.

- In May 1987, Michael Baker, a digital communications expert working on a defence project, crashed through a roadside barrier near Poole and died.

- In March 1988, Trevor Knight, a computer engineer, apparently killed himself with the exhaust gases from his car.

- In August that year, Peter Ferry, a marketing manager working for the company, seemingly killed himself by putting mains electric cables in his mouth and switching on the power.

- The same month, another employee of the firm, Alistair Beckham, a software engineer, was found dead in his garden shed. Wires had been attached to his body and he had been electrocuted.[5]

Investigative journalists strove in vain to find a link, other than their employer, between the men, or with the then current inquiry into the valuable defence contracts awarded to GEC-Marconi. In all probability, there was none. And yet, as coincidences go, it really was quite remarkable.

With all this in mind, I set about examining the circumstances surrounding the deaths of the scientists I had listed. The first stage was to establish which, if any, might be murder. The second would be to look for links with Dr Kelly, and therefore a possible motive. What could possibly link microbiologists across continents and possibly years?

Benito Que was a cell biologist working at the University of Miami's School of Medicine, who appears never to have worked with infectious diseases such as anthrax. Indeed, his line manager at the university, Dr Bach Ardalan, denied that Mr Que had been engaged in any sensitive work. He was found unconscious in a Miami side street. Friends say he was heading for his car when he was attacked by four young men carrying baseball bats. When he was found, his wallet was missing, but his briefcase was still at his side. His car was found several miles away.

There were few signs of violence on his person and his CAT scan showed no trauma, which fuelled suspicion about the explanation that this had been a mugging. It transpired, however, that Mr Que had been suffering from hypertension and indeed that very day, a nurse had recorded his blood pressure as 190/110. She had wanted to admit him to hospital immediately, but Mr Que insisted on returning home. He was to die just over three weeks later from the incident.

Four days after Mr Que's attack, Don Wiley, professor of biochemistry and biophysics at Harvard University's Department of Molecular and Cellular Biology, went missing. His research had focused on the structure of viruses and proteins in the human immune system. This included viruses such as HIV and ebola, and how these and other viruses have evolved to infect different living organisms.

In the United States, he was the foremost expert in using X-ray cameras and mathematical formulae to create high-resolution images of viruses. At the time of his death, he was heavily involved in work relating to the sequencing of DNA. Such work, as well as having potentially important health benefits for humans, would also have been of interest to those developing biological weapons and defences against them.

On 16 November 2001, at around midnight, Dr Wiley left a dinner he had been attending in Memphis. His car, a rented Mitsubishi Galant, was found at 4 a.m., just five minutes' drive away on a bridge on the Mississippi River. The keys were still in the ignition and the petrol tank was full. The hazard lights had not been turned on. Dr Wiley was nowhere to be seen. His body would later be found, on 20 December, caught on a tree some 300 miles downstream.

The official explanation is that Dr Wiley's car had a minor collision with some road signs, there to warn of roadworks on the bridge which reduced traffic to a single lane in either direction. He then pulled over onto the hard shoulder and got out to inspect the damage, whereupon a huge blast of wind from a passing truck swept him over the guardrail into the river.

The county medical examiner, O. C. Smith, said that there were paint marks on the car which matched the paint on the temporary road signs, and that the car had a hubcap missing, most likely as a result of the minor collision. He also said that Dr Wiley had had a few glasses of wine, and pointed out that he also occasionally suffered from a seizure disorder that affected his balance.

Interestingly, he ruled out suicide in favour of a verdict of accidental death on the basis that there was forensic evidence that Dr Wiley had hit a support beam of the bridge before landing 135 feet below in the water. Those who commit suicide here apparently find it easy to clear the support beams, which project only 3 feet beyond the guardrails. Furthermore, those who had been with Dr Wiley that evening maintained that there had been no reason at all to think that he might have been feeling suicidal. The police themselves concluded from their investigations that he had been upbeat and looking forward to his family coming down the next day.

So that was that. Except that there were some curious aspects to the case that have never been explained. First, there is the gap of four hours between Dr Wiley leaving the dinner and his car appearing in the middle of the mile-long bridge. Nobody seemed to know why there was this time gap, or where he had gone. Second, witnesses at the dinner said he appeared perfectly sober, and nobody has been found to say he had been drinking, contrary to the suggestion from the county medical examiner. Third, he was due that evening to stay at his father's home in the Memphis suburb of Germantown, yet the road his car was found on would have taken him in quite the wrong direction, towards Arkansas. Fourth, Interstate 40 out of Memphis at midnight on a Friday evening is a busy road, yet despite this and the single-lane working which would have slowed vehicles down, no witnesses have been found who saw Dr Wiley on the bridge. Fifth, the reported damage to the car's paintwork, and the missing hubcap, were absent from initial reports. Moreover, if a hubcap had been removed from this model of car as part of a collision, this would have caused damage to the sheet metal on either side of the wheel. No such damage was reported. In addition, the paint marks were on the driver's side of the car, but the hubcap was missing from the passenger's side. Sixth, in order for Dr Wiley to have been swept over the guardrail, which was waist high, he would need to have been right up against it and probably already leaning over it. But Dr Wiley was terrified of heights, according to his brother Greg.

In a bizarre twist, the Memphis medical examiner investigating the case was charged in 2004 with possessing an illegal bomb and lying about an allegation that he had been attacked by an unknown assailant. He said that his attacker had wrapped him up in barbed wire, put a bomb around his neck, and then thrown a chemical in his face to blind him. This was indeed how he had been found, at the bottom of a stairwell outside his office on 1 June 2002. Mr Smith pleaded not guilty, and the trial ended with a hung jury unable to reach a verdict.[6]

Vladimir Pasechnik was a Soviet microbiologist with close links to Dr Kelly. He had been heavily involved in the illegal Soviet germ warfare programme, details of which only became known to the west on his defection in 1989. The work had, amongst other things, succeeded in producing a strain of plague resistant to antibiotics. He had also worked on a series of potential biological weapons, utilising anthrax, ebola, Q fever, Marburg virus and smallpox. His revelations, along with those of Ken Alibek, another employee from the Soviet Union's Biopreparat programme who defected to the west shortly afterwards, led to the despatch of an international team of weapons inspectors to Russia. Dr Kelly played a leading role in this effort.

Mr Pasechnik was debriefed by Dr Kelly, who helped him find a berth at Porton Down and eventually start up his own business, Regma Biotechnologies, with a laboratory at Porton Down. He seemed to settle down to English life, living quietly in a Wiltshire village close to Porton Down.

On Wednesday 21 November 2001, Mr Pasechnik was found dead in bed. The death occurred just ten days after the Russian had been in Boston to discuss DNA sequencing with Dr Wiley. The police who were called in described the death as 'inexplicable'. At the subsequent inquest, the pathologist concluded that Mr Pasechnik had died from a stroke, a conclusion accepted by the coroner.

The news of his death was broken by a Dr Christopher Davis. The public relations department at Regma did not issue a statement. Dr Davis was described in the article as being resident in Great Falls, Virginia and having been 'formerly in British intelligence'. Quite why it should have fallen to him to announce the death is far from clear.

In fact, before his retirement, Dr Davis had been the chief scientist and director of biomedical research at the biotechnology company CUBRC, and a recognised international authority on biological warfare and biodefence issues, including DNA sequencing. He was also for ten years a member of the Defence Intelligence Staff and in that capacity was directly responsible for the collation, analysis and assessment of all intelligence on biological weapons. Like Dr Kelly, he had helped debrief Mr Pasechnik on his arrival in the UK.

The stroke explanation had also first come from Dr Davis. According to author Gordon Thomas, a secret post-mortem analysis was carried out by a pathologist working for the British security services.[7] Mr Thomas also quoted a US expert in the field of toxic poisons, Dr Leonard Horowitz, as pointing out that 'there are a number of nerve agents that can mimic a stroke and leave no traces'.[8]

When I spoke to Ken Alibek, he told me he had been surprised to learn of Mr Pasechnik's death. He had been in regular email contact with him, and he had seemed to be in fine fettle. He thought Dr Davis had announced Mr Pasechnik's death 'because he debriefed him'.

Dr Robert Schwartz was a founding member of the Virginia Biotechnology Association, and an expert in DNA sequencing. At the time of his death, he was working on the first online database of DNA sequence information. On Monday 10 December 2001, he was found dead at his secluded farmhouse in Leesburg, Virginia. Police had been alerted after he failed to turn up for work that morning. He had apparently been stabbed.

Subsequently, it was suggested that four young friends had carried out what a prosecutor called 'a planned assassination' on Dr Schwartz, using a 2-foot sword. The microbiologist was stabbed and slashed repeatedly, and an X was carved into the back of his neck. The four appeared to be heavily into black magic and the occult, to the extent of drinking blood and experimenting in self-mutilation, in the case of the ringleader, eighteen-year-old Kyle Hulbert. All were charged with murder. One of the four was in fact Dr Schwartz's daughter, Clara.

Set Van Nguyen worked in a laboratory, which handled microbes such as mousepox, which can be used in certain experiments as a substitute for smallpox. On 14 December 2001, he became trapped in a nitrogen-filled airlock chamber at his place of work, the Australian Commonwealth Scientific and Industrial Research Organisation's animal diseases facility at Geelong, and allegedly died from suffocation.

On closer examination, however, it transpired that Mr Van Nguyen was only a member of the laboratory's technical support team, and not a research scientist. There would therefore appear to be no sinister motive for murder which stands up to scrutiny.

Now we return to England and the death of Dr Ian Langford, a scientist at the University of East Anglia, on 11 February 2002. He was described by his colleague Professor Kerry Turner, the director of the university's Centre for Social and Economic Research on the Global Environment, as 'one of Europe's leading experts on environmental risk, specialising in links between human health and environmental risk'.

Dr Langford was found dead at his home, where police found the walls blood spattered. The house, in a terrace, seemed to have been ransacked and the external doors were locked. His body was naked from the waist down and partly wedged under a chair. It had sustained some wounds. The police concluded that the death was not suspicious, and that the injuries must have been self-inflicted or sustained accidentally. The post-mortem failed to conclude how Dr Langford had died.

On the face of it, although this death is unusual, it is difficult to see a link between it and that of Dr Kelly. Dr Langford did not even appear to have been engaged in the same sort of work. It is all the more surprising, therefore, that no less a person than John Eldridge, editor of the specialist periodical *Jane's Nuclear, Biological and Chemical Defence*, should have indicated to the *News of the World* that the two deaths may be linked: 'If I was a microbiologist, I would be worried,' he told the paper.[9] So far as can be ascertained, Mr Eldridge has made no further statements on this matter. When I rang him to pursue it, he slammed the phone down on me.

Dr Paul Norman's death is separated by some time from the others considered above, but is notable in that Dr Norman was a close colleague of Dr Kelly's at Porton Down. Like Dr Kelly, he toured the world, imparting his knowledge of weapons of mass destruction. At the time of his death, Dr Norman was chief scientist for chemical and biological weapons research at the establishment.

His death came on 27 June 2004, almost a year after that of Dr Kelly, when the light aircraft he was piloting crashed near the Devon village of Beacon, shortly after take-off from nearby Dunkeswell airfield. Dr Norman was an experienced pilot and had completed 628 flying hours, including 172 in the type of plane he was that day piloting, a leased Cessna 206. On an earlier flight in the aircraft that day, the alternator warning light had come on, but otherwise the flight had been uneventful. A maintenance check had been carried out just an hour and ten minutes before the fatal flight.

According to the official accident report, the aircraft's engine began to lose power and the pilot was unable to maintain height. In attempting a forced landing, the aircraft clipped the tops of several tall trees and crashed steeply nose down into a sloping grass field. Witnesses said the plane's engine had been 'coughing and spluttering'. It turned out that the same plane had, under the control of a different pilot a week earlier, experienced a problem when the throttle was opened: there was no immediate response and the engine began to run roughly. On that occasion the pilot returned safely to land.

The accident report was extremely thorough, and was carried out by one principal, and three senior, inspectors from the Air Accidents Investigation Branch. While the cause of the crash could not be definitively identified, there was no suggestion of any sabotage. Official figures from the Department for Transport show that there were five incidents between 2002 and 2006 involving a Cessna 206 which resulted in an investigation by the AAIB.[10] Of these, only the incident involving Dr Norman produced fatalities.

The inquest into Dr Norman's death was due to be heard by the Devon coroner, Dr Elizabeth Earland, on 1 November 2006, but this was postponed. Eventually on 3 August 2007 Dr Earland returned a verdict of accidental death.

What can be concluded from all this? It is certainly interesting that a number of the scientists were involved in cutting-edge work on DNA sequencing, that two of them – Don Wiley and Vladimir Pasechnik – appear to have met shortly before their demise, that the deaths themselves were close together in time, and that each had certain singular features. Michael Ruppert, in his book *Crossing the Rubicon*, suggests that Dr Wiley, Robert Schwartz and Benito Que also had a further matter in common, namely that they had been working for medical research facilities that received grants from the Howard Hughes Medical Institute. According to Mr Ruppert, the institute has long been used by the CIA for 'black-ops' medical research.[11] One theory is that the work the scientists were engaged upon might have led to the development of ways to treat diseases such as smallpox or anthrax without a requirement to use conventional vaccines or antibiotics. Such a breakthrough would not have been popular with those companies who produce vaccines.

And producing vaccines is big business. According to a 2003 report from Reuters, sales of vaccines were expected to top $10 billion by 2006.[12] The year before, President Bush had signed into law the Public Health Security and Bioterrorism Preparedness and Response Act, which anticipated a spend of some $4.6 billion, much of which would be used to produce and stockpile vaccines.

The deaths of all the scientists considered above, with the exception of Paul Norman, came shortly after the arrival of anthrax-contaminated letters at news media offices and the offices of two US Senators, Tom Daschle and Patrick Leahy. This anthrax, it was subsequently confirmed, was all derived from a single bacterial strain, the Ames strain, and was traced back as originating in an American military laboratory, specifically the US Army Medical Research Institute of Infectious Diseases in Fort Detrick, Maryland.[13] The crime remains unsolved.

In 2001, the US government announced that it intended to offer a vaccine manufactured by a Michigan-based pharmaceutical company, BioPort, to thousands of people who might have come into contact with the US-manufactured anthrax.[14] This was a curious move, given that vaccines are designed to be taken before exposure rather than after. Furthermore, it transpired that the vaccine in question had not been subject to proper testing. Moreover, the choice of BioPort itself, while unsurprising given the company's then position as the sole producer of anthrax vaccine, was nevertheless controversial. In 1998 its factory had been forced to halt production for failing to meet Food and Drug Administration standards, including breaching cleanliness standards, contamination problems, and suspicious changes made to quality assurance records.[15]

BioPort, whose largest shareholder was the retired chairman of the Joint Chiefs of Staff, Admiral William Crowe, certainly benefited from the attacks of 11 September 2001. Its military orders rose to $60 million.

So here is a link between at least four of the dead scientists considered in this chapter – Mr Que, Dr Wiley, Dr Schwartz and Mr Pasechnik – but it is a leap of faith to then conclude that they might have been involved in some work that would have provided some sort of motive for eliminating them. In any case, there is no obvious way in which all this ties in with Dr Kelly, whose death, after all, came not in the same short period of a few weeks, but more than eighteen months later.

As for the other deaths, it seems overwhelmingly likely that they were not in any way connected, and that the apparent reasons for death are the actual ones. An explanation for Dr Kelly's death would have to be found elsewhere.

15 Project Coast

There is one further death in the series of 'dead scientists' that is worth considering. The investigation of this would lead from an American gynaecologist to the development of chillingly effective biological weapons by the apartheid-era South African government, take in a cottage near Ascot, and link in with David Kelly.

Dr Larry Ford ran a company called Biofem Pharmaceuticals in Irvine, California with his business partner, James Riley. On 28 February 2000, Mr Riley, having parked his car, was walking towards the front door of Biofem's building when a masked stranger appeared and shot him in the face. The bullet entered his cheek, gashed his cheekbone and exited just above his lip. He survived.

Fortunately, a witness recorded the number plate of the van in which the assailant had escaped, and it turned out to belong to a Dino D'Saachs, a long-standing friend of Dr Ford. Police discovered from telephone records that Mr D'Saachs and Dr Ford had that morning spoken on the phone. Dr Ford told police the call had been about a prescription.

Mr D'Saachs was subsequently identified as having driven the gunman to the scene, arrested and put on trial for conspiracy to commit murder. He declined to secure himself a lesser sentence by revealing the identity of the gunman and was sentenced to twenty-six years' imprisonment.

The day after the shooting, police searched Dr Ford's house and shortly afterwards he was found dead with a gunshot wound to the head. He had left what appeared to be a suicide note, denying any involvement in his business partner's death. Those who knew him found it difficult to believe that he had killed himself. Dr Ford, a Mormon, had himself been subject to an unsuccessful gun attack by an unidentified hitman back in 1978.

The search, inspired by anonymous telephone tip-offs, turned up large numbers of weapons, including over forty hunting rifles and shotguns hidden under floorboards, which even his activity as an avid hunter could not really justify. They also found beneath a concrete slab next to the swimming pool twenty-seven sealed canisters containing military explosives, a massive collection of automatic rifles and other weapons, and several thousand rounds of ammunition. None of the weapons appeared to have been used in the shooting of Mr Riley.

The police, however, were to find material that proved to be even more sinister than the cache of weapons. The telephone tip-offs had suggested that there were canisters of HIV-related material buried somewhere on the property. What they found was a vast array of highly toxic and infectious substances which, had they been released, would have had appalling consequences for huge numbers of people. Twenty-five jars of unidentified substances removed from Dr Riley's house were found to contain live cultures of cholera and salmonella. Even more alarming, there were also more than 250 bottles and phials of live cultures, holding botulism and typhoid fever, amongst others. A sealed container was found to hold a large quantity of potassium cyanide.

Where had all these weapons, military-grade explosives and biological substances come from?

Dr Ford told his friends that he worked for the CIA. His doctor believed he had done so for about twenty years. The *New York Times* appeared to back up this suggestion. It reported that police officers deployed to search the property were forewarned that Dr Ford was reported as having worked on developing biological weapons for the CIA, although it was later denied that the police had been so warned.[1] The CIA also denied that he had worked for them, though such denials are standard practice, whether true or not.

There were also reports that Dr Ford, in his role as a gynaecologist, had carried out unauthorised experiments on some of his patients. On one occasion he is said to have infected a student with whom he had been having an affair with an 'alpha toxin' that caused neurological damage and led to her having brain surgery.

What is certain, however, is that Dr Ford had strong links with the apartheid government of South Africa, and this provides by far the most likely explanation for his ability to secure highly controlled and dangerous substances. In particular, he was indisputably involved with Project Coast, the highly unpleasant chemical and biological warfare programme run by the Pretoria government from 1981 onwards. The programme was deeply secret, with only a handful of people knowing of its existence. It was answerable to the Defence Minister.

Project Coast was one piece of the jigsaw designed to keep the white supremacist government in power in South Africa. Its aims included the creation of a biological weapon designed to attack the black population whilst leaving the whites unscathed. The key to this is DNA sequencing, which of course Dr Ford and some of the scientists referred to in the previous chapter were engaged upon. DNA sequencing exploits the idea that substances can be developed that will work to the genetic characteristics of a person, or group of people. Benignly, this holds out the prospect that drugs can increasingly be targeted at specific genes responsible for particular conditions. The likely health benefits are potentially enormous. Less benignly, pathogens can be developed to target individuals based on their racial characteristics, their sex or even their eye colour.

According to the *Los Angeles Times*, Dr Ford had acted as a consultant to the South African Defence Force, providing advice on matters connected with biological weapons.[2] He was certainly a regular visitor to South Africa, undertaking dozens of trips between 1984 and 2000. Mike Odendaal, a microbiologist who worked at the Roodeplaat Research Laboratories where Project Coast work was undertaken, told the South African *Sunday Independent*: 'Ford spent an entire day showing us how to contaminate ordinary items and turn them into biological weapons.'[3] These ordinary items included pornographic magazines and teabags. From the Truth and Reconciliation Commission hearings in South Africa, we also learnt of chocolates and cigarettes contaminated with anthrax, milk infected with botulism, and salmonella germs in sugar.

The exotic techniques of murder hit the headlines again in the summer of 2007 when, at the end of a trial in South Africa, former police minister Adriaan Vlok and the then police chief, Johan van der Merwe, were found guilty of attempting to kill a black activist, Rev. Frank Chikane, by impregnating his underpants with a nerve toxin. No doubt if anyone had suggested such a scenario prior to Mr Vlok's arrest, they would have been called a conspiracy theorist.

It also became clear at the Truth and Reconciliation Commission hearings that those involved in Project Coast had spent a great deal of time and effort developing a number of innovative ways to carry out assassinations without leaving a detectable trace. Dr Schalk van Rensburg, the director of the Roodeplaat Research Laboratories, told the commission:

The most frequent instruction we obtained . . . was to develop something with which you could kill an individual that would make his death resemble a natural death, and that something was to be not detectable in a normal forensic laboratory. That was the chief aim of the Roodeplaat Research Laboratories' covert side.[4]

One further creation was an organism, *Hormoconis resinae*, intended to attack aircraft fuel, clog fuel lines and cause engines to splutter and fail. It is unlikely that even the thorough investigations carried out by the Air Accidents Investigation Branch of the Department for Transport ever considered that this might be the cause of a crash.

Dr Ford was close friends with General Niels Knobel, the surgeon general of the South African Defence Force, who theoretically had overall operational responsibility for Project Coast. In practice, General Knobel was happy to provide large sums of money without very much explanation to the man who really drove Project Coast forward, Dr Wouter Basson, described by South African papers variously as 'the South African Mengele' and 'Dr Death'. It was General Knobel who introduced Dr Ford to Dr Basson in the mid-1980s. And it was Dr Basson (and a Dr Swanepoel) who issued the instructions to Dr van Rensburg referred to above.

The end of the apartheid era and the formation of a government under Nelson Mandela eventually led to Project Coast being officially closed. However in his book *Elimination Theory*, the American T. J. Byron, who had worked as an 'informant agent' for both the CIA and South African intelligence at the time of Project Coast, claims that the programme was not really shut down at all, and in particular that the huge store of chemical and biological agents was simply moved to other sites in South Africa, and also to sites abroad. He also alleges that Project Coast was supported at arm's length by successive US administrations, even to the extent that they turned a blind eye to the free movement of deadly bacterial strains and pathogens between the two countries.[5] If true, it is likely that the UK would have had a similar policy.

It must be more than possible, therefore, that the haul of toxins found in Dr Ford's house was part of the material that had originally been held in South Africa. Certainly much of the material was quite old, according to the FBI, which would be consistent with material produced prior to the official closure of Project Coast in 1993. We also know that Dr Ford was not averse to carrying such material across the world himself. His laboratory assistant Valerie Kesler said that she had once travelled with him to South Africa when he had had a phial in his jacket pocket. He handed it to a South African official upon arrival.

According to the writer Gordon Thomas, the Israeli secret service, Mossad, believes that Dr Ford had links with Dr Kelly. In an article for the *Sunday Express*, Mr Thomas pointed out that three of the cultures in particular found at Dr Ford's house – cholera, botulism and typhoid fever – were ones Dr Kelly had been working on at Porton Down.[6]

Dr Kelly had certainly met Dr Basson. It appears he visited Porton Down at least once. It also seems that Dr Kelly, with official sanction, visited Delta-G, South Africa's equivalent of Porton Down, around the time of the fall of the apartheid regime. Dr Basson was a frequent visitor to Britain, and for years used a cottage in Watersplash Lane, in the village of

Warfield, near Ascot. It is clear that this was not a holiday home.

In 2001, a glimpse into the world of Dr Basson was provided when a former secretary of his dramatically revealed what her job had entailed. If Patricia Leeson had expected that she would just be typing or filing, she was to get a rude awakening. Rather than taking a letter, she found herself taking £50,000 in cash to Heathrow airport to hand over to a man called 'Roger'. In true spy style, she had to wear a bright red dress with a distinctive brooch to aid recognition. She was to answer to the name Vanessa. Her ten months' employment, in 1987, was filled with codenames, false passports, bundles of cash and circuitous routes to shake off anyone who might be following her.

On one occasion, she was asked to leave her house in Ascot for the day to enable a secret meeting to take place. She returned to find Jan Lourens, a colleague of Dr Basson's, looking extremely pale. He explained that he had nearly killed himself with a poisoned umbrella. Mr Lourens would go on to tell the Truth and Reconciliation Commission that on one occasion, he delivered two phials containing toxins and a screwdriver containing a biological poison to Watersplash Lane.[7]

Dr Basson's cottage was one of a pair of semi-detached three-bedroom properties, originally built to house farm workers. The pair sit some considerable distance from the next nearest property. Dr Basson's neighbour, John Stockton, still resides there. He told me that Dr Basson was 'a very nice person'. They had been good neighbours and Mr Stockton had regularly been in Dr Basson's house. There had also been a steady stream of South African visitors and the occasional American. He found it difficult to believe that the house might have been used for any illegal activity.

After the fall of the apartheid regime, Dr Basson established contacts with Libya, a development that concerned both the United States and the UK. He was in fact interviewed by a team from both countries. It is likely Dr Kelly would have been part of this process.

In August 2007, I tracked Dr Basson down to the hospital in the Western Cape where he was working as a cardiologist, saving lives. He was both friendly and helpful, almost disarmingly so. I could understand why his neighbour had reached the view he had.

Dr Basson told me that he had first met Dr Kelly in 1985 at Porton Down and the two continued to meet occasionally until the late 1990s, and to speak on the phone thereafter, including to discuss the Iraqi capability in weapons of mass destruction. Dr Basson was in no doubt that there was nothing to be found in the country and told me that he went on South African television two weeks before the invasion to say so. Pertinently, he formed the view that Dr Kelly doubted that there was much to be found in terms of weapons of mass destruction, but he thought that he may have internally suppressed those doubts.

I asked him if he thought Dr Kelly had been murdered. He paused, as if choosing his words carefully, then replied that he did not know for sure, but Dr Kelly 'didn't seem the sort to commit suicide'. He was in no doubt, however, that the UK, and indeed other western countries, have a capacity for assassination. He seemed to know what he was talking about.

It is clear that there was substantial contact between the white government in South Africa and both Britain and the United States in respect of chemical and biological weapons. There is no doubt that Dr Kelly's contacts, and those of his colleagues at Porton Down, were officially sanctioned. The official position was set out in a parliamentary answer in June 2006:

> The then Conservative Government were aware of the existence of legitimate South African chemical and biological defence programmes from the 1980s. Initial reports indicating offensive chemical and biological weapons activities, later known as Project Coast, were not received until 1993, but they were inconclusive. There were also unsubstantiated claims of chemical weapon use by South African forces in Angola, Mozambique and Zimbabwe in the 1980s and 1990s. More detailed evidence of previous offensive activities was received in the years leading up to the truth and reconciliation hearings in 1998, when further details of the offensive activities emerged. In 1994, we understood that the South African government had terminated offensive chemical and biological weapons activities.[8]

The government also stated, in response to another parliamentary question, that it had 'no reason to doubt' that the stores of biological materials assembled by Project Coast had been destroyed,[9] and, in response to a third parliamentary question, that there was 'no record' of collaboration between Ministry of Defence officials and the Roodeplaat Research Laboratory,[10] which is of course not the same as denying that such contact existed. It did concede that UK officials had attended a meeting with the South African surgeon general and Dr Basson in 1995, which, according to T. J. Byron, was the year the United States pressurised the Mandela government to re-employ Dr Basson, so that he could be brought under military control again, following his dealings with Libya.

Interestingly, the official answer from the armed forces minister, Adam Ingram, ended with the following sentence: 'I am not in a position to comment on the activities of Her Majesty's Government-funded institutions outside the Ministry of Defence.' In other words, he could not speak for Porton Down.

It is no secret that the Thatcher government was sympathetic to the white administration in Pretoria, and openly opposed sanctions on the regime. Its continued dealings with Pretoria may therefore have reflected this, or a belief that it was necessary to sustain the white government to ward off communism or anarchy in South Africa. That was certainly the view of the United States. Alternatively, the decision to keep channels open may have been based on the pragmatic view that a degree of contact would at least allow a continual assessment of South Africa's capabilities in this most sensitive field to be undertaken. Whatever the reason, it is likely that Dr Kelly would have known much of what South Africa had been up to, and also the complicit nature of the response at the time from Washington and London.

Dr Basson told me that from 1985 until the late 1990s, he was allowed to move around the UK unhindered, provided he did not 'push anyone under a train'. He seems to have been regarded as a useful asset, and told me of regular meetings with those he termed 'your secret intelligence guys', who were particularly interested in what he could tell them about Iran.

Then in 1998, while he was in Pretoria, he received a minimalist letter from the British Home Secretary, Jack Straw, which told him that he was no longer welcome in Britain. No specific reasons were given. A similar ban was put in place by the United States. The ban has been rigorously enforced – he has not been allowed even to use Heathrow airport for transit purposes. He says that he sold his cottage in Watersplash Lane at around the same time as the ban came in.

In his book *Gideon's Spies*, Gordon Thomas asserts that the week before Dr Kelly died, the weapons inspector had been told that he was to be questioned by MI5 about his involvement in bringing Dr Basson to Porton Down.[11] If true, it is probable that this development would have come about as a by-product of the heightened interest in Dr Kelly amongst British intelligence, which may have uncovered the historic link between the two men. In terms of a motive for the murder of Dr Kelly, it is possible therefore to speculate that somebody did not want this interview to take place for fear of what Dr Kelly might say. Dr Basson told me this suggestion was 'rubbish', and added: 'The only person who knows about Project Coast is me, and I'm not talking.'

But what could Dr Kelly say? Certainly any revelations about co-operation between the apartheid regime of South Africa and the British government might have been embarrassing for the latter. They might have shown that the British were not only breaking the established sanctions regime but actually aiding the South Africans to develop an offensive chemical and biological weapons capability, and one designed, in the most heinous way, to target the majority black population.

On the other hand, the events in question all occurred some ten years earlier, and under a government of a different party. Moreover, there seemed to have been attempts in the 1990s to help close Project Coast down, so it should not have been politically impossible to smudge the whole thing over.

Could those who were involved from the South African side have feared what Dr Kelly might say? It seems unlikely. The Truth and Reconciliation hearings allowed the truth to emerge in a way that enabled the majority of those involved to put the matter behind them. As far as Dr Basson himself was concerned, he had been arrested in 1999 in South Africa and put on trial, but he had been found 'not guilty' of all charges brought against him, and was continuing to receive an income from the South African authorities.

Moreover, if anyone with experience of Project Coast had been involved in his death, they would doubtless have managed to make a more professional and convincing job of it, particularly given the experience they had chillingly built up. After all, the main focus of the Roodeplaat Research Laboratories had been to develop assassination techniques which left no trace.

The whole truth about Project Coast and the links with Britain in general and Dr Kelly in particular has yet to come out, but on the basis of what we know, it seems unlikely that this was a telling factor in the death of Britain's leading weapons inspector.

At this point, it is also worth considering Dr Kelly's links with Israel. Here too was a country with a capability in respect of chemical and biological weapons, and one well hidden from the world at large. And Israel, like the apartheid-era South Africa, had muted links in this area with both the USA and the UK.

Information regarding Dr Kelly's links with Israel relies heavily on one source, Gordon Thomas. There is little doubt that he is very well connected to Mossad, the Israeli secret service, and *Gideon's Spies* reads like a semi-official biography of the organisation. Nevertheless, it would be satisfying to be able to corroborate what he has written and said using alternative sources, but I have not been able to do so.

When we spoke, Mr Thomas told me that Dr Kelly had, early in his career, been asked to assist Mossad, and had become familiar with its London chief. He also is said to have been one of the few outsiders allowed to visit the Israel Institute for Biological Research, officially a government defence research establishment specialising in biology, medicinal chemistry and environmental science. Unofficially, my own research suggests that this centre is the focus for work by the Israelis on chemical and biological weapons. A glimpse of this came in 1992, when El Al flight 1862 crashed in the Netherlands. It transpired that the plane's cargo included 190 litres of dimethyl methylphosphonate, en route to the research centre. This compound is listed in Schedule 2 of the Chemical Weapons Convention and is used in the manufacture of sarin nerve gas. It also transpired that the cargo originated from a US chemical plant and carried a proper US Department of Commerce licence. Here was clear proof of the activities of the Israeli government at this plant, and the co-operation that existed, and doubtless still exists, between the two countries.

It is striking to note in passing the double standards applied to the possession and use of such material. Israel, with the help of the United States, appears to have exempted itself from a raft of international requirements. For example, before the 2003 invasion, Iraq had violated or ignored sixteen UN Resolutions, and the UK and the USA were telling the world that enough was enough. Israel, with rather less of a commotion, appears to have violated or ignored sixty-eight. And Israel, unlike Iraq, most certainly does have weapons of mass destruction: chemical, biological and nuclear.

Mr Thomas alleges that Dr Kelly first became involved with Mossad in 1995, when he attended a meeting in New York with Mossad agents, as well as ones from the FBI and the Canadian Security Intelligence Service. The purpose of the meeting, he relates, was to nail down the illegal movement of 32 tons of bacterial growth medium from Iraq to Montreal.

Could the Israelis have been responsible in some way for Dr Kelly's death? It is common knowledge that the Israelis do carry out assassinations; indeed it is a policy they openly admit to. The Kidon (meaning 'bayonet'), a specially trained elite unit within Mossad's highly secret Metsada department, is tasked with these killings. Rafael Eitan, a near-legendary former Mossad hitman, has spoken of being an executioner on numerous occasions, killing people at close enough range 'to see the whites of their eyes'.[12] Notwithstanding the capability, however, there is no evidence that Israel was in any way connected with Dr Kelly's death. Indeed, the evidence such as there is points in exactly the opposite direction. From what we can tell, Dr Kelly had been helpful to the Israelis and trusted by them.

So another potential explanation for Dr Kelly's death can almost certainly be ruled out.

If neither South Africa nor Israel could provide an explanation for David Kelly's death, what about Russia?

Back in January 1991, Dr Kelly had been a member of the team of US and UK inspectors that would conduct the historic first inspection of plants established by the old Soviet Union. Russia maintained that they existed only for defensive purposes, but a sub-group of British inspectors was to prove otherwise.

The group included Dr Kelly and Dr Chris Davis, the man who, a decade later, would communicate news of the death of the Russian defector Vladimir Pasechnik. It was they who, in a complex at Obolensk, near Moscow, found a test chamber that, upon inspection, had clearly been used to test biological weapons for offensive purposes. This was just the beginning. In Siberia, the Vektor laboratory, near Novosibirsk, proved to be a huge centre for the production of viral agents for biological weapons. It contained samples of virtually every virus that existed, in multiple strains. Here too the Russians would rue the presence of Dr Kelly. It was he who discovered that work was being undertaken on smallpox, contrary to the global agreement reached in 1983, after the virus had been eradicated, that the remaining samples would be kept in just two locations, at laboratories in Atlanta and Moscow. The Russians had been caught red-handed, in clear breach of an international treaty.

On the next inspection trip, over the cold Russian winter of 1993–4, Dr Kelly would again succeed in cutting through obfuscations and diversionary explanations to get to the truth. He and his colleagues discovered a huge capability to produce vast quantities of biological weapons at short notice.

It is not clear how much first Mikhail Gorbachev and then Boris Yeltsin knew of the activities of these plants, but the work of Dr Kelly and his colleagues shone a harsh spotlight on them, and without doubt helped put a brake on the offensive work carried out by the Russians.

Could there have been resentment, if not from the state itself then from individual Russians, at the role Dr Kelly had played, resentment enough to generate a murder? The Russians, after all, had invested huge sums of money in developing their biological weapons capability, almost certainly in the incorrect belief that the Americans too were cheating on the terms of the Biological Weapons Convention.

Just how much time and effort had been invested was laid bare for all to read when in 2005, former KGB agent Aleksandr Kuzminov published his book *Biological Espionage*. He even suggested that the illegal activities that Dr Kelly and his colleagues had unearthed may have been reactivated. 'Can you imagine such power being abandoned just because of détente and democratisation?' he said in an interview to launch his book. 'Would all the efforts and money expended in training and developing our people be forgotten?'

Apart from his role in uncovering Russia's offensive work with biological weapons, Dr Kelly also played a leading role in debriefing the defector Vladimir Pasechnik and may well have been seen to have a hand in the subsequent defection of another pivotal player, Kanatzhan Alibekov, who became a US citizen and westernised his name to Ken Alibek.

Loyal patriotic Russians working in this field had reason to resent the efficiency and effectiveness of Britain's leading weapons inspector. Those less loyal to the motherland, on the other hand, were rumoured to be angered by Dr Kelly's refusal to help them defect. One curious suggestion, contained in *Gideon's Spies*, is that some of these disaffected scientists were in contact with agents from the Russian embassy, and that Dr Kelly, shortly before his death, had been given details of car number plates to look out for, specifically Russian diplomatic cars bearing the combination 248D. Gordon Thomas further alleges that a Land Rover bearing such a number plate had been spotted a week before Dr Kelly died in a village not far from Southmoor. Even if true, of course, that proves nothing.

There is no evidence provided in the book to back up these claims, and suggestions of Russian involvement have not, so far as I can ascertain, appeared elsewhere. Furthermore, it seems highly unlikely that the anger towards Dr Kelly would be such as to simmer for a decade and then explode just as the man had become a very public figure. In the absence of further evidence, it seems a safe conclusion to discount any suggestion of Russian involvement in Dr Kelly's death.

It is interesting to note in passing that Russia appears to have had its own strange sequence of 'dead scientists' to deal with. January 2002 saw Andrei Brushlinsky, the director of Moscow's Institute of Psychology, attacked in his own home, and Ivan Glebov, an expert in biological and agricultural terrorism, fatally mugged in St Petersburg. The next month, Professor Valery Korshunov, the head of the microbiology facility at the Russian State Medical University, was attacked in the street near his home. He had, according to *Pravda*, been working on a vaccine for a biological weapon. The same month, his colleague Boris Svyatsky was shot three times near his home. In early 2003, Viktor Frantsuzov, the deputy head of Moscow's Institute of Chemical Technologies, was shot by unknown gunmen, and Sergei Bugaenko, the head of the Centre for Nuclear Security, was battered to death in the stairwell of his Moscow home.

At this distance, it is impossible to establish whether there are any sinister links between these deaths, though the overwhelming probability must be that they simply reflect the violent society that modern Russia has become.

16 Mai Pederson

If South Africa, Israel and Russia were peripheral to David Kelly's work in his last five years, the United States was bang in the middle.

Dr Kelly had long had very close links with the United States, which reflected the long-standing foreign policy collaboration between the US and UK governments. He had worked side by side with US personnel on weapons inspections in Russia and Iraq. He was clearly held in high regard by the Americans and, unusually, his Ministry of Defence security clearance from 2000, a copy of which I have obtained (see Plate 11), gave him access for a period of seven years to material of both UK and US origin classified as 'Top Secret', even if some of the access was, in a phrase redolent of the Cold War, 'subject to indoctrination'.

One particularly close relationship he had, the subject of considerable press speculation after his death, was with Mai Pederson, a sergeant in the US Army. Variously described as charismatic and exotic, Ms Pederson was an Arab–American linguist whom Dr Kelly had met in Iraq. She was born in Kuwait with the name Mai al–Sadat, before her parents moved to the USA when she was three years old. She is bilingual in Arabic and English, perhaps not surprisingly, and also fluent in German and French.

Ms Pederson has been married twice, once to a US Special Forces soldier, Cameron DeHart, known as 'Duke', and then to a US Air Force sergeant called Jim Pederson. Both men have stated that Ms Pederson was an intelligence operative, or, in common parlance, a spy. Both have also remarked, almost in awe, it seems, on her ability to bewitch men.

Mr DeHart first came across her when she was performing an Egyptian belly dance at a US Air Force talent show. In a 2003 newspaper interview he said: 'Mai is a charmer. Her eyes are so beautiful that when she looks at a man, she can wrap him around her little finger.' In the same piece Jim Pederson was quoted as saying: 'Mai was always going away for months at a time. She was proficient with a gun and in basic unarmed combat and worked undercover for long periods . . . in Egypt and I believe Iran. She was a very complex character.'[1]

It was Mai Pederson who introduced Dr Kelly to the Baha'i faith she herself had adopted at the age of nineteen. Within a year of their first meeting in Iraq in December 1998, Dr Kelly himself became a Baha'i. This requires the initiate to accept some basic rules of behaviour, including respect for life, for marriage and specifically for the United Nations, whose role was bypassed by the US and the UK in their determination to invade Iraq.

The two clearly became close. On his frequent trips to the United States, Dr Kelly, when he could, crossed the continent from New York to Monterey in California, where Ms Pederson was stationed. It was a long way to go just to say hello.

An examination of US postal records shows that in the sixteen months prior to Dr Kelly's death, Ms Pederson was registered at three different addresses where Dr Kelly was also registered as living. In March 2002, the two are recorded as living in a bungalow in Springfield, Virginia. In June 2003, each appears on the list of those using the post collection service at the post office servicing the Maxwell air force base in Montgomery, Alabama. And in July 2003, the month of Dr Kelly's death, they show up together on the register for a house which had just been purchased by Ms Pederson in Quail Ridge Drive, also in Montgomery.[2]

After Dr Kelly's death, Ms Pederson was, through her lawyer, at pains to reject suggestions that her relationship with the weapons inspector had been anything other than a platonic one.

Her lawyer is Mark Zaid. Among my contacts in American civil liberties campaigns he is widely regarded as a talented and effective representative, though also an expensive one, whose bills could not normally expect to be met from the salary of an army master sergeant. In his colourful career, Mr Zaid spent some time working in the House of Commons as an intern for a Conservative MP, Gary Waller, and he represented Mohamed al-Fayed in the United States in the latter's attempts to secure documents relating to the death of Princess Diana.

He is also the executive director for the James Madison Project, a group which challenges secrecy in government. His biography, since removed, on its website stated: 'Mr Zaid often represents former/current federal employees, intelligence officers, whistleblowers and others who have grievances or have been wronged by agencies of the United States government or foreign governments.'[3]

Mr Zaid suggested that the explanation for Dr Kelly appearing at Ms Pederson's addresses may have been that he needed to use her name to secure a loan. The *Mail on Sunday* did in fact report that the Springfield address had appeared on a credit application made by Dr Kelly.[4] On the face of it, this seems an unlikely explanation. He could simply and successfully have used his existing British credit references, unless of course he wished for some reason not to use his own Southmoor address and have related mailings arrive there on a regular basis.

The lawyer accepted that Dr Kelly had visited his client in Springfield, but professed himself mystified how he would have known the two subsequent addresses. He also denied that his client had ever received any post for Dr Kelly, which rather seems at odds with his suggestion of the use of at least one of her addresses for credit application purposes.

Notwithstanding the last change of address, in the month before Dr Kelly's death, Mr Zaid maintained that Ms Pederson could not 'recall having any personal contact with Dr Kelly in the immediate weeks before his death'. He could not imagine that she would have anything useful to help Lord Hutton's inquiry.[5] In the event, Ms Pederson did speak to Thames Valley Police, but she did not appear at the Hutton inquiry. Nor did she provide a written statement for the inquiry.

When I queried this with Lord Hutton, he told me that he had first learnt of Ms Pederson through press reports. He had then, of his own volition, asked Thames Valley Police to seek to interview her in the United States, which they did (and which, one assumes, they would not have done without his request). Two detectives flew out to Montgomery and spent two days interviewing her. A record was kept of the interview, but Ms Pederson declined to make a formal statement.

She did, however, offer to appear at the Hutton inquiry if she could do so with her identity protected, a facility which was made available for Rod Godfrey, for example. She was told that this was not possible, though not, it seems, by Lord Hutton, who appears not to have been consulted on the matter. He was subsequently told by Thames Valley Police that 'she had nothing significant to add concerning Dr Kelly personally, professionally or as a member of the Baha'i faith that was not available from other sources'.[6] Lord Hutton added, in his letter to me, that he had been told by the police that Ms Pederson had given a statement (by which they presumably meant there existed a record of the conversation with her) on the express condition that it would not be supplied to his inquiry, and he had therefore not seen it.

This was not unique, it turns out. There were seventeen people who had similarly made statements to the police on condition that they were not passed on to Lord Hutton. He was not even made aware of the identities of those who had given these statements.

Lord Hutton presumed that Ms Pederson's reluctance to allow her statement to be made available to him represented a desire to avoid media interest in her. That may well be true, particularly if she really is a spy, as her two husbands have suggested. But is it not also possible that, contrary to the assurance given to Lord Hutton that she had nothing of interest to say, the opposite was in fact the case? After all, she would appear to have been uniquely well placed to offer insights into Dr Kelly's personality and frame of mind, given their closeness. She probably understood him better than most.

In fact, Ms Pederson did offer an insight immediately after his death to her local Baha'i group. She is said to have broken the news of his death to them, and indicated that they should not believe all they read in the newspapers.[7]

She disappeared from sight following Dr Kelly's death and remains below the radar to this day. Some months on, however, she did surface once to give an interview to the *Mail on Sunday*. Her stated reason for doing so was to quash the scuttlebutt that had spread far and wide, suggesting that she and Dr Kelly had been having an affair. They were very close, like brother and sister, she insisted, but no more.[8]

That was interesting, but other comments in her interview were electric. She said bluntly that she did not believe Dr Kelly had committed suicide. The paper quoted her: 'I told the police that the fact that he was found dead in the woods was not surprising. The fact that they said he committed suicide was.' She also claimed that Dr Kelly had told her that he was convinced he would be murdered. He even predicted that he would probably be found dead in the woods one day – the very same phrase he used to the diplomat David Broucher and which was reported to the Hutton inquiry. She asked him to promise not to walk by himself in the woods, but he refused. 'He was very British that way. He had his routines.'

Earlier in the interview, Ms Pederson recalled a conversation she and Dr Kelly had had about suicide, and specifically his mother's death. Would he ever do that, she asked.

'Good God, no, I couldn't imagine ever doing that,' he is said to have replied. 'Why are we discussing it? I would never do it.'

She also revealed that Dr Kelly hated all types of pills and had trouble swallowing even a headache pill. (He is, let us remember, supposed to have swallowed twenty-nine coproxamol tablets to aid his suicide, according to the official version of events.)

She said that she had last spoken to Dr Kelly on 9 July, when he told her, in apparently a relaxed and slightly humorous tone, that he had to 'evacuate' his house, given the press interest that had sprung up.[9] The conversation on this date contradicts the statement from Mark Zaid that Ms Pederson could not 'recall having any personal contact with Dr Kelly in the immediate weeks before his death'.

Ms Pederson may have spoken to the police in confidence, but the day after her interview, a story appeared in the *Times* suggesting she was having an affair with Dr Kelly. Why had someone leaked this story? Was it simply the irresistibility some people feel when they can pass on salacious information to others; was it for money; or was there a more sinister motive, such as to divert attention onto the trivial?

If Ms Pederson is a spy, then it is always possible that her version of events is one produced for other purposes, but it is difficult to imagine what those could be, or what advantage the US Army or US administration would derive from making public a suggestion that Dr Kelly did not kill himself. Logic suggests that Ms Pederson is telling the truth, if perhaps not the whole truth.

One would have thought that an exploration of each of these points might have been helpful to Lord Hutton's inquiry, and it is difficult to understand how Thames Valley Police, if Ms Pederson had repeated all or even some of the above to them, could have concluded that she had nothing of importance to say.

Interestingly, Mr Zaid indicated, after the publication of the Hutton inquiry report but before the Oxfordshire coroner had ruled out reopening the inquest, that Ms Pederson would be willing for the record of her conversation with Thames Valley Police to be given to the coroner, and willing also to testify under oath, provided her identity were shielded. Perhaps she was as unimpressed with the Hutton report as many others were.

It is unclear if this offer was passed on to the coroner, but he was certainly aware of the existence of the interview and interested in it. The *Times* reported that he wanted to see the record of her interview and other statements taken by the police but not passed on to Lord Hutton. 'What the motives might be for not handing over their statements I have no idea but I think I ought to see them,' he told the paper.[10] Whether he was able to do so is not known.

Some support for Ms Pederson's viewpoint came from Gabriele Kraatz-Wadsack, a German weapons inspector who was also a friend of Dr Kelly's. She and Dr Kelly had travelled around the world giving joint presentations to scientists and others on Iraq's weapons of mass destruction. The two were in regular email contact. They were obviously close, and had even exchanged emails on the morning of Dr Kelly's death. After his death, Thames Valley Police found a two-page handwritten note in his briefcase entitled 'Gabriele concerns'. They said that it appeared to relate to Iraq and weapons of mass destruction, but it has been withheld on the grounds that it is a personal document.

Ms Kraatz-Wadsack also disappeared from sight following Dr Kelly's death. Refusing to speak at length to the press, she alleged she had been gagged by the Berlin Defence Ministry and said, referring to Dr Kelly's death: 'Things would be very bad for me if I became involved in this. I don't want to end up like him.'[11]

Thames Valley Police spoke to Ms Kraatz-Wadsack and declared that she too had nothing of interest to say. They also took a statement from Colonel Terence Taylor, then head of the Washington-based International Institute for Strategic Studies and former UN chief weapons inspector. He had worked with Dr Kelly at Porton Down. He also expressed doubts about the suggestion that Dr Kelly had taken his own life. That statement was not passed on to Lord Hutton either.

Chief Inspector Alan Young, who was heading the investigation for Thames Valley Police, gave this perspective to the *Times*: 'It was not actually tested whether Lord Hutton had the full powers of a coroner and whether the inquest part of the inquiry had the right to see the statements. It is not 100 per cent crystal clear.'[12]

Those signing statements were in fact offered an opt-out. At the end of the statement they were asked the following question: 'Do you agree for your statement to be released to Lord Hutton for use in his inquiry?' If the answer given was no, then the statement was not passed on. Here is another example of the inadequacy of a non-statutory inquiry. These statements, which may well have contained valuable and relevant material, were simply filed away under lock and key, never to be used.

What then was the relationship between Mai Pederson and David Kelly? It was certainly one of which Janice Kelly was aware, and indeed, Pederson had actually visited Dr and Mrs Kelly at their cottage in Southmoor (see Chapter 2). She had agreed with Dr Kelly shortly before his death that she would do so again in the autumn of that year.

The only reference in open session to Ms Pederson in the whole of the Hutton inquiry actually came from Mrs Kelly, who, referring to her husband's conversion to the Baha'i faith, of which incidentally she was unaware for quite some time, said: 'He read widely on the subject and met a number of people. I think there was one interpreter, Mai Pederson, who in fact later became a family friend, who was quite influential there.'[13] So unknown was the diminutive Ms Pederson that the Hutton team's official transcript recorded her name as 'Mike Peddison'.

Details of her army life did appear, however, in one of her local papers, the *Monterey County Herald*. Buried deep inside the article, which refers, amongst other matters, to various staff changes at the local district attorney's office and a special student attending the Foothill Elementary School, is a short biography of her time in the area between 1997 and 2001. According to this piece, Ms Pederson was on the staff of Air Force Squadron 311 at the top security Defense Language Institute during this period. Her duties included serving as chief of the Air Force commander's support staff and supervisor of 'satellite personnel activities for the squadron'. In 1998, she was awarded the Joint Service Achievement Medal at the institute.[14] She was then assigned to the Pentagon, where she was 'involved in Air Force re-enlistments as chief of enlisted skills management'. She was apparently in the building when it was hit on 11 September 2001.

For the US army sergeant, it is possible that getting close to Dr Kelly was part of an official assignment, according to her ex-husband Jim Pederson. 'Part of her military training was to cultivate anyone who might be able to help her in her intelligence work,' he said. 'It may well have been that she zeroed in on Dr Kelly. She undoubtedly viewed him as a potential intelligence source.'[15]

At one level, the relationship may have been simply this. It is also possible to imagine that the US authorities, aware that Dr Kelly's expertise and the respect in which he was professionally held meant he would have access to much sensitive material, including some of US origin, thought it prudent to keep a close eye on him. After all, the Bush administration would not have wanted comments unhelpful to its policy position on Iraq coming from authoritative sources.

For her part, Mai Pederson described herself as a close platonic friend to Dr Kelly, despite the existence of the shared postal addresses. They were certainly an odd couple – he giving all the appearance of a cultured boffin, in his glasses, baggy sports jacket and jeans; she fabulously attractive, seductively dressed and sixteen years his junior.

There is, however, some evidence that Dr Kelly was seriously considering moving to the United States. The journalist Tom Mangold wrote that Dr Kelly was considering taking 'a post-retirement post in Washington or California . . . which would have meant leaving his family in Britain while also making the maintenance of his relationship with Pederson somewhat easier'.[16] Then there are the words of Dr Christopher Davis, making yet another cameo appearance in the story. He recalled:

I vividly remember how on Tuesday June 4th 2002, David gave a seminar about Iraqi biological weapons in Washington DC. Afterwards . . . we were standing on the street chatting . . . He said he was thinking of moving to the US. He said, 'Some friends have said they could get me a position here in the US at a university . . .' It occurred to me later that he hadn't mentioned his wife, Jan, once.[17]

Part of Dr Kelly's thinking does seem to have involved a desire to spend more time with Ms Pederson, platonic relationship or not. But he may well also have been motivated by the linked matters of money and prestige.

The Hutton inquiry heard that Dr Kelly had been dissatisfied with his salary scale, which he felt had graded him at the wrong level. This evidence came from Dr Richard Scott, the director of the Defence Science and Technology Laboratory, an agency of the Ministry of Defence, who from July 2000 onwards had officially been Dr Kelly's line manager. He told Lord Hutton that he had some sympathy with Dr Kelly's complaint that his level had been incorrectly set.[18] Some improvement to the position occurred in 2002, but Dr Kelly was still uncertain about his salary level. Unfortunately, a letter that confirmed the improved position did not reach him before his death.

His salary was that of an upper-middle-ranking civil servant, £61,038 a year. That was certainly a comfortable amount, but he may well have thought, with some justification, that it was meagre for someone who was a highly respected and world-renowned expert on biological weapons. It is also worth noting that dealing with highly toxic substances on a daily basis is in itself not without risk. This misgrading, and the insensitive and unimaginative management of him by the Ministry of Defence, would also have adversely affected his prestige. A move to the United States could have corrected both these matters.

Dr Kelly, then, appeared comfortable in, and with, the United States, even to the extent that he was actively considering taking up employment there. He had high-level clearance to see documents of US origin, and had successfully and harmoniously worked side by side with American nationals for many years. Could there be any motive for anyone across the Atlantic to wish to have him killed?

The instinct of many people will be to conclude without much thought that it would be absurd to suspect the United States of any involvement in his death. It is only right, however, that the idea should be tested, and on two levels: first, to establish if the United States has carried out assassinations, and specifically if that was their policy in July 2003; and second, to establish if there was any reason why the US authorities would have wanted Dr Kelly dead.

The second question is covered in Chapter 18. The answer to the first, meanwhile, is somewhat disturbing. It is now accepted that throughout the twentieth century, elements within the US establishment did indeed regard it as legitimate to seek to assassinate those whom they regarded as opponents of the United States. There were, for example, numerous attempts to kill Fidel Castro, as noted in the preface to this book.

After the turmoil of Watergate and the Nixon presidency, a ban on extra-judicial killings was imposed, but the events of 11 September 2001 changed all that. A joint resolution of the two Houses of Congress, passed a matter of days after those terrible events, gave the President sweeping new powers. He was henceforth 'authorised to use all necessary and appropriate force against those nations, organisations or persons he determines planned, authorised, committed or aided the terrorist attacks that occurred on September 11th 2001'.[19]

The same month, President Bush overturned the 25-year ban on state assassinations and gave the CIA permission to eliminate individuals designated by the President.[20] This followed the publication of a top-secret paper from the CIA entitled *Worldwide Attack Matrix*. Its proposals were intended to give the CIA 'the broadest and most lethal authority in its history'.[21] The document contained a 'Memorandum of Notification', which would effectively hand the agency carte blanche to conduct political assassinations abroad. And in August 2002, the *Guardian* reported that the US government was planning to send elite military units on missions abroad to carry out targeted assassinations and kidnappings without necessarily informing the relevant governments.[22]

Other US-directed killings may have taken place under a different guise. One government lawyer, quoted by the

Washington Post, argued that killing an al-Qaeda person wouldn't be assassination, but self-defence, while Donald Rumsfeld, then US Defence Secretary, was quoted in the *Guardian* as saying: 'The only way to deal with terrorists is to take the battle to them and find them and root them out and that's self-defence.'[23]

This argument was important. If assassination could be classified as acting in self-defence then even the flimsy safeguards in place would not apply, and instead the very wide authority would be that under the resolution of both Houses granted to the President on 18 September 2001 as quoted above. Three days after that joint resolution, according to a report in the *Washington Post*, the largest covert CIA programme since the height of the Cold War kicked into action. Known by the initials GST, and apparently comprising dozens of highly classified individual programmes, it allowed the organisation to capture individuals suspected of posing a threat to the United States, to maintain secret prisons abroad, to use questionable interrogation techniques and to maintain a fleet of aircraft for the purposes of facilitating extraordinary rendition. The article quoted A. John Radsan, assistant general counsel at the CIA until 2004, as saying: 'In the past, Presidents set up buffers to distance themselves from covert action. But this President, who is breaking down the boundaries between covert action and conventional war, seems to relish the secret findings and the dirty details of operations.'[24]

Since 2001, some of the consequences of all this have seeped out. There were, and are, the orange-jumpsuit regime at Guantanamo Bay, where alleged terrorists are held indefinitely but never brought to trial; the pictures graphically showing the humiliation and mistreatment of uncharged prisoners held at Abu Ghraib, for which nobody any distance up the command chain was held responsible; and the 'extraordinary rendition', in layman's language routine kidnapping, of individuals and their onward despatch to hellhole prisons in countries such as Egypt, where, according to Amnesty International, severe torture is still systematic. In the United States itself, we learnt that the National Security Agency was given powers by the President to eavesdrop on American citizens without the need to secure a warrant first.

This has been the brutal reality of 21st-century America, as fashioned by the neocons who have run the administration since the end of the Clinton era. Fortunately, the worst may be over, as the Democrats, now back in charge of both Houses, and the Supreme Court apply the brakes.

In July 2007, President Bush issued an executive order setting new limits for CIA interrogation methods, which eliminated some of the most objectionable techniques such as 'waterboarding', where drowning is simulated. However, critics declared the new order full of loopholes, and the CIA stated it would maintain the ban on the Red Cross visiting detainees in agency hands.[25] Moreover, the order does not cover those in military detention. Before it came into effect, fourteen high-profile terrorist suspects were transferred from secret CIA prisons to Guantanamo Bay, which is run by the Defense Department.

Respect for international law and for the safeguards built into the American constitution and into the world order of international agreements – largely shaped after the Second World War by the Americans themselves – was at an all-time low in 2003. Based on the approach adopted by President Bush and his colleagues after 11 September therefore, it would be naïve to conclude that, had they perceived Dr Kelly as a real threat to their interests, they would necessarily have baulked at removing him.

But is there any evidence that he was perceived in this way?

17 Much too professional, much too neutral

As time went on, it became clearer than ever that the motive for David Kelly's killing must be rooted in his role as a weapons inspector, and specifically his activities in Iraq. After all, if there were some motive unconnected with Iraq, then it would qualify as a huge coincidence that he should have died in the middle of the maelstrom that monopolised the international headlines in 2003.

We saw in Chapter 9 how the Bush administration was preoccupied, even obsessed, with Saddam Hussein and Iraq, particularly after the events of 11 September 2001, and had clearly decided at an early stage that it was going to bring about regime change. The question of a link between Iraq and the September 11th attacks, and the spectre of the threat from Iraqi-held weapons of mass destruction, were not determinants of US policy in the period before the invasion, but rather supporting material to bolster a case for war, the decision for which had already been taken.

In that context, whether those around the President ever actually believed that Saddam was in some way responsible for the September 11th attacks, or that Iraq was still producing and stockpiling WMD, does not really matter. What they clearly did believe, however, was that any attempt to prove false their assertions about either of these two matters was most unwelcome and had to be dealt with. So we saw in Chapter 8 the revenge wreaked on Joseph Wilson for his debunking of the suggestion that Niger was supplying uranium to Iraq, when his wife, Valerie Plame, was outed as a CIA agent and her career effectively finished.

But Dr Kelly was also to prove an irritant to the White House and the Pentagon. The Bush administration had never really trusted the United Nations' weapons inspectors, even those from the United States and its allies. As a body, they were much too professional and much too neutral for its liking. For that reason, it had long been US practice to embed CIA operatives within the weapons inspection team. Rod Godfrey, the leading UK chemical weapons inspector with UNSCOM, said: 'It did become clear to me . . . that there were people associated with the mission who had functions which were not explained to the rest of us . . . People would travel in with us and out with us but nobody ever explained quite what they were doing with the mission.'[1]

On 29 May 2003, President George W. Bush announced to the world that two trailers found by US troops were the much-awaited 'mobile biological laboratories', the existence of which had long been predicted by the White House. Here, at last, almost two months after Saddam had been defeated, was the evidence that the allies had been looking for. 'We found the weapons of mass destruction,' declared Bush. 'We found biological laboratories.'[2] The existence of mobile laboratories had been central to the US case for war. It had featured prominently in the presentation made by Secretary of State Colin Powell to the UN on 5 February 2003.

However, on 27 May, two days before Bush's announcement, a three-page summary of a secret authoritative report, commissioned by the administration itself, had been delivered to the Defense Intelligence Agency (DIA). It concluded precisely the opposite. The full 122-page report, *Final Technical Engineering Exploitation Report on Iraqi Suspected Biological Weapons-Associated Trailers*, would be delivered three weeks later, stamped 'secret' and promptly filed away as quickly as possible in a deep recess.

The authors of the report comprised nine US and UK experts. It did not take these experts more than a matter of moments to conclude definitively that the trailers were not mobile laboratories but almost certainly intended for the manufacture of hydrogen for weather balloons, just as the Iraqis had said.

Hamish Killip was one of the UK weapons inspectors flown out to Baghdad following the fall of Saddam as part of the Iraq Survey Group, formed by the CIA in June 2003 to look for Iraqi weapons of mass destruction. He inspected the trailers and was not impressed by the capacity of the trailer equipment to make biological weapons. 'We were in hysterics over this,' he said. 'You'd have better luck putting a couple of dustbins on the back of the truck and brewing it [a biological weapons concoction] there.'[3] Another member of the team called them 'the biggest sand toilets in the world'.[4]

None of this stopped the CIA and the DIA jointly publishing, on 28 May, the first formal assessment of the trailers, in a report entitled *Iraqi Mobile Biological Warfare Agent Production Plants*. The assessment said that the CIA and the DIA were 'confident' that the trailers were used for 'mobile biological weapons production'. The hydrogen production explanation was a 'cover story', part of Iraq's 'sophisticated denial and deception methods'. As late as February 2004, the CIA's then director–general, George Tenet, was still arguing that the trailers might have been used for this purpose, despite, we now know, the overwhelming expert opinion to the contrary. Mr Killip was to resign in March 2004, unhappy that the CIA was perpetrating a fiction. He is now back home on the Isle of Man.

The Iraqi Study Group's report, published in September 2004, concluded that the trailers were designed and built at the Al Kindi General Establishment at Mosul as hydrogen generators for Republican Guard artillery units. It turned out that the balloons, an artillery meteorological system, had actually been sold to the Iraqis by the British back in 1987.

Dr Kelly was himself to have inspected the trailers, and left London for Iraq via Kuwait on 19 May 2003. He did not, however, get into the country. It seems that he incorrectly assumed that the Ministry of Defence had organised his visa for

Kuwait, and was allowed to board the plane in London. On arrival, however, he was not allowed into Kuwait, was searched, physically restrained and kept overnight in a hotel. His mobile phone was removed. He was forced to return home the following day via Dubai, bewildered and angry. This unexpected twist meant Dr Kelly could be in London on 22 May to meet Andrew Gilligan for the now notorious conversation at the Charing Cross Hotel.

Dr Kelly had been to Iraq close on forty times, so it seems peculiar that this sort of mix-up with visas should have occurred on this occasion. He was, however, to make a further, and this time successful, trip to Iraq between 5 June and 11 June, when he was able to inspect and photograph the trailers. On his return, Dr Kelly spoke off the record to the *Observer* in candid terms, and his comments appeared in that paper's next edition, on Sunday 15 June. Billed as 'a British scientist and biological weapons expert, who has examined the trailers in Iraq', he was quoted as saying: 'They are not mobile germ warfare laboratories. You could not use them for making biological weapons. They do not even look like them. They are exactly what the Iraqis said they were – facilities for the production of hydrogen gas to fill balloons.'[5] It was confirmed at the Hutton inquiry that this quote came from Dr Kelly.

There had in fact been other stories in the British and American media that month casting doubt on the veracity of the mobile laboratories claim. One such piece appeared in the *New York Times* on Saturday 7 June, under the byline of Judith

Miller. Dr Kelly emailed her on 11 June, having read the article, to say that 'the article fits in with my thoughts'.[6] As we saw in Chapter 12, it was another email he sent her which of course attracted rather more attention, the now notorious one sent on the morning of his disappearance referring to 'dark actors playing games'.

Ms Miller had actually had her own experiences of dark actors playing games. On 12 October 2001, she received a hoax anthrax letter at the *New York Times* office, the only journalist to receive such a package in the spate of anthrax letters sent out that autumn which killed five people and seriously affected twenty-two others. Ten days earlier, on 2 October, she had had published a book on bio-terrorism, entitled *Germs: Biological Weapons and America's Secret War*.[7] And the month before, she had written a newspaper article revealing Pentagon plans to develop a more potent variety of anthrax.[8] The anthrax in the malicious letters we now know was definitely of US military origin.

Shortly after receiving the anthrax package, Ms Miller wrote material much more helpful to the White House. Another *New York Times* article quoted an Iraqi defector, a 43-year-old chemical engineer called Adnan Ihsan Saeed al-Haideri, who claimed that he was familiar with more than twenty hidden weapons sites, including in private villas, underground wells and even under the Saddam Hussein hospital in Baghdad.[9] This was just what the White House wanted and the article was seized upon by the hawks as proof of Iraq's WMD activities. Here was justification for a pre-emptive strike on Iraq.

After the invasion, the sites in question were searched. Nothing was found. Eventually, on 26 May 2004, the *New York Times* conceded that the information it had published about the sites had instead been the product of disinformation. In an editorial, it wrote: 'In this case it looks as if we, along with the administration, were taken in.'[10] Other pieces questioning the official line on the trailers had appeared in the *Observer* on 8 June 2003 and in a *Newsnight* report from Susan Watts on 2 June.

We know that Dr Kelly talked to Ms Watts on 30 May and discussed the alleged mobile laboratories. He told her: 'We've seen on the mobile labs that the politics of that is so strong that it deflects all practical objectivity.' In respect of the joint CIA/DIA report, he told her: 'That was a funny report. To me it looked like it had just been pushed out at a whim overnight.' Privately, he described the CIA assessment to colleagues as 'roguery'.[11]

The CIA/DIA report had stated: 'The design, equipment, and layout of the trailer found in late April is strikingly similar to descriptions provided by a source who was a chemical engineer that managed one of the mobile plants.'[12] This source was clearly more highly rated than the nine US and UK experts who had unanimously concluded that the function of the trailers was to produce hydrogen. An unnamed US intelligence officer, when challenged after the *Washington Post* had revealed the existence of the advice given by the nine experts on 27 May 2003, subsequently put it like this: 'You don't change a report that has been co-ordinated in the [intelligence] community based on a field report. It's a preliminary report.'[13]

What, then, was the point of sending an urgent party of experts out to Iraq to assess the trailers, if its unanimous voice was to be ignored? Doubtless if the experts had come back with evidence to support the administration's assertions, they would not have been ignored. As so often in this period, on both sides of the Atlantic, intelligence was only useful, and only wanted, if it reinforced preconceived policy positions.

On the *Newsnight* report on the mobile labs which followed the conversation between Dr Kelly and Ms Watts, Labour MP Malcolm Savidge described the consequences as 'extremely grave', even suggesting that this 'could be the Prime Minister's Watergate'.

The private response of the British government was doubtless one of embarrassment. Publicly, the Prime Minister stonewalled, telling Parliament on 20 June that, in respect of the trailers, 'investigations into their role are continuing'.[14] The Defence Secretary, Geoff Hoon, was more bullish and openly supportive of the official US line. He told the House of Commons: 'The mobile laboratories were wholly consistent with the description of mobile laboratories given by Secretary of State Colin Powell in his evidence to the United Nations Security Council.'[15] Had he not been given a copy of the report submitted to the DIA on 28 May? If not, that would suggest that the UK was being treated less than honestly by the United States. But if he had seen the report, how could he in all honesty make that statement to Parliament?

It seems Dr Kelly was not prepared to allow the spin emanating from either the White House or Downing Street to go uncorrected. Within the space of a couple of weeks, he had briefed Andrew Gilligan on his doubts in respect of the UK government's dossier, and the 45-minute claim in particular, and flatly contradicted the official line from the White House in respect of the trailers found in Iraq. He was thus involved to some degree with both the major stories that June which were damaging to Bush and Blair.

Dr Kelly must have known that by making the contacts he did, he was challenging the authority and integrity of both Bush and Blair, on the issue of the day most central to their agenda. Given the dishonest manipulation of intelligence for political purposes, many will agree that he was right to act in this way. To do so was, however, brave, if not foolhardy. The presentation of the truth was leading Dr Kelly down risky avenues.

At this point, it is worth considering whether there were indeed weapons of mass destruction being made or stored in Saddam Hussein's Iraq. The automatic assumption prior to invasion was that such weapons of course existed. Nobody really doubted or even questioned this. Equally, now, the automatic assumption is the exact opposite – that there were no such weapons.

In my investigations into the death of Dr Kelly, I deliberately set out not to conclude automatically either that he had committed suicide or that he had been murdered. The only responsible course, it seemed to me, was to examine the evidence and see where it took me. Similarly, merely because the zeitgeist is now that there were, after all, no WMD in Iraq is not a reason to accept that view. It must be tested.

There seems little doubt that neither the United States nor the UK expected to find vast stockpiles. The confidential Downing Street minutes, referred to in an earlier chapter, categorised the risk from Iraq in this regard as less than that posed by Libya, North Korea or Iran. Even so, it was a reasonable expectation that some residual matter might be found, material that had escaped the detailed attention of the UN's diligent weapons inspectors. Dr Kelly himself, in his discussions with Mr Gilligan and then when giving evidence before the Foreign Affairs Committee, put the likelihood of Iraq possessing chemical weapons at about 30 per cent.[16]

It is also the case that it is not difficult to hide biological, as opposed to chemical, weapons, even in large quantities, as Dr Larry Ford demonstrated all too vividly. You do not need a trailer. A few test tubes and a fridge will do. As it turned out, however, Dr Ford had more in the way of biological weapons in his house and under the concrete slab in his garden than could be found in the whole of Iraq. Perhaps the weapons inspectors might more usefully have been deployed in California.

That nothing at all was found by the inspectors and US forces combing the country after the fall of Saddam is genuinely surprising, given Saddam's long history of developing chemical and biological weapons. It was a history that benefited from some considerable help from western nations. The preparedness of the UK and the US to arm Saddam in the 1980s as a counter-balance to Iran is well known. What is less appreciated is that Saddam was able to secure considerable help in his efforts to develop a chemical and biological weapons capability under the guise of academic research.

A British weapons inspector told me that, in the 1980s, scientists from Baghdad University wrote around the world to ask for strains of biological material, with some considerable success. Organisations such as the Institut Pasteur in Paris readily obliged. 'Academic freedom was the over-riding concept,' the inspector told me. It was a concept that was ended not long before the Iraqi invasion of Kuwait, after it had slowly dawned that the concept of free exchange was being abused. This was a time when dangerous strains would be sent by post inside nothing more than a balsa block. This is, for example, how plant pathogens would arrive at Kew Gardens.

Iraq also benefited from the openness that came from the declassification of patents. UN inspectors found in Iraq UK patents from this country's abandoned biological weapons programme, patents which had been bought from the British Library. They had been listed obliquely, and it was necessary to know exactly what to ask for, but the Iraqis clearly did.

They also secured declassified patents in the United States relating to war gases.

So why were there no weapons of mass destruction found in Iraq? Undoubtedly the US and UK underestimated the effective job done by the UN's weapons inspectors, including Dr Kelly. At the same time, they had overestimated Saddam's WMD capability and misread his politics. Saddam had been screwed down by a combination of the UN inspection regime and sanctions, and so much of his talk about weapons of mass destruction was most likely for internal consumption to maintain his position.

But this cannot be the whole picture. There were, after all, plenty of paper trails suggesting weapons manufacture and storage. One explanation for these trails might be that the records were created by those charged with developing biological weapons, solely to be able to demonstrate to Saddam that his demands, however unreasonable and indeed unachievable, had been met. After all, telling Saddam that his orders had not been carried out was not to be recommended if one wanted to stay alive. There could, therefore, have been plenty of paper evidence of such weapons, without any actually existing. It may also be the case that Iraqi scientists twigged that one way to secure funding was to present Saddam with programmes for weapons development, for which such records may have been useful. That strategy, though, was clearly a high-risk one.

Another credible explanation for the failure to find weapons of mass destruction might be that Saddam, anticipating an attack, had taken steps to move his WMD capability, such as it was, out of the country prior to invasion. There are certainly experts around who believe that this may well be the case. The leading US weapons inspector Dr Richard Spertzel told me that there most certainly had been material and an ongoing capability. He referred to a moveable, as opposed to mobile, laboratory which he had seen and which he maintained had been used for the manufacture of mustard gas. The aim apparently was to introduce mustard gas and Sarin into perfume sprayers destined to be shipped to Europe and the United States.[17] Dr Spertzel believes that Saddam's remaining material and capability was moved out of the country in late 2002, probably to Syria.

Ken Alibek, formerly involved in the Soviet germ warfare programme (see Chapter 14), is now the president and chief scientific officer of AFG Biosolutions Inc., based in Gaithersburg, Maryland. However, he was in Ukraine when I tracked him down. He too was convinced that there must have been something to be found in Iraq. 'It's hard to believe that the Iraqis had stopped work completely,' he told me. He also thought it possible that material had been moved abroad.

Mr Alibek pointed out that whilst the infrastructure needed for chemical weapons could not be easily hidden, the manufacture and storage of biological weapons needed only a small laboratory with a fridge. He also confirmed that such material would decay and deteriorate and there was therefore a limited shelf-life for the bulk of such weapons, with the exception of anthrax, which remains effective for a much longer period.

The colourful Australian weapons inspector Richard Butler is also on record as believing that there was an established relationship between Iraq and Syria when it came to weapons of mass destruction. While he was in Iraq between 1997 and 1999, he saw intelligence which indicated that containers filled with banned materials were transported between the two countries.

And David Kay, the former head of the Iraq Survey Group, writing after the invasion, also referred to the role of Syria: 'We know from some of the interrogations of former Iraqi officials that a lot of material went to Syria before the war, including some components of Saddam's WMD programme. Precisely what went to Syria, and what had happened to it, is a major issue that needs to be resolved.'[18] A clear enough statement from an expert in the field, yet the allies appeared to be completely uninterested, at least publicly, in pursuing the matter with Syria. A good US source did tell me, however, that both the CIA and MI6 had subsequently been conducting clandestine operations in the country, though whether this was on account of Syria's involvement with weapons of mass destruction was not clear.

I asked the British government for its assessment of the likelihood that WMD were moved from Iraq to Syria prior to invasion, but was told simply that no comment is made on security matters.[19] That, of course, was not the approach when dossier after dossier was published on Iraq. The mute response does tend to suggest that the threat from chemical and biological weapons was not the most important matter when Iraq was invaded. If it were, presumably we would now be hearing about the dangers from Syria.

The public nonchalance was perhaps not matched by the level of concern felt behind closed doors.

Dr Jill Dekker is an American bio-defence expert based in Belgium who has acted as a consultant for NATO and the European Union. She is particularly knowledgeable about the Syrian angle and has spoken about this publicly. In March 2007, for example, she gave a lecture titled 'Calculating the Syrian Biological Weapons Threat and Regional Security' at the Intelligence Summit meeting in Florida. Her appearance there, in her capacity as an academic, was not welcomed by the CIA, who seemed paranoid about what she might say. She was warned not to attend, but chose to ignore that warning.

Dr Dekker's lecture was delivered in tightly controlled conditions. All were searched on the way in, no recording equipment was allowed and no copies of her speech were made available. I have, however, obtained a copy. Dr Dekker supported the view that Iraqi weapons of mass destruction had been moved to Syria, even giving specific locations where they could apparently be found.

In her dramatic contribution, she warned that Syria was working on a wide range of biological warfare pathogens, including anthrax, plague, botulinum, ricin and, most worryingly of all, smallpox. She assessed that Syria had been sold a weaponised strain of smallpox by the former Soviet Union or possibly North Korea. Dr Dekker pointed the finger at specific establishments, including the Scientific Studies and Research Center in Damascus, which she alleged is the primary location for biological weapons research, and said that production facilities had been built with the help of western firms. Syria, in her view, now possesses the entire suite of capability necessary for a robust biological weapons programme.

The smallpox capability particularly worries Dr Dekker, and in her lecture she pointed out that in the 1972 outbreak in Yugoslavia, each affected person contaminated on average a further thirteen, so that one index case took nearly 19,000 doses of vaccine to control. She also suggested that most of the Syrian military had been inoculated against the disease. In April 2000, she told her audience, the Syrian defence minister General Mustafa Talas published a lengthy article entitled 'Biological (Germ) Warfare: A New and Effective Method in Modern Warfare'. She believes that Syria's ultimate objective is to mount biological warheads on all varieties of long-range surface-to-surface missiles.

When she returned home, Dr Dekker says that she was subject to a campaign of harassment and intimidation by the CIA. They would follow her relentlessly and park vehicles outside her house, such as cars with darkened windows, headlights blazing even in daylight, and on one occasion a hearse, which raced off at remarkable speed when approached.

I have met Dr Dekker on two occasions and had a number

of long exchanges with her. She does not strike me as the sort either who would frighten easily, or who would ginger up her story for effect. Rather, she is a somewhat hard-nosed, intelligent and knowledgeable woman who has succeeded well in a profession where men predominate. I therefore took it seriously when she emailed me on 23 March 2007 with this message, clearly meant for the eyes of the CIA: 'I've informed all my diplomatic friends that not only am I not suicidal, and looking forward to my children growing up and my up-coming interviews but also my great career – much like other people who suddenly were found dead in woods or having accidents.'

In a further email to me eight days later, she wrote:

The US State Dept and their surrogates the CIA continue to intimidate me and my family – every day they are outside my home – they tail me 24/7 – I believe they could try to kill me so I don't reveal any more of my research on Syrian biological weapons. I want to tell you this so you understand how very very serious it is indeed. It is shocking to me as an academic to have this happening. It looks like they have tipped off Syrian agents in Damascus so they will do the hands-on work the CIA wants to avoid. Please retain this email.

By 12 April, she was rather more feisty: 'I refuse to be intimidated by anyone who uses the tactics they used – so unprofessional even people inside can't believe how they have acted here – it's like *Johnny English* [a 2003 James Bond spoof starring Rowan Atkinson as an inept spy], really so amateurish. Our services just aren't what they used to be.' Dr Dekker called the Belgian police in, and that action, and also perhaps her determination not to be intimidated and her willingness to make others such as myself aware of the position, meant that the intimidation stopped a month or so later.

It can be seen that a number of leading experts believe that WMD material was transported from Iraq to Syria, and even that Syria is acquiring such material from elsewhere as well. Dr Dekker told me that the United States is desperate to avoid discussion of this matter, but why?

Then on 6 September 2007, the Israelis launched Operation Orchard, a military attack on an unspecified target in Syria. Unusually, no details were given of the nature of the target, and a strict news blackout was imposed in both Israel and Syria. Speculation in the media centred on the possibility that it was a nuclear target, but in the light of Dr Dekker's paper, and also the strong suggestion that Iraqi chemical and biological weapons were moved into Syria in 2003, perhaps the strike was more to do with that. Even so, this still cannot explain the curious stance of the United States and Israel to say as little as possible at the time, although the Israeli opposition leader, Binyamin Netanyahu, subsequently admitted Israel's involvement.[20]

Perhaps David Kelly shared the view of some of his weapon inspector colleagues that Syria had acquired a capability, which doubtless would have dismayed him, given his determined and effective work over the previous decade and more to reduce the threat the world faced from biological weapons in particular. If he did share that view, then perhaps it was another subject on which he would be prepared to speak publicly.

Finally, the most Machiavellian reason given for a failure to find weapons in Iraq relates to the relationship at that time between the White House and the Pentagon on one side, and the CIA and the Iraqi Study Group on the other.

That there was a division is hardly in dispute. In both Washington and London, a kind of Messianic grip on the President and the Prime Minister blinded the leaders to the intelligence the professional elements of their governments were providing. In London, it was the Foreign Office, MI6 and the Defence Intelligence Service that were cold-shouldered. In America, it was the State Department, the CIA and the DIA. In both countries, the great reservoirs of knowledge were disregarded because they provided an analysis that was unwanted.

In the United States, the President paid more attention to a small group of self-selected analysts working out of the Pentagon called the Office of Special Plans. It worked on the premise that it was a given that Iraq held weapons of mass destruction and had links with al-Qaeda. If the CIA and DIA could not find those links, then axiomatically they were not doing their job properly.

The consequence of all this was not only that intelligence in both countries was twisted and stretched for political purposes, but that the agencies began to write papers justifying their position, rather than simply providing hard intelligence and analysis. Naturally, this bred resentment, and some I have spoken to have suggested that one consequence was actually a deliberate collusion between the CIA and MI6 not to find any weapons of mass destruction in Iraq so as to embarrass or even destabilise the White House and Downing Street respectively.

There is certainly a view that the Iraq Survey Group was under the firm direction of the CIA, so such a policy was in theory deliverable. Dr John Gee, the Australian weapons inspector who resigned because the Australian government would not acknowledge that there were no weapons of mass destruction in Iraq, has written that the Iraqi Study Group was 'run by the CIA to protect the CIA'.[21]

Without doubt, the attempts to find weapons of mass destruction in Iraq were fundamentally flawed. In particular, the US obsession with trailers was gravely misplaced. The lessons from Russia and the Biopreparat programme is that inspections of possible sites which might have been home to latent programmes would have been more sensible. Yet apparently, not even the Veterinary Vaccine Research Institute in Baghdad was checked, even though it was known that it had been working on camelpox, which can be used in experiments as a substitute for smallpox.

Why the criteria that had delivered the goods in Russia were not applied in Iraq is difficult to justify. Was this incompetence, with the United States blithely led off towards fictitious mobile laboratories by information from Iraqi defectors, or something more sinister?

There is also a suggestion that the Iraqi Study Group failed to follow up reliable leads relating to possible sites where weapons of mass destruction might be found. The *New York Sun* reported that David Gaubatz, a special investigator for the Pentagon in 2003, maintained that he had found four sealed underground bunkers in southern Iraq, but was rebuffed when he asked weapons inspectors to assess the sites. He was told that the sites were not safe, that the Iraqi Study Group lacked the personnel or equipment to break into them – they had concrete walls five feet thick and all tunnels to the bunkers had been deliberately flooded – and in any case they were concentrating on the north of the country.[22]

If, as seems the case, the inspection process was faulty, for whatever reason, that is not something which someone with the commitment and moral backbone of Dr Kelly is likely to have accepted easily. In general, morale amongst the weapons inspectors appears to have been at a low. The *Independent* reported, some months after the fall of Saddam Hussein, that the United Nations' inspectors were locked in a dispute about pay, which had caused a delay in inspections. One inspector told the paper: 'They wanted to pay us half what we were earning at the UN. I would rather work for nothing than accept those terms.'[23] There was also, it seems, a feeling that the United States was disinclined to allow the United Nations, through its inspectors, to take any credit for the unearthing of weapons.

The inspection process might also have been helped if there

had been an examination of prisoners held under Saddam who alleged they had been used in experiments, or the corpses of those who did not survive imprisonment, to establish what substances, if any, had been tested on them. That would have given a clear indication of what areas, if any, Saddam's regime had been working on. But bewilderingly, no such examinations took place.[24]

That it can even be suggested that the CIA (and its friends in MI6) might have had a policy not to find weapons – and the experience of Mr Gaubatz, referred to above, could perhaps be seen as supporting evidence for such a claim – shows up the dysfunctional nature of the US administration in 2003. But it also shows up something else: the enormous influence wielded by those Iraqi dissidents who were feeding what turned out to be false information to the United States.

18 Britain and America

Who would have had a reason to want to keep David Kelly quiet? Previous chapters have ruled out a number of theoretical possibilities. Is there any evidence that the US or UK might have had a reason to decide that Dr Kelly had to be killed?

We do know that the United States has been prepared to use assassination as a political tool, that that tactic was given a new fillip by President Bush, and that Dr Kelly, in July 2003, was clearly identified as making statements which undermined the case for invasion of Iraq as set out by the United States and the UK. He would also be likely to have had a reasonable inkling of the biological weapons capacity of other countries such as Syria and North Korea, which for some reason it seems not to have suited the United States to have made public.

There is also support in the brutal way in which the US administration dealt, at around the same time, with Joseph Wilson and his wife, Valerie Plame (see Chapter 8), and how Bush himself subsequently intervened to ensure that those responsible could escape prison. Mr Wilson had also noticed the close juxtaposition of the outing of his wife and the death of Dr Kelly four days later. In his book he wrote:

I received several calls from friends wondering, first, whether it had been a suicide; and if not, was I watching my own security? . . . I too wondered about Kelly's death . . . I was horrified that I could actually harbor suspicions . . . that a democratic government might actually do bodily harm to a political opponent.[1]

There is also the fact, according to Tom Mangold, the CIA were present at the scene where Dr Kelly's body was found.[2] On the face of it, therefore, the premise that the United States might have taken Dr Kelly out is certainly one worth investigating.

The writer Sterling Seagrave used to cover the White House for the *Washington Post* and has been an investigative journalist for fifty years. He has developed a particular expertise in the use by states of exotic poisons to carry out assassinations. It was he who in the 1980s uncovered the Yellow Rain scandal, in which a highly toxic substance was deployed as a weapon in south-east Asia in the 1970s. Mr Seagrave alleges that within the Pentagon there exists a private army of professional assassins who go by the name of the Grey Ghosts, and it is this body, rather than any CIA employees, which these days carries out 'wet operations'. He further alleges that the origin of the Grey Ghosts was a refusal by Donald Rumsfeld to work through the CIA, instead relying on a black ops system provided through private security organisations such as Blackwater and Halliburton.

Halliburton is possibly the best-connected company in the United States and one which is benefiting enormously from the aftermath of the invasion of Iraq. According to Mr Seagrave, it was Halliburton that carried out the looting of the Baghdad museum, while US troops were ordered to back off. For its part, Blackwater hit the news in September 2007 when it faced accusations that it had been responsible for the killing of seventeen Iraqi citizens. Blackwater claimed that its contractors 'acted lawfully and appropriately in response to a hostile attack', while Iraqi officials said they opened fire indiscriminately.

Mr Seagrave was keen to draw a parallel between Dr Kelly's death and that of a young American journalist called Danny Casolaro, who had been investigating the activities of US-based private security firms including Halliburton. Mr Casolaro was found dead one morning in a hotel room near Harper's Ferry in Virginia. He was in the bath, naked, with his wrist slashed. There were no signs of bruising or other marks on the body. The police concluded that he had committed suicide.

Dr Christopher 'Kit' Green was for decades the CIA's chief forensic pathologist. It was he who discovered that the BBC's Bulgarian employee Georgi Markov had been shot in the leg with a device concealed in an umbrella that implanted a jeweller's watch-bearing in which two tiny tunnels had been hollowed out and filled with ricin.[3]

Dr Green participated in Mr Casolaro's autopsy. In a conversation with Mr Seagrave in 2006, he revealed that the official version of events was totally false. Dr Green told him that the hotel room had been the scene of a violent struggle, that the young journalist had been killed before being stripped, put in a full bath, and his left wrist slashed in precisely the manner in which Dr Kelly's had been. And as with Dr Kelly, there was remarkably little blood, bar a small amount smeared on the edge of the tub, suggesting that the wrist had been slashed after the heart had stopped pumping. Mr Seagrave says that the United States will carry out assassinations abroad with or without the approval and permission of the host country and could have done so in Dr Kelly's case.

That may be so, but it strikes me as more likely that, if the United States were involved at all, it would have forewarned the British Prime Minister, though not necessarily sought permission. Of course, knowing what we know of Tony Blair's subservient approach to George Bush, if he had received a call asking for permission, one can well believe that he might have said yes.

Another explanation comes from John Simkin, an historian specialising in the covert activities of the CIA. He too believes that Dr Kelly may have been murdered by the Americans, and suggests that the motive may have been to apply heavy pressure on the British government, the kind of intimidation that some have concluded can be read into the despatch in the United States of anthrax letters to difficult opponents of the administration.

Specifically, the object would have been to ensure there was no undermining of the occupation of Iraq, either through admission that the grounds for invasion were flawed – the UK government was of course being robustly challenged on this in July 2003, not least because of Dr Kelly's actions – or through any commitment to scale down troop levels in Iraq. Mr Simkin also makes the Machiavellian suggestion that the pressure could have been maintained by a threat to Blair from the Americans to leak information about the death in a way that would have implicated the British government if Blair failed to follow the Bush line on the so-called 'war on terror'.

It is certainly the case that Blair's relationship with Bush was a peculiar, even unhealthy, one. British Prime Ministers since 1945 have, with the exception of Edward Heath, worked hard to ensure they stick close to the American President and administration of the day, but have managed to combine that with a healthy degree of independence. Harold Wilson, for example, resisted the strong pressure to send British troops into Vietnam, for which we can all be thankful.

It is not the fact that Blair wanted to be close to Bush that is so strange, even allowing for the fact that Bush is the most right-wing and US-supremacist president in living memory and Blair is, theoretically at least, of the left. It is rather that the Prime Minister appeared to be willing to give ground where none had to be offered, to cause problems for himself when that could have been avoided, and to behave submissively when it was not necessary to do so.

What are we to make of the instruction sent by Downing Street to Sir Christopher Meyer, the British ambassador in

Washington, to 'get up the arse of the White House and stay there'?[4] Is this normal behaviour for a Prime Minister? Again one has to ask: if the White House had held information on Blair that, had it been released, would have forced him to resign, and if the White House had made Blair aware that it held such information and intended to release it unless he fully co-operated, in what way would he have behaved differently from how he did? Indeed, so inexplicably submissive was Blair towards Bush that a wild story – passed on to me by two separate and unconnected sources – is circulating that that was exactly the situation, and that the Americans were aware of a deeply personal scandal involving Blair dating from the early 1980s.

There are, however, strong reasons to doubt any US involvement in the death of Dr Kelly. First and foremost, although Dr Kelly's actions were doubtless unwelcome to the United States, the problems they caused were predominantly for the British government and so would not have necessitated a US response. Second, if the United States had wanted to prevent Dr Kelly from making further unhelpful comments, perhaps about Syria, there were other levers to pull. Dr Kelly could have had his pension position threatened, for example. Third, if the United States really did have something on the Prime Minister, they would have no need to apply pressure in this way.

I have spoken to a number of individuals in the United States well connected to the CIA as part of my investigations. None is aware of the names of the others I have engaged. Nor could any be reasonably characterised as advocates for the

White House. Each, separately, has come back to me to say that the inside track does indeed report Dr Kelly as having been murdered, but that the United States was not part of it.

★

Then there was the letter that arrived one morning at my constituency office in Lewes. This letter was from an individual who described himself as 'a member, now ex, of the Intelligence Services'. It was anonymous, with no method of making contact provided. The writer provided certain other details about himself but I have withheld these to seek to prevent him from being identified. I took him to be a hands-on soldier rather than a desk officer from MI6 headquarters at Vauxhall Cross.

The letter was not particularly well written, with a number of spelling and grammatical mistakes (which I have corrected for the purposes of the quoted sections below). Yet something about it spoke of authenticity. My correspondent alleged that David Kelly was murdered

> because he was about to go public with certain info he had about government lies regarding Iraq. He had forewarned the government that Iraq had no WMD and was going to make his views known through a national paper. . . . It was discussed by British security whether to erase him or not. It was decided against, but the intelligence services knew that Iraqi agents were after him, but offered him no protection, letting agents from

303

Iraq carry out their dirty work. The Prime Minister was aware of all operations regarding Kelly. . . . Kelly was murdered by this government by association.

My correspondent also alleged that a letter had been left in Dr Kelly's pocket by the Iraqis to 'try to bring down the government' – he did not specify what was in it – but that it was removed by an officer from Thames Valley Police as Dr Kelly's body lay in the woods. However, the police have formally denied to me that any letter was found on Dr Kelly.[5]

Anonymous letters are inherently unsatisfactory and need to be treated with scepticism. This one seems to me to be a touch contradictory in another way too, in that it gives a reason why Dr Kelly was wanted dead, but the beneficiaries in this scenario would appear to be the British government, rather than the Iraqis, who the writer (and indeed others) says were directly responsible. On the other hand, it does tend to corroborate the theory that there was some foreknowledge of Dr Kelly's demise amongst the British, most obviously in the start-time for Operation Mason.

At this point it is worth asking whether there were elements in the intelligence services, or indeed within 10 Downing Street, who would have wanted Dr Kelly dead. It is difficult, frankly, to think that anyone in the government could have thought this to be in their interest, even if one accepts that morally they were prepared to bring it about, and many would challenge that. The aftermath of Dr Kelly's death presented

Tony Blair with his greatest political challenge, and returned the political focus firmly onto Iraq, which cannot be where the government would have wanted it. For a time, it even seemed, if only to some excited commentators, that the government might fall.

It might be argued therefore that for the Prime Minister or other senior elements in the government to have been prepared to sanction the assassination of Dr Kelly can only be explained if the information Dr Kelly might have imparted was even more dangerous to the government than the consequences of the discovery of his body in the woods; if the Prime Minister or others were under external pressure, probably from the Americans, that they could not resist; or if a catastrophic misjudgement had been made.

Against that can be set the fact that the Prime Minister, Geoff Hoon and Alastair Campbell at least had shown themselves to be uncaring, if not callous, in their handling of Dr Kelly's situation both before and after his death, notwithstanding the findings of the Hutton report. Before his death, Dr Kelly was treated as a pawn to be played in the game against the BBC. What he was feeling, or what he was owed in the way of decent treatment, never seemed an issue for this trio and others around them.

Even after his death none seemed particularly chastened. As we have seen, Campbell spent the weekend after working the phones to shore up his own position; Hoon went off to enjoy himself at the motor racing; and the Prime Minister's spokesman began briefing journalists that Dr Kelly had been a 'Walter Mitty' figure.

The idea of a catastrophic misjudgement should also not be ruled out. After all, the invasion of Iraq itself qualifies for that label, and as his length of stay in Downing Street increased, the Prime Minister did appear to develop the dangerous trait of convincing himself of whatever he had to be convinced of at that moment, believing that he alone could solve problems, and that even when everybody else disagreed with him, they must all be wrong.

Of course it is in principle possible that there was involvement, tacit or otherwise, from MI6 or elements within the Joint Intelligence Committee, without either knowledge of or approval from politicians, with the possible exception of the Prime Minister. That would chime in with the letter I had received, purporting to be from a recently retired member of the intelligence services. But for any official, whether in MI6 or the Joint Intelligence Committee, to have either commissioned or, more likely, done nothing to prevent the assassination of Dr Kelly, should have required political clearance at the highest level.

What would the possible motives be for elements in the intelligence services to allow Dr Kelly to be killed? Two of the three generic motives already referred to might apply – to prevent him from making any further damaging revelations, as my anonymous letter writer suggests, or as a warning to others to stay in line. There is actually another possible motive. We have seen how in the United States there was a breakdown between the CIA and the administration, and it was suggested that the efforts to find Iraqi biological and chemical weapons might have been made deliberately unsuccessful so as to put pressure on the White House.

Here in Britain, too, relations had become strained between the government and the intelligence services, including both MI6 and the Defence Intelligence Service, on account of the misuse and abuse of intelligence for political purposes. Might it have suited some in intelligence to teach the government a lesson? Might MI6, with its close links to the CIA, have been happy to follow a similar line to that organisation?

A case can certainly be made that there was some official foreknowledge of Dr Kelly's demise amongst the powers that be in Britain. I have already referred to the start time of Operation Mason, which, I had been told, indicated that this foreknowledge had come late, too late to stop the murder. Alternatively If the contents of the anonymous letter I had received are to be accepted, then elements in the police were not alerted to his impending murder too late to stop it, but rather were simply preparing for what they knew was going to happen.

It was also very convenient politically for the Prime Minister that Dr Kelly's body should have been found less than a day after Parliament broke up for its long summer holiday, and at a time when Blair himself was out of the country, far away. And it is striking how quickly the political process swung into action, which saw an inquiry announced and Lord Hutton appointed in astonishingly quick time to head it. It is almost as if there were a prearranged plan which was seamlessly set in train.

On the other hand, for there to have been British involvement, even if it were limited to obscuring the real cause of death, certain key people would need to have been in the loop and willing to co-operate. It is, however, almost impossible to believe that those involved, professional police officers and medical specialists, for example, would agree to be part of any plot to kill Dr Kelly.

But just suppose that the position was indeed as had been suggested, that the police were warned of a likely assassination attempt, but were not in time to stop it. Suppose also that subsequent to this, they were told that Dr Kelly had been murdered by Iraqi elements, but that in the interests of Queen and country, it was vital that this not come out, given the possible destabilisation of both Britain and Iraq that could result. That it was their patriotic duty to allow the impression to be formed that Dr Kelly had killed himself. They might just buy that.

19 Iraqi connections

As I reviewed my notes, it became clear that there were a number of people who worked with David Kelly who suspected some sort of Iraqi involvement in his death.

David Broucher told the Hutton inquiry that he had asked Dr Kelly what would happen if Iraq were invaded (see Chapter 12). Dr Kelly replied that he 'would probably be found dead in the woods' – as indeed he was. Mr Broucher told Lord Hutton that he himself interpreted the phrase to mean that 'he was at risk of being attacked by the Iraqis in some way.'

Mai Pederson recorded that she and Dr Kelly had discussed the dangers of working in Iraq, and the personal threats that resulted (see Chapter 16). She confirmed that he had received death threats from supporters of Saddam Hussein, something he acknowledged but refused to be cowed by, in a very British stiff-upper-lip way. During her interview with Thames Valley Police, Ms Pederson told the two detectives who had flown out to Alabama to speak to her that Dr Kelly had expressed fears that he could be killed by enemies from Iraq.[1] Dr Kelly had himself also passed on such concerns to Colonel Terence Taylor, head of the International Institute for Strategic Studies.

Dick Spertzel was the most senior biological weapons inspector in the United States. When I rang him, he was relaxing at his home in Jefferson, Maryland. He had worked closely with Dr Kelly in Iraq and believes that he may have been murdered by elements from the Saddam regime. He felt that these elements might well have pursued a vendetta against Dr Kelly, and that he was probably a victim of the Iraqi intelligence services, because of the long-standing enmity towards him. 'A number of us were on an Iraqi hit list,' he volunteered in a rather matter-of-fact way. 'I was number three, and David was a couple behind that.'

The Iraqis would have regarded Dr Kelly as an enemy on account of his success at uncovering Iraqi weapons programmes, Dr Spertzel said. His involvement in the production of the UK government's dossier would have antagonised the Iraqis still further. Saddam Hussein's regime knew that the United States was looking for a reason to attack, and regarded all the talk of weapons of mass destruction as merely a ploy to that end. By participating in the dossier's production, Dr Kelly would have been seen as being a tool of Bush and Blair.

I suggested that it was unlikely that the Iraqis would have maintained a desire for revenge, or that they would have known what Dr Kelly's role was in the writing of the dossier, but Dr Spertzel sharply disagreed. 'Revenge is a big factor in Iraqi society,' a fact which he said had been evident even during the inspection process. He recalled that the only way into the Rashid Hotel in Baghdad, where the weapons inspectors and journalists would stay, was to walk across a specially laid mosaic of George Bush Snr. Such an arrangement of course constitutes a great insult in Arab culture. 'And Saddam Hussein's intelligence people were superb,' Dr Spertzel went on. 'They knew more about us than we knew ourselves, including our movements in the United States and the United Kingdom.'

On one occasion, a colleague of his had been asked by an Iraqi how his move had gone from Miami to Minneapolis – a move that nobody had talked about. The question, in Dr Spertzel's view, was just to let the inspectors know that they were being closely monitored at home. He believed that Iraqi informants had been embedded within the United Nations inspection system itself. He added that there was 'no question' but that Saddam's people were still active after the fall of their leader, perhaps even more so.

I had also spoken to George Pulley, who used to play cribbage regularly with Dr Kelly at the Hind's Head in Kingston Bagpuize. Dr Kelly told Mr Pulley that a fatwa had been issued against him following his work in Iraq. The timing of this was two or three years before his death. There had, apparently, been an incident when he ended up in an argument with a leading Iraqi, whom Dr Kelly is said to have branded a liar. He was subsequently warned to leave Iraq and not come back, but that if he did, he would pay with his life.

Now of course this could all have been bravado on the part of the Iraqi in question, and certainly Dr Kelly did subsequently visit Iraq without incident. It is also the case, of course, that Dr Kelly was found dead in an English wood, rather than on Iraqi soil. Nevertheless, the perceived Iraqi threats, and the juxtaposition of the joint US/UK invasion, suggested that it might be useful to examine more closely how all this tied in together.

That Dr Kelly had created resentment and made enemies amongst Saddam's supporters is unquestionable. He had led the first ever biological weapons inspection back in 1991 and was a regular and key participant in inspections for the rest of the decade until Saddam brought the process to an abrupt halt in 1998. His most regular colleagues were Richard Spertzel, Rod Barton and Hamish Killip. All have paid tribute to his stamina and his effectiveness in uncovering that which the Iraqis were desperate to hide.

Dr Kelly used logic, argument and guile to trap the Iraqis. He even managed to outwit the formidable Dr Rihab Taha, also known as 'Dr Germ', the woman in charge of Saddam's 'defensive' biological research programme. His style was rather British, quiet and polite, and all the more effective for it. Dr Spertzel recalled one occasion when Dr Kelly had forced Dr Taha into contradictory statements, causing her to shout that he had insulted all the women of Iraq. Dr Kelly's response was to say quite calmly: 'Dr Taha, please stop.'[2] He also made a strong enemy out of Dr Amer al-Sa'adi, Saddam's chief scientific adviser, who gave himself up to the Americans three days after Saddam's statue was pulled down.

Then there were the dissidents, the informers who worked closely with the Americans. In that regard, 'Curveball' is a word that those in the Bush administration may prefer to forget. It was the codename given to the Iraqi dissident who provided information that was sensational and, as events would turn out, wildly distorted and in most regards simply plain false.

In the manner of US codenames of the time, the suffix '-ball' represented a source with information on weapons. The prefix 'curve-' was arbitrary though, as it turned out, somewhat apposite, given that the source in question was not exactly straight with his debriefers. In 1999, he landed at Munich airport on a tourist visa and promptly applied for political asylum, saying that he was wanted for embezzlement of Iraqi government money. He was sent to a refugee centre, but then changed his story. Now he maintained that in Iraq he had led a team that equipped trucks to produce biological weapons. In retrospect, the change of story should have rung alarm bells, but it did not.

Curveball was debriefed by the Germans, who guarded their asset jealously and would not allow him to be interviewed by the Americans until March 2004, who thus had to rely on what the Germans sent them. The information he provided via the Germans seemed, superficially at least, to tie in with what the Americans thought they already knew, and they failed to notice, or chose to ignore, the gaps and inconsistencies in his information.

According to the *Los Angeles Times*, MI6 was rather more grounded, and warned the CIA that it was 'not convinced that Curveball is a wholly reliable source'.[3] It also pointed out that satellite images of the building where he had claimed to be working were at odds with what he had described. Indeed, elements in the CIA itself, including its European intelligence chief, Tyler Drumheller, were uncertain about Curveball's credibility.

Yet Curveball's fantastic snippets were lapped up by the Bush administration and regurgitated. They were the basis of Colin Powell's allegations made before the UN Security Council, when he talked of 'firsthand descriptions' of mobile biological factories. In that presentation, Mr Powell referred to the source for his information:

> The source was an eyewitness, an Iraqi chemical engineer who supervised one of these facilities. He was actually present during biological agent production runs. He was also at the site when an accident occurred in 1998. Twelve technicians died from exposure to biological agents ... His eyewitness account of these mobile production facilities has been corroborated by other sources.

These other sources, three in number, were, according to Mr Powell, an Iraqi civil engineer, an Iraqi major and someone 'in a position to know'.[4]

If Colin Powell is to be believed, nobody told him of the doubts that existed within the CIA before he weighed in hawkishly. It was only on 8 February 2003, three days after his

UN speech, that Curveball's allegations were actually checked out on the ground in Iraq and found to be false. Six weeks later the invasion began.

As for Curveball himself, his information and readiness to talk had dried up in 2001, after he succeeded in being granted asylum and negotiating a small income stream from the German government. His motive all along seems simply to have been to find a way to stay in Germany. Subsequent investigations by the United States following the invasion revealed that Curveball, who bears an uncanny resemblance to a young Engelbert Humperdinck, had actually come bottom in his engineering class, that he had been fired in 1995, and that he had thereafter been driving a taxi in Baghdad. Here were the foundations of sand on which were built Mr Powell's authoritative call to war at the UN.

Abram Shulsky was the director of the Pentagon's Office of Special Plans, which, we have seen, decided what it wanted to find in the way of WMD in Iraq and then declared it had found them. He once wrote about defectors in a 1991 textbook on intelligence: 'It is difficult to be certain that they are genuine. [They] may be greedy; they may desire to avenge what they see as ill treatment by their government; or they may be subject to blackmail.'[5] In other words, they have every reason to tell those debriefing them exactly what they want to hear.

Shulsky's book provides a sound analysis. It is a pity he appeared to have forgotten its contents while there at the Office of Special Plans.

But what of the three other sources Mr Powell referred to? All three were eventually confirmed as fraudulent, and interestingly, two of them had links to another Iraqi of even greater influence in Washington at this time, Ahmed Chalabi.

At the end of the first Gulf War in 1991, the first President Bush asked the CIA to initiate a programme that would facilitate the removal of Saddam from power. This was no throwaway wish – $100 million was allocated to the project. The CIA contracted the matter out to a shadowy public relations organisation called the Rendon Group, at the time operating out of a London office in Catherine Place, near Buckingham Palace. The organisation, established by John Rendon, specialises in 'perception management' and, according to *Rolling Stone*, has been authorised access to the most secret information held by the US government, whether from interceptions, satellite imaging or old-fashioned espionage.

Mr Rendon himself was living in Washington's Kalorama district, conveniently 'just around the corner' from Donald Rumsfeld, US Defense Secretary at the time of the invasion of Iraq. At a dinner at a private Washington club, Mr Rendon is reported to have said: 'We've worked in ninety-one countries. Going all the way back to Panama, we've been involved in every war, with the exception of Somalia.'[6] At a conference on information operations in London in 2005, he warned that news organisations reporting on the Iraq war had often been able to 'take control of the story ... We lost control of the context. This has to be fixed for the next war.'[7]

The Rendon Group, like other private sector companies, is almost entirely unaccountable through the democratic process, allowing any administration, American or British, to outsource tasks where they would wish to have deniability. Part of the scheme to effect regime change in Iraq involved the creation of an anti-Saddam grouping, which is where Chalabi came in.

Born in 1944, Chalabi comes from a rich and influential Shiite family. His father was president of the Senate and adviser to the King, and his grandfather held posts in nine cabinets. The latter, in the manner of a Middle Eastern Sheriff of Nottingham, is also said to have run a private prison into which he threw serfs who failed to pay the requisite taxes to him. The family was forced into exile when the King was deposed in 1958 and the young Ahmed attended boarding school in England.

In 1977, he started what was to become the second largest bank in Jordan, but a financial crisis twelve years later forced him to flee to England. Some $158 million had disappeared from the bank's accounts. In his absence, Chalabi was found guilty of a multiplicity of charges, including embezzlement, currency speculation, forgery, theft and making false statements, and sentenced to twenty-two years' hard labour. He claimed that the prosecution was political and that he had been stitched up.

Shortly afterwards, he emerged as the CIA's favourite Iraqi opposition politician, leading the newly formed Iraqi National Congress. Even the name was created by the Rendon Group. Over the next twelve years, the US government would make more than $100 million available to the Iraqi National Congress, with the level of funding moving up a gear with the arrival of the Bush administration in 2001.

It is not at all clear what positive benefits, if any, the Americans got for their money. There was a particular disaster in 1995 when Chalabi, with CIA money, assembled thousands of Kurds in northern Iraq for an uprising. Saddam sent in the army and the result was all too predictable. The CIA cut off his funds the next year, but he simply secured money from the Pentagon instead.

There was an inherent flaw in the arrangement between Chalabi and the United States. The Americans were desperate for an Iraqi opposition to Saddam and were prepared to overlook quite a lot to keep one on track. Chalabi was desperate for American military action in Iraq and happy to tell the Americans what they wanted to hear.

He seems to have played his cards well. The *New Yorker* reported a conversation that took place in London in 1998 between the US weapons inspector Scott Ritter and Chalabi, pursuant to a search for a vast quantity of anthrax which the inspectors believed Saddam had not neutralised. Chalabi had claimed he had people inside Saddam's circle who could help.

Mr Ritter told the *New Yorker*: 'I should have asked him what he could give me. Instead, I let him ask me, "What do you need?" ... We made the biggest mistake in the intelligence business. We identified all our gaps.' Mr Ritter also said that Chalabi talked of a time when he would be President of Iraq and control all the oil concessions. When the *New Yorker* put this to Chalabi's office, they branded Ritter a 'liar'.[8]

In the same year, the Republican-controlled US Congress passed an astonishing piece of legislation, the Iraq Liberation Act, largely inspired and lobbied for by Chalabi. Here was official approval for regime change, five years before it occurred. Meanwhile, Chalabi continued to provide the Americans with details of Saddam's alleged weapons capabilities, directly or indirectly. Curveball, for example, was believed to be the brother of one of his senior aides.

Chalabi's fingerprints can also be found in the now notorious *New York Times* article by Judith Miller, which quoted a source who alleged he was aware of twenty or more sites in Iraq associated with chemical and biological weapons (see Chapter 17). Subsequent searches showed this allegation to be without foundation, but at the time, the article provided just the smoking gun the Bush administration was looking for. It was also the smoking gun Chalabi was looking for, in his quest to pull the United States into military action. It was he who had brought the informant in question, Adnan Ihsan Saeed al-Haideri, to Thailand, where he stayed for several days with a spokesman for the Rendon Group, Zaab Sethna.

According to the award-winning journalist James Bamford, who has extensively studied both the Rendon Group and the Iraqi National Congress, it was normal practice for the INC to coach defectors on their stories.[9] The preparation was for a lie detector test, to be carried out by a CIA official. Despite the coaching, the print-out from the detector showed that the informant had lied, indeed that the whole story was a fabrication.

That, however, was a mere detail. Before the CIA official was back in the United States, Chalabi and Mr Sethna were on the phone to Ms Miller with the informant's now disproven story, which duly appeared writ large in her paper.

Why did the CIA, with access to the polygraph print-out, not correct the story? Perhaps, as with Geoff Hoon and the totally misleading UK newspaper headlines covering the 45-minute claim, they did not think they had any duty at all to do so. Or perhaps it was because they were paying the Rendon Group vast sums for effective 'perception management'.

Chalabi himself made no secret of his wish to drag the United States into Iraq. BBC journalist Christopher Dickie recalled that when he had interviewed him on Radio 4's *The World Tonight*, he had put it to him that 'a lot of people in the CIA and the State Department say you would do anything to drag the USA into a war with Saddam Hussein'. Chalabi had looked him in the eye and replied: 'Yes, absolutely.'[10] Naturally, those like Dr Kelly who, by sticking to the facts, weakened the case for invasion beforehand and discredited those who had exaggerated it afterwards were unhelpful to Chalabi and his Iraqi National Congress colleagues. The last thing they wanted was the sober truth to prevail.

After the invasion, the Pentagon flew Chalabi and hundreds of his supporters into Iraq, in preparation for his playing a major role in the new post-Saddam regime. He was given a position on the Iraqi interim governing council by the Coalition Provisional Authority, heading the important finance committee, where his Jordanian banking experience will doubtless have come in useful. He served as president of the council in September 2003.

In an interview with the BBC's *Breakfast with Frost* in July that year, ten days after Dr Kelly's death, Chalabi painted a rosy picture of life in Iraq for the interviewer, Peter Sissons: 'There are difficulties with services, it is true. But the point is you have to balance that against the complete lack of repression. People are free. People are free and they celebrate that every day.' The Iraqis themselves, with good reason, seemed unconvinced. A poll in Iraq in August 2003 revealed that he was the only candidate for President with a negative poll rating.

Later, relations between Chalabi and the United States turned sour, amid allegations of fraud involving Iraqi currency and the passing of US secrets to Iran. In May 2004 funding for the INC was suddenly discontinued. The next day, Iraqi police and US soldiers raided Chalabi's home and documents and computers were removed. An arrest warrant for counterfeiting followed on 8 August. Oddly, he was never arrested and charges were dropped. Subsequently, he bounced back and on 28 April 2005 became Deputy Prime Minister and simultaneously Oil Minister. His long-standing wish to be involved in oil concessions, revealed to Scott Ritter, was realised.

He also kept his contacts in good shape with a visit to the United States in December 2005, when he met, amongst others, Dick Cheney, Donald Rumsfeld and Condoleezza Rice. He was one of a very select few to be given an invitation to attend the prestigious Bilderberg Conference in 2006 in Ottawa.

In February 2007 Chalabi assumed a new role, as the official intermediary between Baghdad residents and the Iraqi and US security forces. He was helping Iraqis arrange reimbursement for damage to property resulting from the aggressive counter-insurgency campaigns being waged across the city. Less encouragingly for him, he appeared at number eleven on a hit list of sixty-one individuals targeted for assassination, issued on 5 September 2006 by the Iraqi Ba'ath Party.

Also appearing on that list, in twenty-fourth place, was Iyad Allawi, another Iraqi who also played an interesting role in the 1990s through to the overthrow of Saddam and beyond. Allawi was born in 1945 into a Shiite family, and is related by marriage to Chalabi, who is his second cousin. Over the years, the two have developed their careers in parallel, sometimes jostling each other like runners round a track. They even attended the same school, the Jesuit-run Baghdad College.

Allawi began his politics early by joining the Ba'ath party when he was just twelve years old. The *New Yorker*, in an analysis piece on Allawi, reported an allegation that he had been present at the torture of communist youths in Iraq in 1963. One victim, who certified that Allawi had been there, had been hung by his arms from the ceiling while being beaten. Allawi denied the allegation to the publication.[11]

He became friends with Saddam Hussein and helped with the 1968 coup that put the Ba'athists back into power. He moved to London in 1971, ostensibly to continue his medical studies – he is a qualified neurosurgeon – though others claim he had been sent to London by Saddam and actually headed up the European division of the Mukhabarat from the Iraqi embassy.

A former CIA agent, Vincent Cannistraro, seems in no doubt. He told the *New Yorker*: 'If you're asking me if Allawi has blood on his hands from his days in London, the answer is yes, he does. He was a paid Mukhabarat agent for the Iraqis, and he was involved in dirty stuff.'[12] Mr Cannistraro, who is now a consultant on intelligence and terrorism, told me that this included reporting on opponents to Saddam, who would then face torture and death when they returned home.

Mukhabarat, the Arabic word for 'intelligence', is short for *Jihaz al-Mukhabarat al-A'ma*, which translates as Iraqi Intelligence Services. The organisation was extensive, with twenty-eight directorates. It is believed to have been responsible, in Saddam's time, for assassinations abroad and the massacre of whole villages inside Iraq. In 1978, Allawi himself was subject to an assassination attempt, when two men broke into his London home. He was hit on the head with an axe, and spent a year in hospital. His wife was also badly injured. He believes the attack was ordered by Saddam.

In the 1980s began his fruitful relationship with MI6, for whom he remained an asset until passed on to the Americans in the 1990s. Allawi himself says that MI6 set him up with some oil deals in Yemen to allow him to generate an income stream. He took British citizenship and, in 2003, was living in a house in west London with his second wife and their three children, two daughters and a young son.

After the Gulf War, Allawi created a new organisation to oppose Saddam, the Iraqi National Accord. This happened about the same time as Chalabi was forming the Iraqi National Congress, and, like that body, it was generously funded by the CIA.

Allawi's organisation, just like Chalabi's, was responsible for eye-catching but groundless intelligence. In the case of the Iraqi National Congress, it had been the twenty or so sites in Iraq where WMD could be found. In the case of the Iraqi National Accord, it was reports passed to MI6 in the spring and summer of 2002, including the 45-minute claim that fed through to the British government's dossier with such dramatic effect. Allawi admitted this in an interview on the BBC's *Breakfast with Frost* when he said: 'We have the person who gave the story to the *Telegraph* as one of the reliable people, officers who have knowledge of such matters occurring in Iraq.'[13] His spokesman, Nick Theros, later said that the information had been passed on to MI6 'in good faith. It was for the intelligence services to verify.' He accepted that the information now looked like 'a crock of shit'.[14]

There are plenty of people who tell of Allawi's violent

history, working alongside Saddam Hussein and playing a key role in the Mukhabarat. Like many of us, Allawi may have mellowed and adopted a different approach, with the real possibility of power looming.

An examination of his approach to more recent matters, however, suggests that this may be open to question. In June 2004, just a fortnight or so after he had been named as Prime Minister in the new interim Iraqi government, and a week or so before the handover of power from US administrator Paul Bremer to the new Prime Minister, Allawi was reported in the Australian press to have been involved in a shocking and gruesome incident at an Iraqi police station, an allegation which he has strongly denied.

According to eye-witness accounts, seven prisoners were lined up against a courtyard wall next to the maximum security cell block at the Al-Amariyah security centre. They had been handcuffed and blindfolded. The Interior Minister, Falah al-Naqib, is then said to have remarked that he would like to kill them all on the spot, whereupon Allawi apparently replied that each prisoner had killed as many as fifty Iraqis and 'deserved worse than death' and then personally shot each of them in the head from close range with a pistol. One was hit in the neck and survived. The others were killed. The Interior Minister congratulated his Prime Minister. 'This is how we must deal with terrorists,' Allawi is said to have told his stunned audience of close to thirty people, which included twelve policemen and four US security personnel.

Before the shootings, Allawi is said to have told the policemen present in the complex that they must be courageous, and that if they killed insurgents, he would protect them from any repercussions. 'We must destroy anyone who wants to destroy Iraq and our people,' he is reported to have said.

The story was broken by Paul McGeough of the *Sydney Morning Herald*, which had secured separate interviews with two of the witnesses, neither of whom was paid and neither of whom had contacted the paper. The information each gave corroborated that provided by the other in all key respects. Each was in fact supportive of the actions Allawi is alleged to have taken.

The newspaper contacted the then US ambassador, John Negroponte, who was not prepared to issue a denial of the story, only tersely commenting: 'If we attempted to refute each [rumour], we would have no time for other business. As far as this embassy's press office is concerned, this case is closed.'[15]

The Americans seemed unconcerned by reports of multiple murders carried out by their nominee for Prime Minister in front of US citizens. But then Mr Bremer, appointed by President Bush to head the Coalition Provisional Authority in May 2003, had advocated relaxation of the CIA guidelines which restricted working with individuals or groups with a record of human rights abuses.

Strangely, the whole story received remarkably little follow-up in the British or American press. Allawi himself totally denied it, even that he had visited the complex in question. His office said they were rumours instigated by enemies of the interim government.

It has been suggested that this account was designed to bolster Allawi's reputation as a 'hard man' in Iraqi politics. However, Jon Lee Anderson, a reporter for the *New Yorker*, wrote in a piece published in January 2005 that in a visit he undertook to Jordan, 'a well-known former government minister told me that a US official had confirmed that the killings had taken place'. The official had allegedly said: 'What a mess we're in – we got rid of one son of a bitch only to get another.' According to the article, the Americans apparently referred to Allawi as 'Saddam Lite'.

In an interview with Mr Anderson for the article, Allawi told the reporter that he had never killed or tortured anyone. But then added: 'But to kill in self-defence, yes. I've issued orders to my police to kill terrorists when they are unable to take them otherwise.' When asked about the abuse and degradation of Abu Ghraib, he replied: 'Well, you know, it happens in war, this kind of thing. It should not, but it does.'

Allawi is described by those who know him as a man with a temper. His cousin Ali Allawi added: 'Iyad is a man whom the French would call "a man of the shadows". He understands the Mukhabarat culture of intimidation.'[16]

After Allawi became Prime Minister, he reintroduced the death penalty and gave himself the power to declare martial law. As we have seen, he also took early steps to re-establish a secret police force, the General Security Directorate. He displayed an early intolerance for a free press, at one point going so far as to close down the Iraqi offices of Aljazeera. A former Mukhabarat officer, Ibrahim Janabi, was appointed to head the new media regulator.

Allawi spent a week in the United States in September 2004, when, according to the *New York Times*, he

> parroted Mr Bush's absurd claims that the fighting in Iraq was an essential part of the US battle against terrorists that started on 9/11, that the neocons' utopian dream of turning Iraq into a modern democracy was going swimmingly, and that the worse things got over there, the better they really were.[17]

In January 2005, when the Pentagon was considering deploying what the *Times* termed 'El Salvador-style death squads' of Kurdish and Shia fighters in Iraq to tackle the insurgency, Allawi was reported by the paper as being 'one of the most vigorous supporters of the plan'.[18]

His helpful gestures towards the United States were no recent development. In the months before the invasion, he had helped prepare the way for US forces in the Anbar province by securing agreement from the military officers not to fight coalition troops, according to Sheikh Majed Abdelrazzak al-Suleiman, a tribal chief from the province.[19] Perhaps most significantly, he took steps in the important area of oil that will have hugely pleased the Americans who installed him. Under guidelines he issued to the Supreme Council for Oil Policy about three months into his tenure, all oil fields not then currently in production would have to be developed by private, and largely American or British, companies. The state-owned Iraq National Oil Company would thus be limited to just seventeen of the eighty known fields. Even so, it would also be part-privatised. Allawi's guidelines also made clear that speed was of the essence and that the Iraqi authorities should not bother negotiating the best possible deals with the oil companies, but accept whatever the companies proposed. Renegotiation could always come later, it was suggested.[20]

At best, this shows a touching belief in the altruism of oil companies, that they might voluntarily surrender some of their rights because somebody in the future asked them to do so. One has to ask in what way these guidelines would have been different had they simply been written by the Americans themselves, but then again, perhaps they were.

Allawi appeared to have calculated, perhaps at a very early stage, that provided he kept the United States happy, he could achieve what he wished.

Interestingly, after the elections of January 2005 which saw the Iraqis firmly reject Allawi and his colleagues, who should appear as chair of the Iraq Energy Council but Ahmed Chalabi. It was he who, in 2002, had said: 'US companies will have a big shot at Iraqi oil.'[21]

The US attitude to Iraqi oil in fact only mirrored its approach to other Iraqi assets. The Coalition Provisional Authority, under Paul Bremer, issued 100 orders binding on the Iraqi people. Order 39 allowed for the privatisation of around 200 state-owned enterprises and 100 per cent foreign ownership of Iraqi companies. Order 17 granted foreign contractors, including private security firms, full immunity from Iraq's laws. Order 81 prohibited farmers from using the farming methods they had employed for centuries. Farm-saved seed is now illegal in Iraq. All of these moves, and many others, clearly benefited American companies, which hit the jackpot when commercial contracts for reconstruction were awarded. Only 2 per cent of the contracts awarded in 2003 went to Iraqi companies.

In December 2004, Mr Bremer was awarded the Presidential Medal of Freedom, America's highest civil award, for his 'especially meritorious contributions to the security or national interests of the United States'.

Both men – Chalabi and Allawi – wanted US intervention in Iraq, and both wanted to benefit personally from that. It was in the interest of neither for unfounded claims of Iraqi capability to be challenged, let alone disproven. One Iraqi, quoted in the *Observer*, summed it up neatly: 'We wanted the Americans to remove Saddam. We had no interest in making an inspections regime work. The worse it got, the better for us.'[22]

Following the fall of Saddam, Allawi became chairman of the Iraq Governing Council security committee, a role which required him to maintain close and friendly relations with the Americans. In December 2003, he flew to CIA headquarters in Langley, Virginia to discuss setting up a new domestic secret service. Agents were to be recruited from the ranks of Saddam's murderous Mukhabarat.

No doubt this was all helpful to his emergence as the first Iraqi Prime Minister in the summer of 2004, a development that surprised many. In the battle for power, Allawi had beaten Chalabi hands down.

20 A very strange death

It was a normal day in Westminster. The House was sitting and the parliamentary estate was full of the usual collection of weary MPs traipsing from one meeting to the next, researchers veering in appearance from anxious to lackadaisical, and primly dressed men in tights harrumphing around the place. My diary for that morning was filled with a succession of short meetings of a motley nature. None looked particularly remarkable.

I left my office in Portcullis House and took the stairs down to the reception area of the new building, where my next appointment was waiting for me. I had never heard of him before and the matter he wished to talk to me about was marginal to my portfolio. My mind, therefore, was on the pile of unfinished work on my desk rather than the meeting about to take place, which I assumed would be a short and uneventful one. I couldn't have been more wrong.

The ostensible reason given for the meeting was essentially a pretext. My visitor really wanted to talk about the death of David Kelly.

Let me say here that I subsequently checked out this person's bona fides and was able to confirm them. He was who he said he was, and worked where he said he worked. I cannot publicly reveal his name, nor give clues that would enable him to be identified, for reasons that will become apparent. I have no reason to doubt his honesty, and I have looked for one.

My visitor was nervous and distracted. I began to wonder if he was unwell. Then the pretence of a discussion about a portfolio matter ended abruptly. He had decided to open up.

I have to be very careful with what I say about him, as he clearly believes that he is at risk if he is identified as having produced information. For this reason, I have been able to include only a fraction of what he said to me from my detailed contemporaneous notes and our email exchanges.

He told me of a meeting where members of a UK-based Iraqi circle had boasted of people who claimed involvement in Dr Kelly's death. It seemed that the Iraqis felt that Dr Kelly had besmirched them through his publicly reported actions in doubting the intelligence their organisation had provided to MI6, not least in respect of the now infamous September dossier. There was also concern that Dr Kelly might well have gone public with even more details.

My visitor also provided an explanation for the mysterious start time to Operation Mason, the investigation into Dr Kelly's death begun by Thames Valley Police half an hour before Dr Kelly left for his final walk. He told me that the police or the security services had got wind of a possible plan to assassinate Dr Kelly and Operation Mason was originally set up to deal with this threat. But the police were too late to prevent his murder taking place.

I stayed in contact with this person by rather circuitous means throughout 2006, and one day he undertook to send me some specific material. It never arrived, and he went quiet. When we finally met again, some weeks later, he was even jumpier than on the previous occasion. What he told me was chilling.

The day after he had confirmed to me that he would post me certain material, he kept an appointment, made at short notice. He had been promised certain information, which was to be conveyed to him by a contact. I learnt that at that impromptu meeting he was subjected to an horrific attack by unknown assailants, the full details of which he has asked me not to reveal. After this serious assault he told me he felt very hazy, and could barely feel his arms. His thumbs were entirely numb.

He was found by the local police. When he refused to say what had happened to him, he was taken to a nearby hospital, where he was held for nine hours before being released. Before being taken to the hospital, he had managed to use his phone to call someone he knew for help. This person is a well-known and well-respected national figure. When I spoke to her, she confirmed that she had received the phone call in question, and that its contents were consistent with the story I had been given.

In subsequent correspondence, my visitor made it clear that he was 'in danger', even if the attack had not been linked to our meeting. He stated that he was 'at risk from any rogue elements who thought that I might have been pointing a finger at them should they identify me'. Perhaps not surprisingly, he has been reluctant to get any further involved, though he remains well.

*

In Chapter 12, I suggested three generic motives for killing David Kelly: revenge; to prevent him from making public information which some person or persons would wish to remain secret; or, much less likely, as a kind of warning to others in a similar position to himself not to rock the boat as he did.

In terms of revenge, there are clearly a number close to Dr Kelly who believe that Saddam Hussein's forces would have been looking for an opportunity to eliminate the British weapons inspector, though it seems likely that had they been really determined, they might have taken an opportunity to do so on one of the occasions when he was in Iraq, rather than attempting such a venture on British soil. It would also be something of a coincidence for them to have chosen that July, when Dr Kelly was causing rather more angst more immediately to others, though it might be argued that the glare of publicity had brought him once again into the focus of Saddam's henchmen. Revenge, of course, is a motive that can also be ascribed to Saddam loyalists or to those who might have felt insulted and besmirched by the discrediting of the intelligence the Iraqi National Accord had provided to the British intelligence services.

The other realistic alternative – that Dr Kelly had something in his head which somebody else most definitely did not want out – is consistent with involvement from an Iraqi group with London links, which may have feared what further revelations might have done to its credibility with the US and UK. It is also possible that, had the decision to eliminate Dr Kelly come from the British or the Americans, then Iraqis based in London could have been used, either directly or to arrange the dirty work, to enable the operation to be carried out at arm's length from those who had commissioned it.

The next question is how Dr Kelly actually died, if it was not a result of a cut to the ulnar artery. Alarmingly, there appear to be a large number of ways in which an individual can be killed that are difficult or even impossible to trace. For this, we can no doubt partly thank the work of the South African Project Coast, a key objective of which was to develop exactly such capabilities.

One such method, developed in South Africa, is the use of an organophosphate called parathion, which can be introduced into the body through hair follicles, perhaps under the arm or around the crutch. This causes vomiting, which of course we saw in the case of Dr Kelly, and leads to a respiratory attack. It is extremely difficult to detect traces of such a chemical in the body, unless you know what you are looking for.

A private detective who contacted me suggested that another, gruesome, method would be for the killers to use the equipment employed by an undertaker when blood is removed from the body and replaced with embalming fluid. In this process, a tube is inserted into an artery and an electronic pump engaged to forcibly expel blood. Such a process would cause unconsciousness and death. It might leave some evidence of damage to the artery in question, but this could be missed in any subsequent examination. The loss of blood would also help reinforce the assumption that the victim might have lost a lot of blood through a cut.

The funeral director to whom the detective had spoken said that the draining of blood from a body did not need access to a main artery like the jugular, but could be achieved through, say, the ulnar artery. If that had occurred in Dr Kelly's case, then the incision by a knife into the ulnar artery might have been made to cover up this alternative use.

A former army operative, now living in France, suggested to me that potassium nitrate might have been used. This substance, also known as saltpetre, can in concentration cause rapid heartbeat, coma and death. It also causes vomiting.

A doctor got in touch to suggest that insulin might have been used. He said that if it were injected, it could kill and be virtually undetectable after a while. He also volunteered that injections of potassium and calcium, both naturally present in the body, could be introduced in sufficient quantities to stop the heart.

An anonymous letter, signed by 'Nemesis', alleged that he or she had been told by a 'member of the non-English diplomatic corps' that air had been introduced into Dr Kelly's bloodstream through a needle in a vein. Sufficient air in the major organs will kill and leave no scar. 'His heart and lungs were full of air,' the letter said. At the Hutton inquiry there were only passing references to Dr Kelly's lungs from the pathologist and the forensic toxicologist, which conveyed no information worth speaking of.

Then there is saxotoxin, found in some shellfish and known as the CIA shellfish toxin, after its alleged use by the CIA to kill a target. Even a tiny amount is effective seconds after injection and is completely untraceable after autopsy. Or there is suxamethonium chloride, also known as succinylcholine. This is a white crystalline substance that acts as a muscle relaxant. For less beneficent purposes, it can be used to induce paralysis and cardiac arrest.

In a sense, it is not necessary to know exactly how Dr Kelly was killed. It is sufficient to know that there are methods available which mimic other conditions, such as heart failure, and which are very difficult to trace. It is strange, though, that the death looked so bungled, that there were so many loose ends and inconsistencies – the lack of blood, the cutting of only an obscure and narrow artery, the presence of a pill pack suggesting the ingestion of twenty-nine tablets when the presence of less than one was found in his body, the unfinished water, and so on.

In an earlier chapter, I remarked that if Dr Kelly had wanted to commit suicide, then there were far more effective, guaranteed and painless ways available to him. In a way, the same objections can be raised to an explanation citing murder for the scene that was found on Harrowdown Hill. If the objective had been simply to kill Dr Kelly, then why not use a gun? If for some reason the death had to be disguised as natural

evidence that he left home without a coat (although one was subsequently found on his body in the woods) would tend to corroborate this.

Ruth Absalom was the last person definitely to have seen Dr Kelly alive, at the top of Harris's Lane. She told Lord Hutton that he was heading down the road towards Kingston Bagpuize, which must be Appleton Road. This is in the opposite direction from Harrowdown Hill, but consistent with a circular walk of around half-an-hour's duration to return him to his home. Assuming Ms Absalom's evidence can be relied upon, and her recollections were a little hazy, then it is unlikely that Dr Kelly made his own way to Harrowdown Hill.

Appleton Road is a quiet and rather deserted road with only sporadic development alongside. Draycott Road, into which Dr Kelly might have turned right from Appleton Road as part of a circular walk, is even more deserted, with some derelict buildings part way down. It is a no-through road which peters out into a footpath at the end. On either road, it would have been relatively easy for, say, a couple of men to have forced the 59-year-old weapons inspector into a van without anyone seeing.

One crucial fact is that Dr Kelly's mobile phone was switched off when a colleague from the Ministry of Defence tried to call him between 5 p.m. and 6 p.m. Yet Dr Kelly himself would tell friends that his mobile was always on.[1] Given that Dr Kelly had been in regular contact with the MoD that morning, and the aftermath of his appearance at two select committees was still working its way through, it seems unlikely that he would have, particularly that day, turned his phone off or let the battery run down.

There are really only two possible reasons for the mobile being off. The first is if he did indeed intend to commit suicide. Turning his phone off could be seen as a preliminary stage in that process. The second is that someone other than Dr Kelly turned his phone off. Anyone that might have kidnapped Dr Kelly would have wanted to ensure that his phone was off in order that his movements could not be traced via signal records kept by the phone company.

For reasons explained at length, I do not believe suicide is a credible explanation for his death, which thus leaves us with the alternative explanation for his phone being off. Certainly the timing is consistent with a forcible kidnapping at around 3.30 p.m.

We do not have a very good estimate for the time of death, in part because the pathologist unaccountably waited until the last possible moment to take the body temperature, the measurement of which helps establish this. According to the wide window of time given by the pathologist, Dr Kelly died some time between 4.15 p.m. on the 17th and 1.15 a.m. on the 18th. Also unaccountable is the lack of evidence about rigor mortis, which makes it difficult to pinpoint exactly when the scientist died. It is generally accepted that the stiffening of a body begins six hours after death, reaches a peak at twelve hours and begins to subside after twenty-four hours. There is no mention in the evidence from Vanessa

Hunt, the paramedic who moved Dr Kelly's arm at 10.07 a.m. in order to attach electrodes to his chest, that it was particularly difficult to move. Nor were their any comments in Ms Hunt's oral evidence to the inquiry about the extent of the onset of rigor mortis. From this we might deduce that it had not yet fully set in. This would indicate that Dr Kelly most likely died later than 10 p.m the day before, and probably significantly so.

Clearly, that still leaves a gap of at least seven hours from when Dr Kelly set out from his house until he died. It is worth pointing out that, if he really had left his house intent on committing suicide, and the presence of the pills can only imply premeditation if suicide is accepted, then he is not likely to have taken more than seven hours to have done the deed. There would also be a gap of seven hours or more between the time he was abducted, if this theory is right, and the time he was finally killed.

Why not kill him immediately upon abduction? There would have been no insurmountable obstacles to doing so, after all. Perhaps his abductors wanted an opportunity to take him into the woods under cover of darkness to minimise the chance of being spotted or disturbed.

In practical terms, it would not have been difficult to have given Dr Kelly a shot to render him temporarily unconscious. He might then have been forced, when awake again, to walk to the spot where he was found. He could in theory have been carried unconscious, but it would be a long walk.

The most obvious route to Harrowdown Hill from Harris's Lane would be along Cow Lane to Tucks Lane, past the Blue Boar and down the lane that leads to the track to the hill. If a vehicle were taken down the lane past the Blue Boar as far as the road will allow, that would still leave a walk of between a third and half a mile to where Dr Kelly was found. That walk is also a rather exposed one.

But there is an alternative access, and one that seemingly was not investigated by the police. It is less than 500 yards from the river Thames to Harrowdown Hill. At this point, there is a spot where a boat can be easily moored. The footbridge, wooden signpost and length of rail at this point make it an easily identifiable location. There is also a track that runs from the mooring point into the field that runs up to the wood. It takes about eight minutes to make this walk. There are no houses or other dwellings along this route, so anybody walking here is unlikely to be seen, particularly in the dead of night. The tourist website Waterspace.com describes this part of the river as 'one of the most remote stretches of the Thames'.

The evidence presented to the Hutton inquiry by Louise Holmes and Paul Chapman referred to the presence of some people in a boat nearby, but they were not traced and we do not know who they were or what they were doing. They could of course have been holidaymakers. Or not. If the operation had been planned beforehand, river access may well have been identified as the most suitable, for the reasons given above.

Following this through, it is logical to assume that Dr Kelly was killed at the scene, close to where he was found.

According to the information I have been given, the murder itself was carried out by a couple of not very well-paid hired hands. I was told, in fact, that the Iraqi-backed team had given Dr Kelly an injection in his backside, which perhaps points to succinylcholine or something similar. I asked Thames Valley Police whether they had had the body checked for the presence of this or a similar substance. Their reply, somewhat lacking in punctuation, stated: 'A full toxicology was requested whether that included succinylcholine is not within our knowledge.'[2]

I am dubious as to whether a letter of the sort described to me was indeed found in Dr Kelly's pocket. Be that as it may, let us imagine the reaction of the British government, the security services and the police, leaving aside for a moment the question of whether any of them might be implicated in the death, when Dr Kelly is found dead in the woods, and they know, or at the very least strongly suspect, that Iraqi elements are responsible.

I suggest that the reaction would be one of horror. July 2003 was a time when the controversy over the legality of the war, and over the honesty of the government in its portrayal of the intelligence it held, was at its height.

Then suppose it is reported that Britain's leading weapons inspector has been killed by Iraqi elements. Public opinion would be dangerously unpredictable. The government would look weak, there would be a demand for retribution, and the row over the 45-minute claim would intensify even more. Dr Kelly's views would take on an even greater significance.

We might also conjecture what the reaction of the British government would be if it suspected that an Iraqi operation based in England, for example one connected with Britain's foreign policy objectives at the time, might possibly have been involved.

It is not inconceivable that, under the circumstances described above or a variation of them, there may have been a high-level decision taken to make Dr Kelly's death look like suicide. That would have presented its own problems, but would have avoided the elephant traps referred to. And it would have had the bonus of gently discrediting Dr Kelly, something we have seen that the government was distastefully keen to do, both before and after his death.

But there wasn't much time to arrange matters.

If this scenario is correct, it is necessary to conclude that a small number of senior people knew, or at least strongly suspected, that Dr Kelly was dead, perhaps even before he was reported missing close on midnight that Thursday evening. Given that Operation Mason was set up at 2.30 that afternoon, that is not an unreasonable conclusion.

In this scenario, to create the suicide scene, tablets were removed from Dr Kelly's house, to be planted at the scene. His knife could also have been taken, though he might have naturally carried that with him. If he were to have carried a water bottle and the other artefacts he was found with, he would have needed a coat, so that was also taken. He was, let us remember, reported to have left the house without one. His body may even have been found by the authorities at a much earlier stage and a suicide scene created for the volunteers to find. This would have been before the second search of the Kellys' house, the real purpose of which could have been to remove possessions of Dr Kelly's for placement at the suicide scene.

In the woods, most of the tablets were taken away, leaving the empty blister packs, with one of the thirty tablets left in situ as a helpful clue. It is even possible that a small amount of the tablets were forced into his stomach, using a tube. The pathologist recorded a small bruise on his bottom lip, which is consistent with such an endeavour. His left wrist was slashed, and because the heart had stopped pumping, very little blood was discharged, just enough to soak the arm of his jacket and leave stains on some of the vegetation nearby.

Dr Kelly, if injected, could have been left flat on the ground, vomiting, before he died. When the suicide scene was set, he was placed up against a tree, where he was found by the volunteers. Subsequently, the body could have been moved to ensure its position was in accord with the vomit streaks on Dr Kelly's face, his watch put by his side, and a part-empty water bottle smeared with blood set down near him. No fingerprints were found on the bottle, or the knife.

Not many need have known the truth, though some in authority may have suspected. Very much against etiquette, the pathologist broke ranks on *Channel 4 News* in March 2004 to call for the coroner's inquest to be reopened.

It is even possible to surmise that perhaps both Lord Hutton and Janice Kelly were told, and each asked to go along with the story for the sake of the country, although there is of course no evidence to this effect.

The key question is whether the actions of the Iraqi group were self-generated, and subsequently covered up by the government, or whether a tiny cabal within the British establishment commissioned the assassins to undertake this. Perhaps it was somewhere in between, with a nod and a wink being unofficially offered. That would, after all, be very British.

Epilogue

And so my investigation concluded. What I had naïvely thought might take a year at most ended up taking half as much again. In the course of my work, I had met a number of interesting individuals and emerged rather more cynical about those who rule us.

I had always recognised that brutality, immorality and deception were to be found in totalitarian regimes across the world. What I had not appreciated fully was how those qualities can also be easily found in western democracies too, bubbling just below the surface. We fool ourselves if we think: 'It can't happen here.' It can, and it does.

I began suspicious of the official story of David Kelly's death and unhappy with the decision of the British government to go to war in Iraq. I determined to examine the matter honestly, following the evidence wherever it took me. I ended angry at the moral vacuum that was the Blair government with its lies, spin and lack of humanity in embarking on the invasion of Iraq, contemptuous of the official process that supposedly investigated Dr Kelly's death, and certain that he was murdered.

The explanation I have given may not be correct in all respects, but I suggest that it is rather more credible than the verdict of suicide that Lord Hutton reached. I believe there are enough doubts, enough questions, enough of a smell of stinking fish to justify reopening this episode officially.

As far as the government's actions are concerned, we need a full and independent public inquiry into the events that led us into war, and those that followed in the years after, when British troops were in Iraq.

As far as Dr Kelly is concerned, we owe it to a good man to set aside the farce of a process that occurred, and create a new process that inspires public confidence and examines this matter officially, openly and honestly, and with the rigour that people in this country of ours are entitled to expect.

On 28 January 2004, Lord Hutton published his long-awaited *Report into the Circumstances Surrounding the Death of Dr David Kelly CMG*. The edge had been taken off it by the *Sun*, which had managed to get hold of the contents of the report prior to official publication and had splashed them all over its front page. Even so, there was no hiding the incredulity and anger felt by the population at large as Lord Hutton castigated the BBC essentially for one loose report at 6.07 one morning, while clearing the government and the security services of everything.

Lord Hutton had not just delivered what the government wanted, but, rather more dangerously, had overdelivered. The BBC's board of governors, faced with the report, disgracefully caved in, firstly accepting the resignation of the board's chairman, Gavyn Davies, and secondly forcing the effective Greg Dyke to resign as director general. When Mr Dyke appeared outside BBC Television Centre at White City, astonishing scenes ensued. It seemed as if all the BBC staff had turned out to give him their backing. Banners proclaimed 'Cut the crap, bring Greg back' and 'Hutton take a hike, bring back Greg Dyke'.

As pictures of the spontaneous outpourings of support for Mr Dyke and anger at the BBC's board, the government and Lord Hutton filled the nation's TV screens, it all seemed redolent of Alexander Dubček's Czechoslovakia in 1968 and the last gasps of the Prague Spring.

The government began making noises about how the independence of the BBC was of course respected but no-one really believed it. All they succeeded in doing was convincing people that the government did not want its pressure on the BBC to have these consequences, rather than that it was rejecting the use of pressure in itself.

The BBC's vice-chairman, Lord Ryder, made a public apology to the government of such capitulation that I wanted to throw up when I heard it: 'The BBC must now move forward in the wake of Lord Hutton's report, which highlighted serious defects in the corporation's processes and procedures. On behalf of the BBC I have no hesitation in apologising unreservedly for our errors and to the individuals whose reputations were affected by them.' Lord Ryder, former political secretary to Margaret Thatcher, had in one short statement done the image and independence of the BBC more damage than any other event in its history. It has left the indelible impression that, when the chips are really down, the BBC's integrity and independence will buckle under government pressure.

It emerged in January 2007 that Mr Dyke had demanded his job back a week after he was forced out. The governors refused to reinstate him, board minutes show.

Janice Kelly also appeared to be unhappy with Lord Hutton's report. It was reported that she was consulting her legal team to see what action might be taken to defend her husband's memory. She was reported to be particularly unhappy with Lord Hutton's suggestion that her husband's meeting with Andrew Gilligan had been unauthorised. Even more explosively, the *Times* suggested that she was considering whether to sue the Ministry of Defence for the loss of her husband, his salary and possible future earnings. The government would certainly have wanted to avoid such a scenario.[1] As no writ appeared, it is reasonable to assume that Mrs Kelly and the Ministry of Defence reached some sort of accommodation, though details were unsurprisingly never made public.

The Oxfordshire coroner, Nicholas Gardiner, came under heavy pressure from many sides to reopen his inquest in the light of the lack of confidence felt in Lord Hutton's inquiry. He would have been perfectly within his rights to do so, and had certainly been given a huge amount of ammunition by Rowena Thursby and the group of doctors and other professionals she had assembled. On 16 March 2004, however, he announced that he would not do so, and official consideration of David Kelly's death ended there.

There was still mileage in the Hutton report for the Labour Party, though. At an event held at the Arts Club in Mayfair in May 2006 at which ministers were present, an auction was held for a copy of the report specially signed by Cherie Blair. It raised £400 for party funds. Nobody seems to have reflected that treating an official report into the death of a respected public servant as some sort of novelty item might have been in bad taste. Tony Blair, when challenged on the matter in the Commons, refused to apologise, insisting only that 'no offence' had been intended.

In 2007 came Alastair Campbell's diaries, in which we learnt of the pain and anguish he says he suffered following Dr Kelly's death. We were invited to feel sorry for Campbell, and not worry too much about Dr Kelly. Campbell is rumoured to have scooped a million pounds for his diaries, and he is just one of a number who have profited from their role in the David Kelly episode and the government's illegal war in Iraq.

Among the politicians, none of course resigned and all those closely involved survived in office until Blair's departure in the summer of 2007. Geoff Hoon, whose behaviour at the time was more reprehensible than most, remains in the Cabinet to this day, as Gordon Brown's new chief whip. It is said that chief whips need to be skilled in the black arts.

Among the special advisers and civil servants, there were likewise no casualties. Even those caught red-handed, such as Tom Kelly with his 'Walter Mitty' briefing, just carried on as if nothing had happened. On the contrary, many have since been promoted and awarded honours. John Scarlett, then head of the Joint Intelligence Committee, was rewarded for his co-operation with Campbell and given the job he had coveted, head of MI6. He was given a KCMG in the 2007 New Year's honours list.

David Broucher was still concerned about his role in the David Kelly affair as late as May 2007, when he wrote an official letter to Sir Peter Ricketts, the permanent under-secretary at the Foreign Office, responding to 'the inconsistency between Lord Hutton's findings and my evidence'. After initially stating that no such letter could be identified, the Foreign Office eventually unearthed it and released a copy to me.

In the letter, Mr Broucher wrote:

I was mistaken when I told the inquiry that I met Dr Kelly only once. I prepared my evidence in a hurry, without being able, in the summer holidays, to consult people who might have jogged my memory, and I was recalling events that did not have at the time the significance they subsequently assumed. I later realised that I had met him twice.

The second meeting was the only one of any substance. This took place on 27 February 2003, in Geneva, where Dr Kelly had come unexpectedly after attending a conference in New York. Because this trip was unscheduled, it was not recorded in any way, and until recently there was no way to verify it. It is on this point that the two independent witnesses have now become available.

The content of our discussion in February 2003 was as I described it to the inquiry. The discussion could not, of course, have taken place in February 2002, as Lord Hutton concluded, because several things Dr Kelly and I discussed only came about in late 2002 or early 2003.

I did not recall when I gave evidence that I had also met Dr Kelly briefly on 18 February 2002. He had come to Geneva for a regular annual conference, and we were both present at an early morning briefing. I asked him if he would be free for lunch. He said he would check. He later called at the UK Mission to apologise that his programme was too full, and he promised to meet me at a later date. My PA noted in my diary that he had called.

While this explanation is helpful in taking matters forward, it still leaves some unanswered questions about the 2003 meeting, most specifically why this was not recorded in Dr Kelly's diary.

Mr Broucher also recorded in his letter that he 'rather liked Dr Kelly. He seemed to me to be an honest and knowledgeable person who did what he thought was right.'

At Thames Valley Police, the Chief Constable in 2003, Peter Neyroud, who was largely invisible throughout the whole David Kelly episode, was honoured by the Americans with the Gary P. Hayes Award, given to police leaders who possess a sophisticated understanding of the unique role of police in our society. He is the first non-American to be so honoured. In 2006, he was made chief executive of the National Policing Improvement Agency, and was also invited to Chequers by Blair. Detective Chief Inspector Alan Young, who led the police inquiry but who gave no evidence at the Hutton inquiry, has been promoted to detective superintendent. Assistant Chief Constable Michael Page has retired. At his retirement dinner, the eulogy was given by none other than Lord Hutton himself.

I learnt of this from a police officer at Thames Valley Police who declared himself very surprised that Lord Hutton should have been in attendance and given what he called a long and fulsome speech. I asked Lord Hutton for a copy of his speech but he was unable to provide me with one. He told me that his comments were impromptu: 'I paid a tribute to Mr Page, wished him a happy retirement, and told an Irish legal joke.'[2]

Lord Hutton himself has also retired. His inquiry into the death of David Kelly was his last major endeavour, and is what he will always be remembered for.

As for Iyad Allawi, he was provisionally invited by Tony Blair to be a guest of honour at the 2004 Labour Party conference, but for once, the slumbering giant put its foot down and Blair had to back down. His political ambitions were far from dead, however, despite the comprehensive rejection he had suffered in the 2005 elections, and by 2007 he was again manoeuvring to get back into power in Iraq. To this end, he engaged the help of Barbour Griffith & Rogers, a top Washington lobbying firm, who were contracted for a six-month period for the not insignificant sum of $300,000. Employees of this company include Robert Blackwill, President Bush's former special envoy to Iraq. Condoleezza Rice's former counsellor, Philip Zelikow, is a senior adviser to the firm.

American citizens who played a leading role in planning and executing the illegal invasion of Iraq, with all its terrible consequences, have also been fully honoured by the British government. General Tommy Franks, who led the 2003 invasion and was Commander-in-Chief of the occupying forces, was knighted for 'services to UK–American military co-operation'. Riley Bechtel, the billionaire head of the Bechtel Corporation, which has made a fortune out of the Iraq war, was given a CBE. Honours were also showered on Vice-Admiral Timothy Keating, Rear-Admiral Barry Costello, Lieutenant Colonel Mark Childress and many more besides.

Those who strove to ensure the truth was given to the public have fared less well. At the BBC, Gavyn Davies, Greg Dyke and Andrew Gilligan all lost their jobs. It has been an uphill struggle for them to regain their previous prominence. Inside the government, those who put their heads above the parapet have either now retired, such as Dr Brian Jones, or trod water, such as David Broucher. The key weapons inspectors, who between them had done much to make the world a safer place, have all retired as well, some, such as Rod Barton, in protest at the distorted use of information by politicians.

As for the weapons inspector David Kelly, he paid for his honesty with his life. While those who lied, who spun, whose actions were characterised by cynicism, indifference and amorality have prospered, Dr Kelly lies in the quiet graveyard of St Mary's Church in Longworth.

By playing a leading role in helping to eliminate the

biological weapons capability of Russia, and of course Iraq, it is no exaggeration to say that between 1990 and his death in 2003, Dr Kelly probably did more to make the world a more secure place than anyone else on the planet. Even among the elite group of international weapons inspectors, he was regarded with some awe, as the inspectors' inspector.

It is not too late to pay proper respects to David Kelly. Internal government documents show that in May 2003, he was rightly being considered for a knighthood in recognition of the superb work he had done to help eliminate the biological weapons threat posed by both Russia and Iraq, and much more besides. I believe that that honour should now be awarded posthumously in recognition for all Dr Kelly achieved for this country and for the world.

Appendix: Dramatis personae

Where were they then?

Where are they now?

Government

Tony Blair
Prime Minister.

Envoy for Quartet on the Middle East (USA, EU, UN & Russia)

Alastair Campbell
Prime Minister's director of communications and strategy 2001–3.

Resigned on 29 August 2003, the day after Tony Blair gave evidence to the Hutton inquiry. After leaving No. 10 he wrote a sports column for the *Times*.

Worked for the Labour Party again in the run-up to the 2005 general election as the effective director of communications for the campaign.

Recruited by Sir Clive Woodward to manage press relations for the British and Irish Lions tour to New Zealand in 2005.

In 2007, *The Blair Years*, his diaries which document his time at No. 10, were published.

Geoff Hoon MP
Secretary of State for Defence.

Remained in government while Tony Blair was Prime Minister as Leader of the House of Commons and later Minister of State for Europe within the Foreign and Commonwealth Office.

When Gordon Brown became Prime Minister, became parliamentary secretary to the Treasury and chief whip.

Tom Kelly
Prime Minister's official spokesman.

As the only member of the government side to have made an unqualified apology, kept a low profile following the Hutton inquiry.

In 2004 promoted to Tony Blair's chief spokesman when Godric Smith promoted to head of strategic communications.

Role unclear since Gordon Brown took over in July 2007.

Jonathan Powell
Prime Minister's chief of staff.

Remained in post until Tony Blair left office.

Since July 2007 has been working for Blair in his new job as Middle East envoy alongside Lord Levy's son, Daniel.

Godric Smith
Prime Minister's chief official spokesman.

Announced his intention in May 2003 to leave his job as PM's official spokesman 'at some point later this year' but was persuaded to stay on.

In December 2003 received a CBE and in February 2004 was promoted to head of strategic communications in the No. 10 Press Office, a post he held until February 2006.

Director of communications for the Olympic Delivery Authority since 27 February 2006.

MPs

Donald Anderson
Labour chair of the Foreign Affairs Select Committee.

Stepped down from the House of Commons at the 2005 general election.

Created Baron Anderson of Swansea in June 2005.

Andrew Mackinlay
Member of the Foreign Affairs
Select Committee.

Still an MP and a member of the
Foreign Affairs Committee.

Civil servants/security services

David Broucher
Permanent representative to the
Conference on Disarmament in
Geneva, Foreign and Common-
wealth Office. One of the UK
membership of the UN Security
Council in 2003.

EU Policy Adviser to the presidential
administration in Romania. Based at
Cotroceni Palace in Bucharest.

Sir Richard Dearlove
Head of MI6.

Master of Pembroke College,
Cambridge.
      Honorary fellow of Queens'
College, Cambridge since 2004.

Richard Hatfield
Personnel director, Ministry of
Defence.

Still in post.

Martin Howard
Director general of communications, Ministry of Defence, until
2003.
Deputy chief of defence
intelligence, MoD, 2003–4.

Director general of operational policy
at the MoD since 2004. Received a
CB in the Queen's Birthday honours
2007.

Lee Hughes
Secretary to the Hutton inquiry.
Presided over the practicalities of
the inquiry and provided support
for Lord Hutton.

In 2004, promoted to head of judicial
competitions (Courts Division),
Department of Constitutional Affairs.
      Awarded a CBE for public service
in the Queen's Birthday honours
2004.
      Now head of court appointments.

Dr Brian Jones
Former branch head in the Scientific and Technical Directorate, Defence Intelligence Analysis Staff, Ministry of Defence.

Wrote an article for the *Independent* in which he suggested that not a single defence intelligence expert backed Tony Blair's most contentious claims on WMD: 'In my view the expert intelligence analysts of the DIS were overruled in the preparation of the dossier . . . resulting in a presentation that was misleading about Iraq's capabilities.'

Now retired.

Sir David Manning
Former foreign policy adviser to the Prime Minister; head of the Overseas and Defence Secretariat, Cabinet Office.

Ambassador to the United States since 2 September 2003.

Sir David Omand
Director of GCHQ; permanent secretary at the Home Office; permanent secretary in the Cabinet Office as the first UK security and intelligence co-ordinator.

Retired in April 2005.

A regular speaker on security and intelligence.

Deputy chairman of the Windsor Leadership Trust; visiting professor, King's College London.

John Scarlett
Chair of the Joint Intelligence Committee.

Promoted to the head of the Secret Intelligence Service (MI6) on 6 May 2004, succeeding Richard Dearlove.

Appointed KCMG in the 2007 New Year honours list.

Dr Richard Scott
Programme director for science
& technology, Defence Science &
Technology Laboratory.
David Kelly's line manager,
supervising his secondment to the
MoD and responsible for his
career development and pay.

Still in post.

Richard Taylor
Special adviser to Secretary of
State for Defence.

Unknown.

Pamela Teare
Director of news, Ministry of
Defence.

Deputy director & head of Strategic
Communications Division, Crown
Prosecution Service.

Sir Kevin Tebbit
Permanent secretary, Ministry of
Defence.

Remained in post until 2005.
    Now on the advisory board of the
Centre for Studies in Security and
Diplomacy at the University of
Birmingham; visiting professor, at
Queen Mary, University of London.
    Non-executive director, Smiths
Group; chair of the UK branch
Finmeccanica, which owns Westland
helicopters.

Dr Bryan Wells
Director of counter-proliferation
and arms control, Ministry of
Defence.
David Kelly's line manager within
the MoD.

Still in post.

Lawyers

Andrew Caldecott QC
Counsel for the BBC during the
Hutton inquiry.

Still a QC. A leading specialist in
defamation and breach of confidence.

James Dingemans QC
Counsel for the inquiry.

Still a QC.

His practice is focused on constitutional issues and public law, especially in cases with civil liberties and human rights issues.

Media

Tom Baldwin
Times journalist.

Washington correspondent, *Times*.

Gavyn Davies
Chair of the board of governors, BBC.

Resigned in the wake of Lord Hutton's criticisms of the BBC's reports and has since become somewhat of a critic of the government.

Founding partner of Active Private Equity and Prisma Capital Partners; chairman, Fulcrum Asset Management.

In 2005 set up a $1.35 billion hedge fund to invest in macroeconomic situations.

Writes a weekly column on mathematics and statistics, 'Gavyn Davies Does the Maths', for the *Guardian*.

Greg Dyke
Director general, BBC.

Resigned in the wake of Lord Hutton's verdict in January 2004.

Appointed Chancellor of the University of York in November 2003, for a five-year term with effect from August 2004.

Andrew Gilligan
Reporter for *Today* programme, BBC Radio 4.

Resigned from the BBC in early 2004 and became defence and diplomatic editor of the *Spectator*.

Writes for the *Evening Standard* on defence and diplomatic affairs and on other issues.

Has worked for Channel 4 on the investigative programme *Dispatches*.

Tom Mangold
Journalist and broadcaster.

As before.

Nick Rufford
Sunday Times journalist.

Assistant editor, *Sunday Times*.

Thames Valley Police

Graham Coe
Detective constable.

Still in post.

Peter Neyroud
Chief Constable.

In 2005 won the Gary P. Hayes Award, given to police leaders who possess a sophisticated understanding of the unique role of police in our society. This is the first time in the history of the award that it has been presented to a person outside the United States.

Left Thames Valley Police in 2005; in 2006 appointed chief executive, National Policing Improvement Agency.

Michael Page
Assistant Chief Constable.

Retired January 2006.

Alan Young
Detective chief inspector.

Promoted to detective superintendent, Thames Valley Police.

Notes

Chapter 1

1. The dossier's full title is *Iraq's Weapons of Mass Destruction: The Assessment of the British Government*. Published 24 September 2002.
2. In a letter dated 24 July 2003, the Secretary of State for Constitutional Affairs and Lord Chancellor, the Right Honourable Lord Falconer of Thoroton, acting on behalf of the government, wrote to Hutton asking him to 'conduct an inquiry within the following terms of reference: urgently to conduct an investigation in to the circumstances surrounding the death of Dr Kelly'.
3. Lord Hutton, *Report of the Inquiry into the Circumstances Surrounding the Death of Dr David Kelly CMG*, HC 247, 28 January 2004.
4. Scott Ritter, 'The public must look to what is missing from the report', *Guardian*, 30 January 2004.
5. Michael Meacher, 'The very secret service', *Guardian*, 21 November 2003.
6. Nicholas Rufford, 'Spy, boffin, disgruntled civil servant: this was the David Kelly I knew', *Sunday Times*, 25 January 2004.
7. Letter from Eric Matthew, honours secretary, 23 May 2003, inviting suggestions with David Kelly's name handwritten across the top. Hutton inquiry evidence reference FAM/5/0001-0005.

Chapter 2

1. The BBC issued a statement announcing Davies's resignation that day and one announcing Dyke's on 29 January.
2. The BBC issued a statement announcing Gilligan's resignation on 30 January 2004.
3. *International Statistical Classification of Diseases and Related Health Problems*, 10th revision (Geneva: World Health Organization, 1992–4).
4. *Psychological Reports* (1998), vol. 82, pp. 611–14.
5. Alexander Richard Allan, evidence to Hutton inquiry, 3 September 2003. Hearing transcripts, pp. 12–13.
6. Dr Nicholas Hunt, evidence to Hutton inquiry, 16 September 2003. Hearing transcripts, p. 14.

7. Roy Green, evidence to Hutton inquiry, 3 September 2003. Hearing transcripts, p. 146.
8. Hansard, HC Deb, 13 July 2005, vol. 436, cols 936–42. The parliamentary under-secretary of state for health, Caroline Flint, recommended that GPs find alternatives to prescribing coproxamol, as it was responsible for between 300 and 400 deaths a year, of which a fifth were believed to be accidental. The continued withdrawal of the drug was again debated on 17 January 2007 (Hansard, HC Deb, vol. 455, cols 339WH–341WH).
9. Vanessa Hunt, evidence to Hutton inquiry, 2 September 2003. Hearing transcripts, p. 77.
10. Ibid., pp. 77–8.
11. Dave Bartlett, evidence to Hutton inquiry, 2 September 2003. Hearing transcripts, p. 83; Roy Green, evidence to Hutton inquiry, 3 September 2003. Hearing transcripts, p. 146.
12. 'A conspiracy to deceive?', *Daily Express*, 14 December 2004.
13. Dr Nicholas Hunt, evidence to Hutton inquiry, 16 September 2003. Hearing transcripts, p. 25.
14. 'Kelly death paramedics query verdict', *Observer*, 12 December 2004.
15. Dr Malcolm Warner, evidence to Hutton inquiry, 2 September 2003. Hearing transcripts, p. 6.
16. Dr Nicholas Hunt, evidence to Hutton inquiry, 16 September 2003. Hearing transcripts, p. 26.

Chapter 3

1. Ruth Absalom, evidence to Hutton inquiry, 2 September 2003. Hearing transcripts, p. 4.
2. Karen McVeigh and Paul Gallagher, 'Kelly told wife this wasn't the world he wanted', *Scotsman*, 19 July 2003.
3. Assistant Chief Constable Michael Page, evidence to Hutton inquiry, 2 September 2003. Hearing transcripts, p. 39. The evidence describes an email found on David Kelly's home computer dated 17 July 2003 to Ron Manley, timed at 11.18, wishing him well.
4. Ibid, p. 42. The evidence describes emails found on David Kelly's home computer dated 17 July 2003 to various sources indicating his intention to return to Iraq soon.
5. Janice Kelly, evidence to Hutton inquiry, 1 September 2003. Hearing transcripts, p. 48.
6. Ibid, p. 49.
7. Wing Commander John Clark, evidence to Hutton inquiry, 27 August 2003. Hearing transcripts, p. 139.

8. Tom Mangold, evidence to Hutton inquiry, 4 September 2003. Hearing transcripts, p.73.
9. Tom Mangold, GMTV, 2006.
10. Tom Mangold, evidence to Hutton inquiry, 4 September 2003. Hearing transcripts, p. 61

Chapter 4
1. Detective Sergeant Geoffrey Webb, evidence to Hutton inquiry, 2 September 2003. Hearing transcripts, p. 59.
2. Letter from Thames Valley Police, dated 27 February 2007.
3. Assistant Chief Constable Michael Page, evidence to Hutton inquiry, 2 September 2003. Hearing transcripts, p. 20.
4. Janice Kelly, evidence to Hutton inquiry, 1 September 2003. Hearing transcripts, p. 54.
5. Hansard, HC Written Answers, 2 June 2006, vol. 447, col. 40W.
6. Hansard, HC Written Answers, 6 July 2006, vol. 448, col. 1332W.
7. Hansard, HC Written Answers, 13 September 2006, vol. 449, col. 2438W.
8. Letter from Thames Valley Police to Norman Baker, dated 27 February 2007.
9. Letter to me following parliamentary question, 5 July 2006.
10. Assistant Chief Constable Michael Page, evidence to Hutton inquiry, 2 September 2003. Hearing transcripts, p. 23.
11. Rachel Kelly, evidence to Hutton inquiry, 1 September 2003. Hearing transcripts, p. 150.
12. Listed as evidence 'not for release' on the Hutton inquiry website.
13. Janice Kelly, evidence to Hutton inquiry, 1 September 2003. Hearing transcripts, p. 54.
14. Letter from Thames Valley Police to Norman Baker, dated 27 February 2007.

Chapter 5
1. Paul Chapman, evidence to Hutton inquiry, 2 September 2003. Hearing transcripts, p. 28.
2. Ibid.
3. Louise Holmes, evidence to Hutton inquiry, 2 September 2003. Hearing transcripts, p. 14.
4. DC Graham Coe, evidence to Hutton inquiry, 16 September 2003. Hearing transcripts, p. 3.

5. Dr Nicholas Hunt, evidence to Hutton inquiry, 16 September 2003. Hearing transcripts, p. 10.

6. Lord Hutton, *Report of the Inquiry into the Circumstances Surrounding the Death of Dr David Kelly CMG*, HC 247, 28 January 2004, p. 100.

7. Letter from Lord Hutton to Norman Baker MP.

8. Steven Morris and Hugh Muir, 'Mystery of last, lonely walk – final hours', *Guardian*, 19 July 2003; William Langley, 'Torn apart by the wolves of Westminster', *Sunday Telegraph*, 20 July 2003; Simon O'Hagan, Andrew Johnson and Cole Moreton, 'The death of David Kelly', *Independent on Sunday*, 20 July 2003.

9. Karen McVeigh and Paul Gallagher, 'Kelly told wife this wasn't the world he wanted', *Scotsman*, 19 July 2003.

10. Letter from Thames Valley Police to Norman Baker, 27 February 2007.

11. PC Andrew Franklin, evidence to Hutton inquiry, 2 September 2003. Hearing transcripts, p. 34.

12. DC Graham Coe, evidence to Hutton inquiry, 16 September 2003. Hearing transcripts, p. 4.

13. Dr Nicholas Hunt, evidence to Hutton inquiry, 16 September 2003, p. 9.

14. Ian Gallagher, 'We're devastated by David's death', *Mail on Sunday*, 20 July 2003.

15. David Leppard and Gareth Walsh, 'Special Branch seals off Whitehall office', *Sunday Times*, 20 July 2003.

16. Information placed in the Library of the House of Commons in response to a parliamentary question. Hansard, HC Written Answers, 20 June 2006, vol. 447, col. 1710W.

17. Letter from Thames Valley Police to Norman Baker, 27 February 2007.

18. Ibid.

19. PC Andrew Franklin, evidence to Hutton inquiry, 2 September 2003. Hearing transcripts, p. 33.

20. DC Graham Coe, evidence to Hutton inquiry, 16 September 2003. Hearing transcripts, p. 1.

21. Ibid., p. 4.

22. Ibid., p. 6.

23. Assistant Chief Constable Michael Page, evidence to Hutton inquiry, 23 September 2003. Hearing transcripts, p. 202.

24. Hutton report, p. 100.

Chapter 6

1. Norman Baker, parliamentary question to Des Browne. Hansard, HC Written Answers, 13 July 2006, vol. 448, col. 1943W.
2. Francis Beckett and David Hencke, *The Survivor: Tony Blair in Peace and War* (London: Aurum Press, 2005).
3. Norman Baker, parliamentary question to Harriet Harman. Hansard, HC Written Answers, 8 June 2006, vol. 447, col. 828W.
4. Reply from Harriet Harman to Norman Baker dated 12 December 2006.
5. David Amess, parliamentary question to Christopher Leslie. Hansard, HC Written Answers, 5 February 2004, vol. 417, col. 1077W.
6. Letter to Norman Baker from Lord Hutton dated 22 January 2007.
7. Norman Baker, parliamentary question to Harriet Harman. Hansard, HC Written Answers, 27 June 2006, vol. 448, cols 304W–305W.
8. Lord Hutton, 'The Media Reaction to the Hutton Report', *Public Law*, winter 2006, pp. 807–32.
9. Public Administration Select Committee, Session 2003/4, Minutes of Evidence, 25 May 2004, HC 606-ii.
10. Peter Oborne, 'The truth is he lied', *Spectator*, 10 January 2004.
11. On 30 January 1972, thirteen Catholics were killed when soldiers of a British paratroop regiment opened fire during a civil rights march in Londonderry. On Tuesday 21 August 1973 Major O'Neill issued a statement: 'This Sunday became known as Bloody Sunday and bloody it was. It was quite unnecessary. It strikes me that the Army ran amok that day and shot without thinking what they were doing. They were shooting innocent people. These people may have been taking part in a march that was banned but that does not justify the troops coming in and firing live rounds indiscriminately. I would say without hesitation that it was sheer, unadulterated murder. It was murder.'
12. BBC News Online, 'On This Day', 22 August 1973.
13. Letter from Lord Falconer to Norman Baker dated 29 October 2006.
14. Letter from Lord Hutton to Norman Baker dated 22 January 2007.
15. Ibid.
16. Lord Hutton, *Report of the Inquiry into the Circumstances Surrounding the Death of Dr David Kelly CMG*, HC 247, 28 January 2004, p. 2.
17. Letter from Lord Hutton to Norman Baker dated 22 January 2007.

Chapter 7

1. Letter from Lord Chancellor's private secretary to Nicholas Gardiner dated 4 August 2004.

2. Norman Baker, parliamentary question to Harriet Harman. Hansard, HC Written Answers, 13 June 2007, vol. 461, col. 1127W.

3. Norman Baker, parliamentary question to Harriet Harman. Hansard, HC Written Answers, 19 March 2007, vol. 458, col. 620W.

4. Norman Baker, parliamentary question to Harriet Harman. Hansard, HC Written Answers, 24 April 2007, vol. 459, col. 1006W.

5. Home Office, *Death Certification and Investigation in England, Wales and Northern Ireland: The Report of a Fundamental Review 2003*, Cm 5831, 2003, p. 110.

6. Letter from Harriet Harman to Norman Baker dated 6 December 2006.

7. Letter from Harriet Harman to Norman Baker dated 6 February 2007.

8. Coroners' Rules 1984. These have since been amended by Coroners' Rules 2005.

9. Harriet Harman, Hansard, HC Written Statements, 5 June 2006, vol. 447, cols 4WS–5WS; Harriet Harman, Hansard, HC Written Statements, 12 October 2006, vol. 450, cols 26WS–28WS; Harriet Harman, Hansard, HC Written Statements, 18 December 2006, vol. 454, cols 112WS–116WS; Baroness Ashton, Hansard, HL Written Statements, 18 December 2006, vol. 687, cols WS223–WS226; Baroness Ashton, Hansard, HL Written Statements, 20 June 2007, vol. 693, col. WS17.

10. Conversation between Harriet Harman and Norman Baker on 17 October 2006.

11. Norman Baker, parliamentary question to Harriet Harman. Hansard, HC Written Answers, 23 October 2006, vol. 450, col. 1650W.

12. Written Ministerial Statement from the Department of Constitutional Affairs, Official Report, 29 March 2007, Col 121WS

13. A programme of reform to the coronial and death certification service was established in 2003. Proposals on how to take it forward were announced in a position paper in March 2004. On 6 February 2006, further plans were announced in an oral ministerial statement and a briefing note was published. A draft Bill was published on 12 June 2006 and consultation responses published on 27 February 2007.

Chapter 8

1. Andrew Marr, *Today*, BBC Radio 4, 16 July 2003.

2. *Iraq's Weapons of Mass Destruction: The Assessment of the British Government*, published 24 September 2002.

3. Ibid., Executive Summary, para. 6.

4. Nicholas Rufford, 'Revealed – Saddam's secret "Chernobyl" radiation bomb', *Sunday Times*, 29 November 1998.

5. Nicholas Rufford, 'Kelly had evidence of Iraq "dirty bomb"', *Sunday Times*, 3 August 2003.

6. Richard Norton-Taylor and Julian Borger, 'Threat of war: dossier: Secrets of Saddam's hidden arsenal', *Guardian*, 5 September 2002.

7. Lord Hutton, *Report of the Inquiry into the Circumstances Surrounding the Death of Dr David Kelly CMG*, HC 247, 28 January 2004, pp. 107–8.

8. Sir Richard Dearlove, evidence to Hutton inquiry, 15 September 2003. Hearing transcripts, p. 87.

9. Jack Straw, Foreign Affairs Committee, *The Decision to Go to War in Iraq*, Ninth Report, Session 2002/3, HC 813-III, Oral Evidence, 24 June 2003.

10. Robin Cook, 'Blair and Scarlett told me Iraq had no usable weapons', *Guardian*, 12 July 2004.

11. Lord Butler of Brockwell, *Review of Intelligence on Weapons of Mass Destruction: Report of a Committee of Privy Counsellors*, HC 898, 14 July 2004, p. 127.

12. Jack Straw, *The Decision to Go to War in Iraq*, Oral Evidence, 27 June 2003.

13. George Jones, 'We had doubts on 45-minute claims', *Daily Telegraph*, 20 December 2006.

14. Press conference with Ari Fleischer and Condoleezza Rice, aboard Air Force One en route to Entebbe, Uganda, 11 July 2003.

15. Foreign Affairs Committee, *The Decision to Go to War in Iraq*, Ninth Report, Session 2002/3, HC 813-I, p. 29.

16. Email from Jonathan Powell to Alastair Campbell and John Scarlett dated 19 September 2002 from the Hutton inquiry evidence, submitted by the Cabinet Office.

17. Geoff Hoon, evidence to Hutton inquiry, 22 September 2003. Hearing transcripts, pp. 82–4.

18. Ibid., p. 84.

19. Alastair Campbell, evidence to Hutton inquiry, 19 August 2003. Hearing transcripts, p. 63.

20. Hansard, HC Deb, 4 June 2003, vol. 406, col. 148.

21. Alastair Campbell, evidence to Hutton inquiry, 19 August 2003. Hearing transcripts, p. 65.

22. Hutton report, p. 153.

23. David Leigh, Richard Norton-Taylor and Rob Evans, 'MI6 and Blair at odds over Saudi deals', *Guardian*, 16 January 2007.

24. Email from Daniel Pruce to Mark Matthews, 11 September 2002, from the Hutton inquiry evidence submitted by the Cabinet Office.

25. Robin Cook, Foreign Affairs Committee, *The Decision to Go to War in Iraq*, Ninth Report, Session 2002/3, HC 813-II, Written Evidence, 17 June 2003.

26. Hansard, HC Deb, 24 September 2002, vol. 390, col. 3.

Chapter 9

1. Ibrahim al-Marashi, Foreign Affairs Committee, *The Decision to Go to War in Iraq*, Ninth Report, Session 2002/3, HC 813-III, Oral Evidence, 19 June 2003.

2. Hansard, HC Deb, 3 February 2003, vol. 399, col. 25.

3. Jack Straw, *The Decision to Go to War in Iraq*, Oral Evidence, 24 June 2003.

4. Ibid.

5. Alastair Campbell, *The Decision to Go to War in Iraq*, Oral Evidence, 25 June 2003.

6. Ibrahim al-Marashi, *The Decision to Go to War in Iraq*, Oral Evidence, 19 June 2003.

7. Antony Barnett, 'Arms and Iraq: secret emails, missing weapons', *Observer*, 15 May 2005.

8. Ibid.

9. Letter from Kim Howells to Norman Baker, 30 September 2006.

10. Email from Charles Duelfer to Norman Baker.

11. Lord Butler of Brockwell, *Review of Intelligence on Weapons of Mass Destruction: Report of a Committee of Privy Counsellors*, HC 898, 14 July 2004, p. 79.

12. Ibid., pp. 82, 114.

13. *Congressional Record: House of Representatives*, vol. 148, no. 5, 29 January 2002, p. H99.

14. Paul R. Pillar, 'Intelligence, Policy, and the War in Iraq', *Foreign Affairs*, March/April 2006.

15. Seymour Hersh, 'Selective intelligence', *New Yorker*, 12 May 2003.

16. President Bush, press conference, 8 July 2002, 5.00 p.m. EDT.

17. Email from Paul R. Pillar to Norman Baker dated 19 June 2007.

18. Michael Smith, 'Blair planned Iraq war from start', *Sunday Times*, 1 May 2005.

19. Select Committee on Liaison, *Oral Evidence Given by the Rt Hon. Tony Blair MP*, Session 2002/3, HC 300-ii.

20. Rod Barton, *The Weapons Detective: The Inside Story of Australia's Top Weapons Inspector* (Melbourne: Black Inc. Agenda, 2006).

21. Pillar, 'Intelligence, Policy, and the War in Iraq'.

22. 'A letter to Blair: Your Middle East policy is doomed, say diplomats', *Independent*, 27 April 2004.

23. Rodric Braithwaite, 'Mr Blair, it is time to recognise your errors and just go', *Financial Times*, 3 August 2006.

Chapter 10

1. Intelligence and Security Committee, minutes of meeting, 16 July 2003, p. 2. Hutton inquiry evidence ref. ISC/1/0003.
2. John Cassidy, 'The Kelly affair: one day in July', *Observer*, 25 January 2004.
3. Evidence supplied to the Hutton inquiry from Andrew Gilligan's personal organiser. Evidence ref. ANG/5/0013.
4. Freedom of Information Act 2000 Decision Notice, 22 January 2007, ref. FS501 12510.
5. Transcript of Gavin Hewitt's report, BBC 10 O'clock News, 29 May 2003. Hutton inquiry evidence ref. BBC/7/0111–0112.
6. *Panorama*, BBC1, 11 July 2004.
7. Dr Brian Jones, evidence to Hutton inquiry, 3 September 2003. Hearing transcripts, p. 139.
8. Brian Jones, 'Hutton report – the aftermath', *Independent*, 4 February 2004.
9. Lord Butler of Brockwell, *Review of Intelligence on Weapons of Mass Destruction: Report of a Committee of Privy Counsellors*, HC 898, 14 July 2004, p. 138.
10. Carne Ross, submission to the Butler review, 9 June 2004.
11. Quoted in Patrick Wintour, 'Hoon admits fatal errors in planning for postwar Iraq', *Guardian*, 2 May 2007.
12. Carne Ross, Foreign Affairs Committee, Session 2006/7, Minutes of Evidence, 8 November 2006, HC 167.

Chapter 11

1. 'In the air', *Evening Standard*, 9 July 2003.
2. Peter Oborne and Simon Walters, *Alastair Campbell* (London: Aurum Press, 2004), p. 188.
3. Memo from John Scarlett to Sir David Omand, 7 July 2003, Hutton inquiry evidence ref. CAB/1/0046.
4. Memo from Dominic Wilson to Kevin Tebbit, Hutton inquiry evidence ref. MOD/1/0044.
5. Minutes of the meetings in the Prime Minister's study on 7 and 8 July 2003, Hutton inquiry evidence ref. CAB/11/0005.
6. Lord Hutton, *Report of the Inquiry into the Circumstances Surrounding the Death of Dr David Kelly CMG*, HC 247, 28 January 2004, pp. 39–40.

7. Norman Baker, parliamentary question to Des Browne. Hansard, HC Written Answers, 29 January 2007, vol. 456, col. 32W.

8. Extracts from Alastair Campbell's diaries, Hutton inquiry evidence ref. CAB/39/0001.

9. Ibid.

10. James Chapman, 'Blair "headed meeting that approved Kelly's exposure"', Daily Mail, 14 October 2003.

11. Christopher Leake, 'Did Hoon demand to see widow's dossier and did she insist it must go to inquiry?', Mail on Sunday, 27 July 2003.

12. James Blitz, Tim Burt and Cathy Newman, 'Blair denies authorising the leak of Kelly's identity, Financial Times, 23 July 2003.

13. Geoff Hoon, evidence to Hutton inquiry, 22 September 2003. Hearing transcripts, p. 27.

14. Mr A, evidence to Hutton inquiry, 3 September 2003. Hearing transcripts, p. 111.

15. Ibid., p. 112.

16. Simon Hoggart, 'Don't blame the MPs; they perform a crucial role', Guardian, 21 July 2003.

17. 'The Kelly affair: one day in July', Observer, 25 January 2004.

18. All quotes in this section from the Foreign Affairs Committee meeting, 15 July 2003.

19. Quentin Letts, 'It was hold-onto-your-sunhats stuff', Daily Mail, 16 July 2003.

20. Simon Hoggart, 'Whisper of confusion tells its own story', Guardian, 16 July 2003.

21. David Hughes, 'Nice day out Mister Hoon?', Daily Mail, 21 July 2003.

22. Alastair Campbell, The Blair Years (London: Hutchinson, 2007), p. 714.

23. Ibid., pp. 714, 715.

24. Paul Waugh, 'No. 10 dismisses Kelly as a "Walter Mitty"', Independent, 4 August 2003.

Chapter 12

1. Letter from Lord Hutton to Norman Baker, 22 January 2007.

2. Sharon Churcher and Annette Witheridge, 'Kelly planned to move to America', Mail on Sunday, 1 February 2004.

3. Helen Hornby (ed.), Lights of Guidance: A Baha'i Reference File (New Delhi: Baha'i Publications Trust, 1988), no. 677, p. 204.

4. Alastair Campbell, evidence to Hutton inquiry, 19 August 2003. Hearing transcripts, p. 168.

5. Neil Michael, 'The Kelly conspiracy', News of the World, 7 September 2003.

6. Rod Barton, *The Weapons Detective: The Inside Story of Australia's Top Weapons Inspector* (Melbourne: Black Inc. Agenda, 2006), p. 231.
7. Quoted in John Cassidy, 'The David Kelly affair', *New Yorker*, 8 December 2003.
8. Andrew Gilligan, 'Those who say David was murdered are so wrong', *Evening Standard*, 24 July 2006.
9. David Broucher, evidence to Hutton inquiry, 21 August 2003. Hearing transcripts, p. 146.
10. Ibid., p. 140.
11. Emails between David Kelly and Judith Miller. Hutton inquiry evidence ref. COM/4/0076.

Chapter 13
1. Sue Reid, 'Was Dr Kelly murdered?', *Daily Mail*, 6 March 2004.
2. Evidence to the Hutton inquiry. Evidence ref: TVP/3/0287.

Chapter 14
1. Rosalind S. Helderman, 'Slaying suspects allegedly talked with victim's daughter', *Washington Post*, 1 February 2002.
2. Paul Sieveking, 'Strange but true – the deadly curse of the bio-researchers', *Sunday Telegraph*, 6 January 2002.
3. Michael Horsnell, 'Mystery death of scientist', *Times*, 13 February 2002.
4. Obituary, *Times*, 13 July 2004.
5. Jon Craig and Barrie Penrose, 'Pentagon quizzes Britain on 22 deaths', *Sunday Times*, 9 October 1988.
6. John Branston, 'Official misconduct', *Memphis Flyer*, 20 May 2005.
7. Gordon Thomas, 'Microbiologists with link to race-based weapon turning up dead', *American Free Press*, 12 April 2004.
8. Quoted in 'Dead Scientists', www.gordonthomas.ie, 21 November 2003.
9. Neil Michael, 'The Kelly conspiracy', *News of the World*, 7 September 2003.
10. Norman Baker, parliamentary question to Douglas Alexander. Hansard, HC Written Answers, 27 November 2006, vol. 453, cols 263W–264W.
11. Michael C. Ruppert, *Crossing the Rubicon: The Decline of the American Empire at the End of the Age of Oil* (Gabriola, BC: New Society, 2004), p. 517.
12. 'Vaccines seen a $10 billion market by '06', Reuters, 7 January 2003.
13. Debora MacKenzie, 'Anthrax attack bug "identical" to army strain', *New Scientist*, 9 May 2002.

14. Sheryl Gay Stolberg and David E. Rosenbaum, 'U.S. will offer anthrax shots for thousands', *New York Times*, 19 December 2001.
15. Rick Weiss, 'Demand growing for anthrax vaccine', *Washington Post*, 29 September 2001.

Chapter 15
1. Jo Thomas, 'California doctor's suicide leaves many troubling mysteries unsolved', *New York Times*, 3 November 2002.
2. Jack Leonard and Jeff Gottlieb, 'Meetings with South African attache under scrutiny inquiry', *Los Angeles Times*, 17 July 2000.
3. Marlene Bruger and Peta Thornycroft, 'Larry the chemical charlatan and the teabags of death', *Sunday Independent* (South Africa), 17 March 2000.
4. Evidence of Dr Schalk van Rensburg, Truth and Reconciliation Commission hearing, 9 June 1998.
5. T. J. Byron, *Elimination Theory: The Secret Covert Networks of Project Coast* (Frederick, MD: PublishAmerica, 2004).
6. Gordon Thomas, 'MI5 to probe Kelly's links to Russian germ war scientist', *Sunday Express*, 27 August 2006.
7. Evidence of Dr Jan Lourens, Truth and Reconciliation Commission hearing, 8 June 1998.
8. Andrew Mackinlay, parliamentary question to Ian McCartney. Hansard, HC Oral Answers, 27 June 2006, vol. 448, col. 123.
9. Andrew Mackinlay, parliamentary question to Jack Straw. Hansard, HC Written Answers, 11 January 2006, vol. 441, col. 675W.
10. Andrew Mackinlay, parliamentary question to John Reid. Hansard, HC Written Answers, 6 March 2006, vol. 443, col. 1185W.
11. Gordon Thomas, *Gideon's Spies: The Secret History of the Mossad*, 4th ed. (New York: Thomas Dunne, 2007), p. 515.
12. David Pratt, 'Eye for an eye', *Sunday Herald*, 15 January 2006.

Chapter 16
1. Sharon Churcher, 'Mai is a beautiful woman', *Mail on Sunday*, 7 September 2003.
2. Sharon Churcher and Annette Witheridge, 'Why was David Kelly registered at three US addresses with his spiritual mentor?', *Mail on Sunday*, 14 September 2003.
3. Quoted in Laura Peek and James Bone, 'Kelly's spiritual mentor to tell of relationship', *Times*, 10 September 2003.
4. Sharon Churcher and Annette Witheridge, 'Kelly planned to move to America', *Mail on Sunday*, 1 February 2004.

5. Churcher and Witheridge, 'Why was David Kelly registered at three US addresses with his spiritual mentor?'.

6. Letter from Lord Hutton to Norman Baker, 22 January 2007.

7. James Bone, 'American was Kelly's spiritual mentor', *Times*, 1 September 2003.

8. Sharon Churcher, 'I'm not surprised David was found dead in the woods', *Mail on Sunday*, 25 January 2004.

9. Ibid.

10. Laura Peek, Dominic Kennedy and David Charter, 'Coroner ready to open new Kelly inquiry', *Times*, 22 January 2004.

11. Churcher and Witheridge, 'Why was David Kelly registered at three US addresses with his spiritual mentor?'.

12. Laura Peek, 'Oxford coroner may go ahead with Kelly inquest', *Times*, 27 September 2003.

13. Janice Kelly, evidence to the Hutton inquiry, 1 September 2003. Hearing transcripts, p. 8.

14. 'More Cast Changes at Law & Order', Monterey County Herald, 6 September 2003

15. Churcher, 'Mai is a beautiful woman'.

16. Tom Mangold, 'David was told: "Keep away from Mai, she's a spy and won't help your marriage"', *Mail on Sunday*, 1 February 2004.

17. Annette Witheridge and Sharon Churcher, 'Kelly planned to move to America', *Mail on Sunday*, 1 February 2004.

18. Dr Richard Scott, evidence to the Hutton inquiry, 15 September 2003. Hearing transcript, p. 114.

19. The Authorization for Use of Military Force Resolution, passed by the United States Congress on 18 September 2001.

20. Bob Woodward, 'CIA told to do "whatever necessary" to kill Bin Laden', *Washington Post*, 21 October 2001.

21. David Pratt, 'Top former CIA agent condemns new terror war', *Sunday Herald*, 27 February 2005.

22. Oliver Burkeman, 'US considers assassination squads', *Guardian*, 13 August 2002.

23. David Gow, 'Bush gives green light to CIA for assassination of named terrorists', *Guardian*, 29 October 2001.

24. Dana Priest, 'Covert CIA program withstands new furor', *Washington Post*, 30 December 2005.

25. Karen DeYoung, 'Bush approves new CIA methods', *Washington Post*, 21 July 2007.

Chapter 17

1. Mark Phythian, 'UNSCOM in the Time of Cholera', *World Affairs* (2000), vol. 162, pp. 51–63.
2. Interview with President Bush by TVP (Poland), 29 May 2003.
3. Bob Drogin and John Goetz, 'The curveball saga', *Los Angeles Times*, 20 November 2005.
4. Joby Warrick, 'Lacking biolabs, trailers carried case for war', *Washington Post*, 12 April 2006.
5. Peter Beaumont, 'Iraqi mobile labs nothing to do with germ warfare, report finds', *Observer*, 15 June 2003.
6. Email from David Kelly to Judith Miller, 11 June 2003. Evidence to the Hutton inquiry, ref. COM/4/0101.
7. Judith Miller, Stephen Engelberg and William Broad, *Germs: Biological Weapons and America's Secret War* (New York: Simon & Schuster, 2001).
8. Judith Miller, Stephen Engelberg and William J. Broad, 'US germ warfare research pushes treaty limits', *New York Times*, 4 September 2001.
9. Judith Miller, 'Iraqi tells of renovations at sites for chemical and nuclear arms', *New York Times*, 20 December 2001.
10. 'The *Times* and Iraq', *New York Times*, 26 May 2004.
11. Susan Watts, witness statement to the Hutton inquiry. Evidence ref. SJW/1/0057.
12. Central Intelligence Agency, *Iraqi Mobile Biological Warfare Agent Production Plants*, 28 May 2003.
13. 'US shelved evidence discounting Iraq's WMD', Reuters (Washington), 12 April 2006.
14. Paul Flynn, parliamentary question to Tony Blair. Hansard, HC Written Answers, 20 June 2003, vol. 407, col. 446W.
15. Hansard, HC Deb, 23 Jun 2003, vol. 407, col. 696.
16. Foreign Affairs Committee, *The Decision to Go to War in Iraq: Oral Evidence Given by Dr David Kelly*, 15 July 2003, Session 2003–04, HC 1025-i, Q. 55.
17. Iraq Survey Group, *Comprehensive Report of the Special Advisor to the DCI on Iraq's WMD*, 30 September 2004, Annex A.
18. Con Coughlin, 'Saddam's WMD hidden in Syria, says coalition's chief weapons investigator', *Sunday Telegraph*, 25 January 2004.
19. Norman Baker, parliamentary question to Kim Howells. Hansard, HC Written Answers, 19 February 2007, vol. 457, col. 400W.
20. Donald MacIntyre, 'Fury as Netanyahu confirms Syria strike', *Independent*, 21 September 2007.

21. Quoted in Marian Wilkinson, 'Weapons cover-up revealed', *Sydney Morning Herald*, 31 August 2006.
22. Eli Lake, 'Ex-officer spurned on WMD claim', *New York Sun*, 8 February 2006.
23. Quoted in Anne Penketh, 'Iraq, the aftermath: hunt for arms "is being hampered by lack of experienced inspectors"', *Independent*, 26 July 2003.
24. Norman Baker, parliamentary question to Kim Howells. Hansard, HC Written Answers, 20 February 2007, vol. 457, col. 641W.

Chapter 18
1. Joseph Wilson, *The Politics of Truth: Inside the Lies That Led to War and Betrayed My Wife's CIA Identity – A Diplomat's Memoir* (New York: Carrol & Graf, 2004).
2. Interview with Tom Mangold, GMTV, 29 June 2006.
3. Nick Paton Walsh, 'Markov's umbrella assassin revealed', *Guardian*, 6 June 2005.
4. Christopher Meyer, *DC Confidential: The Controversial Memoirs of Britain's Ambassador to the US at the Time of 9/11 and the Iraq War* (London: Weidenfeld & Nicolson, 2005).
5. Letter from Thames Valley Police to Norman Baker, 29 March 2007.

Chapter 19
1. Sharon Churcher, 'I'm not surprised David was found dead in the woods. I am surprised police say it was suicide', *Mail on Sunday*, 25 January 2004.
2. Richard Spertzel, 'David Kelly: the interrogator', *Observer*, 25 January 2004.
3. Bob Drogin and John Goetz, 'The Curveball saga', *Los Angeles Times*, 20 November 2005.
4. US Secretary of State Colin Powell, address to the United Nations Security Council, 5 February 2003.
5. Quoted in Seymour Hersh, 'Selective intelligence', *New Yorker*, 12 May 2003.
6. James Bamford, 'The man who sold the war', *Rolling Stone*, 17 November 2005.
7. Ibid.
8. Jane Mayer, 'The manipulator', *New Yorker*, 7 June 2004.
9. Bamford, 'The man who sold the war'.
10. Quoted in Julian Coman and Philip Sherwell, 'Revenge of the CIA', *Sunday Telegraph*, 23 May 2004.

11. Jon Lee Anderson, 'A man of the shadows', *New Yorker*, 24 January 2005.
12. Quoted in Seymour Hersh, 'Plan B – the Kurdish gambit', *New Yorker*, 28 June 2004.
13. Interview with Sir David Frost, *Breakfast with Frost*, BBC1, 14 December 2003.
14. Quoted in David Leigh and Richard Norton-Taylor, 'Iraqi who gave MI6 45-minute claim says it was untrue', *Guardian*, 27 January 2004.
15. Paul McGeough, 'Allawi shot prisoners in cold blood: witnesses', *Sydney Morning Herald*, 17 July 2004.
16. Jon Lee Anderson, 'A man of the shadows', *New Yorker*, 24 January 2005.
17. Maureen Dowd, 'Dance of the marionettes', *New York Times*, 26 September 2004.
18. Roland Watson, 'El Salvador-style "death squads" to be deployed by US against Iraq militants', *Times*, 10 January 2005.
19. Anderson, 'A man of the shadows'.
20. Greg Muttitt, Guy Hughes and Katy Cronin, *Crude Designs: The Rip-Off of Iraq's Oil Wealth* (London: Platform, 2005).
21. Dan Morgan and David B. Ottaway, 'In Iraqi war scenario, oil is key issue', *Washington Post*, 15 September 2002.
22. Julie Flint, 'The weapons row: MI6 duped by Saddam coup plot', *Observer*, 8 February 2004.

Chapter 20
1. Email from David Kelly to Olivia Bosch, 5 July 2003. Evidence to the Hutton inquiry, ref. COM/4/0062.
2. Letter from Thames Valley Police to Norman Baker, 29 March 2007.

Epilogue
1. Laura Peek, 'Widow may decide to seek damages from the MoD', *Times*, 30 January 2004.
2. Letter from Lord Hutton to Norman Baker, 2 May 2007.

Index

The following abbreviations are used in the index:
DK for David Kelly; MoD for Ministry of Defence;
WMD for weapons of mass destruction